RELIGION, SOCIETY AND POLITICS
IN FRANCE SINCE 1789

RELIGION, SOCIETY AND

POLITICS IN FRANCE

SINCE 1789

EDITED BY

FRANK TALLETT AND

NICHOLAS ATKIN

THE HAMBLEDON PRESS

LONDON   AND   RIO GRANDE

Published by The Hambledon Press 1991
102 Gloucester Avenue, London Nw1 8HX (U.K.)
P.O. Box 162, Rio Grande, Ohio 45672 (U.S.A.)

ISBN 1 85285 057 4

British Library Cataloguing in Publication
Religion, society and politics in France since 1789
    1. France. Catholic Church, history
    I. Tallett, Frank.   II. Atkin, Nicholas
    282.44

Library of Congress Cataloguing-in-Publication Data
    Religion, society and politics in France since 1789
    edited by Frank Tallett and Nicholas Atkin
    Includes bibliographical references and index
    1. Catholic Church – France – History
    2. Catholics – France – History
    3. France – Church history
    I. Tallett, Frank. II. Atkin, Nicholas
    BX1528.R42 1991
    282'.44'09034 – dc20   91–4210 CIP

Printed on acid-free paper and bound in Great Britain by
Bookcraft Ltd, Midsomer Norton, Somerset

Contents

Introduction

Frank Tallett and Nicholas Atkin

The study of modern French Catholicism has always been a central concern of historians of France on both sides of the Channel and the Atlantic. To a large extent, this is because religion has played a more obvious role in shaping the development of French politics, institutions and society since the late eighteenth century than it has, for example, in England. On many occasions the history of France and the fortunes of the Catholic church have been inextricably entwined: the failure in the 1790s of the Revolution to capture the hearts and minds of a majority of the population was, in large measure, due to the perceived attack upon the church; the subsequent instability of political life in the first half of the nineteenth century posed problems for Catholics over the attitude to be adopted towards the different regimes; the establishment and consolidation of political stability in the Third Republic was undermined by the persistent quarrels over the role of the church within society; and, as late as 1984, the disagreements over the funding of Catholic schools brought thousands of angry parents onto the streets of Paris and revealed the extent to which religious differences continue to divide French men and women.

In analyzing these developments, historians have displayed a variety of approaches. To begin with they manifested a predominant concern for the institutional question of church-state relations: this resulted in a focusing of attention upon such matters of high politics as the creation of the 1801 Concordat, the delicate links between the Gallican church and Rome, and the Separation Issue of 1905.[1] Because of the sensitivity of these topics and because many of the nineteenth-century historians who examined them were *partis pris*, much of the debate tended to be

---

[1] See, for example, F. Mourret, *Histoire des rapports de l'église et de l'état en France de 1789 à 1870* (Paris, 1898); P. Thureau-Dangin, *L'église et l'état sous la monarchie de juillet* (Paris, 1880); H. de Lamennais, *Les affaires de Rome* (Paris, 1836); J. Maurain, *La politique ecclésiastique du second empire* (Paris, 1930). C.S. Phillips, *The Church in France, 1789–1907* (2 vols., London, 1929–36) is a masterly survey.

polemical in character.[2] Historians generally remained concerned with the elites of the political and religious world: the members of the church hierarchy, the politicians of the various regimes, and in particular the great anticlericals of the late nineteenth century, men such as Jules Ferry, Paul Bert and Emile Combes, who ironically supplanted the great saints of the Counter-Reformation church in the religious historiography of the period.[3] As Jean Delumeau was to note in 1971, for a long time, 'l'histoire religieuse s'est complue sur les sommets'.[4] Only since the 1930s has it been feasible to discern a more objective approach and it still remains possible to detect in the writings of such recent eminent historians as Adrien Dansette, André Latreille and René Rémond the influence of their liberal Catholic philosophy.[5]

The concerns of historians have nevertheless now broadened markedly. No longer are they preoccupied with elites and with church-state relations narrowly defined. The founding father of this new approach was Gabriel Le Bras who as early as 1931 published the first and most important of a series of articles, collectively reprinted in 1955 as *Etudes de sociologie religieuse*.[6] He urged historians to lower their sights from the study of elites, and posed a wide number of questions together with suggestions on source material designed to enable scholars to discover the *chrétien quelconque*, to know how and to what extent he practised his religion and lived out his faith. A

[2] A. Debidour, *L'église catholique et l'état sous la troisième république, 1870–1906* (2 vols., Paris, 1906–9) is very anticlerical; a more nuanced, albeit Catholic perspective, is found in E. Lecanuet, *L'église de France sous la troisième république* (4 vols., Paris, 1907–30).

[3] Amongst the many, largely uncritical, lives of bishops written in the nineteenth century, F. Lagrange, *Vie de Mgr. Dupanloup* (3 vols., 3rd ed., Paris, 1883–84) remains very useful. On Combes see Y. Lapaquellerie, *Emile Combes ou le surprenant roman d'un honnête homme* (Paris, 1929).

[4] J. Delumeau, *Le catholicisme entre Luther et Voltaire* (Paris, 1971), p. 192.

[5] A. Dansette, *Histoire religieuse de la France contemporaine* (2 vols., Paris, 1948–51); A. Latreille, R. Rémond, J.-L. Palanque and E. Delaruelle, *Histoire du catholicisme en France* (3 vols., Paris, 1962); R. Rémond, *L'anti-cléricalisme en France de 1815 à nos jours* (Paris, 1976).

[6] G. Le Bras, 'Statistique et histoire religieuse: pour un examen détaillé et pour une explication historique de l'état de catholicisme dans les diverses régions de France', *Revue d'histoire de l'église de France*, xvii (1931), pp. 425–49, reprinted in *Etudes de sociologie religieuse* (2 vols., Paris, 1955). See also his *Introduction à l'histoire de la pratique religieuse en France* (Paris, 1942). Another pioneer of religious sociology was F. Boulard. See his *Essor ou déclin du clergé français?* (Paris, 1950), *An Introduction to Religious Sociology* (Eng. trans. London, 1960) and, with J. Remy, *Pratique religieuse urbaine et regions culturelles* (Paris, 1968).

glance at François Lebrun's *Histoire des catholiques en France* and Gérard Cholvy and Yves-Marie Hilaire's *Histoire religieuse de la France contemporaine*,[7] both of which are concerned with investigating levels of religious observance, the nature of religious practice and its relationship to existing political structures, demonstrates clearly the way in which religious history has moved in the post-Le Bras period. Another recent emphasis, exemplified in the Beauchesne *Histoire des diocèses* series, has been upon local studies which have both reflected and confirmed the enormous regional diversity of France in the nineteenth and twentieth centuries.

The aim of the present book is to illustrate some of the ways in which Anglo-Saxon historians have contributed and continue to contribute to an understanding of modern French religious history. It also seeks to provide English readers with an introduction to some of the major themes which remain dominant in the historiography. This volume is not therefore preoccupied with the narrow question of the interaction between the institutional body of the church and the state. Instead the essays included here reveal the wider role played by Catholics in French politics and society and place great emphasis on the diversity of opinion within the church. In particular, they display how Catholics have attempted to come to terms with the profound and continuing political changes initiated by the Revolution of 1789, and how they have grappled with the social realities of the modern, secular world of the nineteenth and twentieth centuries.

To a large extent, the fragmentation of Catholic opinion may be dated back to the Revolution. This destroyed the existing symbiosis between church and state, and bequeathed a whole series of intractable problems to the following century. As Frank Tallett suggests, the dechristianizing campaigns of the year II, in particular, left a legacy of mistrust and hatred on the part of many Catholics towards the supporters of the Revolution. In part this division helps to account for the 'mindlessly reactionary politics of Catholics in nineteenth-century France',[8] who retained an obdurate faith in the corporate and hierarchical values of the *ancien régime*. Catholic suspicions of the modern world remained most firmly entrenched in the western *départements*, but they were far from absent elsewhere.

---

[7]   F. Lebrun (ed.), *Histoire des catholiques en France du XVe siècle à nos jours* (Paris, 1980); G. Cholvy and Y.-M. Hilaire, *Histoire religieuse de la France contemporaine* (3 vols., Toulouse, 1985–88).

[8]   R. Gibson, *A Social History of French Catholicism* (London, 1989), p. 52. A work of synthesis, this is the best introduction in English to the religious history of France between 1789 and 1914.

Brian Fitzpatrick demonstrates how in the Second Empire Ultramontane Catholicism emerged as a political force in the Midi, its intransigent style appealing to the southern Catholic outlook. Here Legitimism, far from being a château-based movement, enjoyed long-standing ties with the urban popular classes, as did the clergy. It was not, however, until the Third Republic that the tensions between Catholics and the state became uncontainable. Anxious to place the new regime beyond the threat of a monarchical restoration, Republican politicians set out to undermine clerical influence within French society, particularly in education. In a wide-ranging analysis Ralph Gibson stresses the multi-faceted nature of relations between Republicans and Catholics. He underlines the way in which the Republic presided over a massive increase in state activity and explains why supporters of the regime found it increasingly difficult to tolerate a church determined to defend its independence at all costs.

Two further aspects of the religious history of the Third Republic are considered by Geoffrey Cubitt and Clive Castaldo. Dr. Cubitt demonstrates one way in which the church responded to the modern world in general and the Republic in particular by identifying them both with freemasonry, which was held to be coeval with atheism, humanism, materialism and the broader ideals of the Revolutionary heritage. This is an aspect of Catholic thought and action all too often summarily relegated to the footnotes of the history of antisemitism or the anecdotal records of pious gullibility. By way of contrast, Dr. Castaldo examines what has always been seen as a mainsteam issue in the nineteenth century: the Dreyfus Affair. He demonstrates the problems which Republican anticlericalism posed for French Socialists. Should anticlericalism be used, as Jean Jaurès argued, as a bridge between Socialists and the radical *bourgeoisie*, or was it, as the Marxist Jules Guesde maintained, a mere distraction to the growth of the Socialist movement?

The onset of the First World War and the establishment in August 1914 of the *Union Sacrée* brought about a better relationship between Catholics and Republicans. The post-war spirit of reconciliation, epitomized by Pius XI's condemnation in 1926 of the reactionary movement, the *Action Française*, promised the possibility of a *ralliement* between the church and the Republic. Yet, as Nicholas Atkin shows in his essay devoted to the religious orders in France between 1901 and 1945, this was never to take root. The church was unable to obtain a relaxation of the punitive Republican legislation governing the orders. Even the pro-clerical Vichy government proved unhelpful. Like preceding regimes, Vichy was anxious to maintain some sort of regulatory control over the congregations and the church in general. The theme of regulation and state authority during the dark years of the Occupation is explored further in W. D. Halls' analysis of prelates, theologians and the Vichy regime. Adopting an untraditional approach to the old theme of church-state relations, he illustrates how members of the church hierarchy were out-of-step with lay Catholics in their support for the Pétainist regime. At the Liberation the episcopate escaped wholesale *épuration*, yet in the popular mind the church as a whole had been redeemed more by the actions of the lower clergy and the laity who had gradually turned against Vichy. With hindsight the Occupation may be seen as the hinge on which relations between church and state turned and a new era began. Ironically, the failure of Vichy to generate wide-scale public support revealed to many Catholics the folly of die-hard politics and reconciled them to the ideas of democracy, a majority coming to regard a Republic as the least divisive form of government for France.

In the years immediately following the Liberation, French Catholicism appeared more liberal in outlook and many of the faithful were even able to articulate a relationship with Communism, a process which would have been unthinkable seventy years earlier. In his essay on Catholics and Communists in post-war France, Michael Kelly reveals how Christians and Communists mingled in the ranks of the Resistance and how this experience provided a fillip to many Catholics in evolving fresh concepts of social doctrine and action. These developments, in turn, gave the lower clergy and the laity a sharply enhanced consciousness of their own role and dignity. However, the evolving intellectual and political partnership between Catholics and Communists was interrupted by the Cold War. Even the newly-formed Christian Democratic party, the *Mouvement Républicain Populaire* (M.R.P.), floundered in the austere world of the late 1950s. David Hanley examines why this was so, but concentrates on why recent attempts in the 1980s to revive a centrist party inspired by Christian ideals in France have made little headway.

This volume reveals how the evolution of religious politics in France has not simply been the story of church-state relations. It also underscores the social and cultural environment in which French Catholicism operated. Once again the Revolution of 1789, which was instrumental in bringing about a decline in religious fervour and a marked laicization in religious practice, set the agenda for many subsequent developments. Not least of these was the feminization of religion. This forms the basis of two chapters by Hazel Mills and James F. McMillan, but is a theme which runs through a large number of the essays. Dr. McMillan challenges the traditional picture concerning sexual dimorphism with respect to religious practice in nineteenth-century

France, questioning whether men were rational and irreligious while women remained gullible and pious. He suggests that factors other than gender were more important in determining religious behaviour. Adopting a different perspective on the traditional view of women, Hazel Mills shows how the dominant images of masculinity and femininity in the nineteenth century require careful analysis: it was possible for women to draw upon the moral discourse of the period to legitimate activities outside the home which gave them status, great freedom of action and an outlet for their talents and energies in the public sphere. Finally, Colin Heywood reviews the way in which the Catholic church responded to the growth of industry and commerce in the nineteenth century and brings fresh light to bear on the vexed question of the relationship between Catholicism and business. The church often fulminated against the new industrial society, but this did not prevent entrepreneurs from discovering means by which Catholic theology might be reconciled with the demands of capitalism; indeed, business elements recognized that Catholicism could be put to good use in constructing and maintaining an hegemony over labour.

Although each of the essays in this book is self-contained, they nonetheless provide an introductory overview to the general reader of the key themes in the religious history of modern France, constituting a synthesis of recent research produced by both French and English scholars. In so doing they demonstrate the wide range of the problems confronting French Catholics in their struggle to come to terms with a modern and secular world. These issues have profoundly divided French Catholic opinion and, undoubtedly, will continue to do so.

The essays in this book were originally delivered as papers at a conference on 'Religion, Society and Politics in France since 1789' held in March 1990 under the aegis of the Department of History at the University of Reading. The editors wish to thank the contributors for agreeing to provide papers and for their willingness to see them through to publication. Thanks also extend to all those who attended the conference and whose verbal contributions are reflected in the published essays. Special thanks go to Mrs. Gill Fearon for her indefatigable energy in helping to organize the practical details of the conference and her generosity in typing and retyping the manuscript.

Notes on Contributors

Nicholas Atkin is lecturer in history at the University of Reading. He has published several articles on the French church and France during the Nazi occupation. He is currently writing a biography of Marshal Pétain and a study of Otto Abetz, the German ambassador to Paris in the second world war.

Clive Castaldo was educated at Ealing Grammar School and Trinity Hall, Cambridge. In 1985 he received his Ph.D. for a thesis 'La Foi Laïque and its Critics: Secular Humanism after the Dreyfus Affair'. He is currently head of history at an independent college in South Kensington, London.

Geoffrey Cubitt is currently a college lecturer in modern history at St. Catherine's College, Oxford. He is the author of articles both on French history and on conspiracy theories and is currently preparing a revised version of his Ph.D. thesis, on 'The Myth of a Jesuit Conspiracy in France, 1814–1880', for publication.

Brian Fitzpatrick lectures in history in the University of Ulster at Jordanstown, Northern Ireland. He is particularly interested in the French Right during the nineteenth century, and has published a number of articles on Ultraroyalism and Legitimism as well as a monograph, *Catholic Royalism in the Department of the Gard, 1814–1852* (Cambridge, 1983).

Ralph Gibson lectures in history and French studies at the University of Lancaster. He was educated at Adelaide, Oxford and Lyon. He is the author of *A Social History of French Catholicism, 1789–1914* (London, 1989).

W.D. Halls is a former senior member and onetime supernumerary fellow of St. Antony's College, Oxford. He has published books on French literature, history, culture and education and translated a number of French sociological and anthropological works.

David Hanley is Professor of European Studies at the University of Wales, Cardiff. His special interest is in French political parties. He has written *Keeping Left? Ceres and the French Socialist Party* (Manchester, 1986) and numerous articles in French and British journals.

Colin Heywood is lecturer in economic and social history at the University of Nottingham. He is the author of *Childhood in Nineteenth-Century France* (Cambridge, 1990) and of various articles concerned with the social and economic history of modern France. His current project is a history of the town of Troyes during the nineteenth century.

Michael Kelly is Professor of French at the University of Southampton. He has written extensively on the history of ideas in France and the relationship between literature, art and politics in the 1930s and 1940s. He is the author of books on Emmanuel Mounier and modern French Marxism.

James F. McMillan is senior lecturer in the history department at the University of York. Among his many publications are three books: *Housewife or Harlot: the Place of Women in French Society, 1870–1940* (Brighton, 1981); *Dreyfus to De Gaulle: Politics and Society in France, 1898–1969* (Cambridge, 1985); and *Napoleon III* (London, 1991). He is currently working on a social history of women in Europe between 1780 and 1945 and on a study of Catholicism and Nationalism in twentieth-century France.

Hazel Mills is a fellow of Fitzwilliam College, Cambridge, where she teaches modern European history. She is presently completing a D.Phil. and a book on Women and Catholicism in Provincial France during the first half of the nineteenth century.

Frank Tallett is a lecturer in history at the University of Reading. He has published articles on the religious history of *ancien régime* France. His book on *Armies and Society in Western Europe* is shortly to be published by Routledge.

List of Principal Abbreviations

A.A.	Archives Archiépiscopales
A.C.A.	Assemblée des Cardinaux et Archevêques
A.C.J.F.	Action Catholique de la Jeunesse Française
A.D.	Archives Départementales
A.M.	Archives Municipales
A.S.M. & C.F.	Association for the Study of Modern and Contemporary France
A.S.S.R.	Archives des Sciences Sociales des Religions
C.D.	Centre Démocrate
C.D.P.	Centre Démocratie et Progrès
C.D.S.	Centre des Démocrates Sociaux
C.D.U.	Christlich-Demokratische Union
C.F.T.C.	Confédération Française des Travailleurs Chrétiens
C.G.T.	Confédération Générale du Travail
C.N.I.	Centre National des Indépendants
C.N.R.	Conseil National de la Résistance
C.S.U.	Christlich-Soziale Union
D.R.A.C.	La Ligue des Droits des Religieux Anciens Combattants
F.E.N	Fédération de l'Education Nationale
F.G.D.S.	Fédération de la Gauche Démocrate et Socialiste
F.N.	Front National
I.P.S.A.	International Political Science Association
J.O.C.	Jeunesse Ouvrière Catholique
L.V.F.	Légion des Volontaires Français
M.R.P.	Mouvement Républicain Populaire
Ö.V.P.	Österreichische Volkspartei
P.C.F.	Parti Communiste Français
P.P.E.	Parti Populaire Européen
P.P.F.	Parti Populaire Français
P.R.	Parti Républicain
P.S.	Parti Socialiste
P.S.F.	Parti Socialiste Français

P.S.d.F.	Parti Socialiste de France
P.S.D.F.	Parti Socialiste Démocratie Français
R.I.	Républicains Indépendants
R.M.I.	Revenu Minimum d'Insertion
R.P.R.	Rassemblement pour la République
S.F.I.O.	Section Française de l'Internationale Ouvrière
S.N.I.	Syndicat National des Instituteurs
S.T.O.	Service du Travail Obligatoire
U.D.C.	Union du Centre
U.D.F.	Union pour la Démocratie Française

1

Dechristianizing France:
The Year II and the Revolutionary Experience

Frank Tallett

During the course of the year II much of France was subjected to a campaign of dechristianization, the aim of which was the eradication of Catholic religious practice, and Catholicism itself. The campaign, which was at its most intense in the winter and spring of 1793–94, but which began as early as the summer of 1793 in some regions,[1] and continued after the fall of Robespierre in August 1794 in a few areas, comprised a number of different activities. These ranged from the removal of plate, statues and other fittings from places of worship, the destruction of crosses, bells, shrines and other 'external signs of worship', the closure of churches, the enforced abdication and, occasionally, the marriage of constitutional priests, the substitution of a Revolutionary calendar for the

---

[1] Thus the *société populaire* at Nerondes destroyed statues of the saints and other religious emblems in the local church early in August 1793: M. Vovelle, *La révolution contre l'église: de la raison à l'être suprême* (Paris, 1988), pp. 237–8. It was typically the arrival of a *représentant-en-mission* in an area which triggered off a comprehensive campaign of dechristianization, although the more radical elements in the clubs might well have been pressing for harsher measures to be taken against Catholics and the constitutional church well before the *représentant*'s arrival. Cf. for example J. McManners, *The French Revolution and the Church* (London, 1969), pp. 87–8; Y-G. Paillard, 'Fanatiques et patriotes dans le Puy-de-Dôme: la déchristianisation', *Annales historiques de la révolution française*, 233 (1978), pp. 379–87.

Gregorian one, the alteration of personal and place names which had any ecclesiastical connotations to more suitably Revolutionary ones, through to the promotion of new cults, notably those of Reason and of the Supreme Being.

All historians of the Revolution, and certainly those with an interest in religious history, have described the dechristianizing campaign and sought to provide some analysis of it, yet in many respects it still remains, as Richard Cobb has suggested, 'one of the most baffling and least understood phenomena of the Great Terror'.[2] The origins of the movement, in particular, have been the subject of much acrimonious debate. There has been wide disagreement over the extent to which dechristianization was a genuinely popular movement, as opposed to one foisted on people by politicians at Paris and by the *représentants-en-mission*, for example; disagreement too over whether the campaign was born out of the exigencies of warfare, an 'expedient of national defence' as Aulard put it, whether it was the brain-child of corrupt politicians seeking to cover their tracks, or whether it emanated from long held and deeply entrenched anticlerical sentiments which predated the outbreak of the Revolution.[3] There has, however, been a much more substantial measure of agreement over the effects of dechristianization, and Cobb's assessment of the campaign as intense, destructive and irresistible in the short term, but without an important long term legacy, has been generally accepted.[4] In this essay I shall not attempt any discussion of the origins of dechristianization, but I will suggest that our view of the effects of the campaign need to be substantially revised: that in the short term

[2] R. Cobb, *Les armées révolutionnaires, instrument de la terreur dans les départements* (2 vols., Paris, 1963), vol. 2, p. 636.

[3] A. Aulard, *Le culte de la raison et de l'etre suprême* (Paris, 1892), esp. pp. 19–20; *Le christianisme et la révolution* (Paris, 1925), p. 115. A. Mathiez suggested that friends of Danton were responsible for initiating the campaign: *Robespierre et la déchristianisation* (Le Puy, 1909). A similar view is expressed in D. Guérin, *La lutte des classes sous la première république* (3 vols., Paris, 1968) vol. 1, p. 305. There is a good overview of the historiography on Revolutionary dechristianization in B. Plongeron, *Conscience religieuse en révolution* (Paris, 1969), ch. II.

[4] Cobb, *Les armées révolutionnaires*, pp. 660, 667; J. Solé, *La révolution en questions* (Paris, 1988), pp. 287–93. A different conclusion is to be found in J. de Viguerie, *Christianisme et révolution* (Paris, 1986), pp. 259–60. The different senses in which the term dechristianization has been interpreted are explored in B. Plongeron, 'La déchristianisation, a-t-elle une histoire?', *Sciences religieuses*, 16 (1987), pp. 205–20 and G. Le Bras, 'Déchristianisation, mot fallacieux', *Cahiers d'histoire*, ix (1964), pp. 92–97.

it encountered much more popular resistance, and was less successful than is often imagined; that its impact upon the religious sensibilities of French men and women needs to be assessed within the context of the Revolution as a whole; and that in the longer term its legacy was a very profound one.

The aspect of dechristianization which undoubtedly achieved least success was the attempt to substitute Revolutionary cults for Catholicism. It is true that during the nineteenth century a vague, moralizing deistic outlook, similar to that encapsulated in Robespierre's cult of the Supreme Being, remained dominant amongst many sections of the intellectual bourgeoisie; but during the Revolution neither this cult, nor those of Reason or of the *décadi*, achieved any substantial following, and all were short-lived. At Besançon, for example, by the beginning of 1794, members of the local *société* had begun to appear each *décadi* at the Temple of Reason to propound the virtues of the new cult, but there were no attenders outside the ranks of the *clubistes*, and even they were not wholehearted in their support. There was little response when the club at Quingey called upon its members to send their children to the local Temple of Reason for instruction, and parents withdrew their children from the school at Fontaine when the teacher refused to teach them the sign of the cross and instead sought to lecture them on the virtues of the Supreme Being.[5] In the Ille-et-Vilaine, admittedly a department where the *Montagnards* had little support during the Terror, Temples of Reason were to be found only at Rennes, Saint-Malo and Redon, and one local official subsequently painted a sorry picture of the *fêtes décadaires* in the department when he wrote that 'le petit nombre de citoyens qui s'y présentent, soit par aversion, soit par insouciance, les rendent extrêmement tristes'.[6] The Revolutionary cults' lack of popular appeal was hardly surprising. Not only were they being promoted by a régime which was widely detested, but they fulfilled none of the essential functions of *ancien régime* Catholicism which they were supposed to replace. Cold and abstract, the cults were based on reason, whereas life in the eighteenth century, and perhaps most especially during the Revolution, was an irrational and capricious lottery, in which food

---

[5] C. Brelot, 'Besançon révolutionnaire', *Annales littéraires de l'université de Besançon*, 77 (1966), p. 133; J. Sauzay, *Histoire de la persécution révolutionnaire dans le départment du Doubs de 1789 à 1801* (10 vols., Besançon, 1867–73), vol. 6, pp. 119–20; A.D. Doubs L2237, report of 2 December 1794.

[6] J. Delumeau (dir.), *Le diocèse de Rennes* (Paris, 1979), pp. 172–73.

shortage, accident, disease and death might strike in random fashion. Catholicism, with its rituals, festivities and therapeutic saints designed to protect people and crops against misfortune, ease the anguish of childbirth and provide solace in the hour of death, was closely attuned to popular needs, fears and expectations, while in contrast the cults brought no magic to assist with the grizzly business of living, and no consolation to the act of dying.

Attempts to enforce observance of the Revolutionary calendar, published in November 1793, by fining those who worked on the *décadi* for example, met with similar lack of success.[7] From every side reports indicated that the *décadi* was widely ignored and that Sunday continued to be treated as the day of rest. 'Seulement les patriotes chôment les décadis', noted the constitutional curé of Russey. *Représentant* Mallarmé reported in March 1794 that at Thionville, 'l'imbécile lambeau du papisme, le çi-devant dimanche, était religieusement observé, et le repos national avili'. His colleague Guyardin wrote from Privas in the same month that, 'L'empire de l'habitude . . . est tel qu'il maîtrise l'homme . . . la plupart des habitants restent encore dans l'oisiveté les jours qu'ils étaient accoutumés de chômer.'[8] One problem for the authorities in securing observance of the *décadi* was that it cut across established patterns of work, leisure and even courting rituals, yet to be successful it required the cooperation of a wide social spectrum: factory owners and shopkeepers had to close their premises on the same day, and masters give their apprentices and servants the same day off, for example. This broad measure of consent was simply not forthcoming.[9] Of course, the general popular refusal to work on a Sunday did not simply derive from habit as Guyardin implied, nor

[7] That the new calendar was envisaged primarily as a dechristianizing measure is clear from the remarks of Fabre d'Eglantine, cit. in A. Latreille, *L'eglise catholique et la révolution française* (2 vols., Paris, 1946–50), vol. 1, pp. 154–55.

[8] Abbé Monnier, *Monographie de Russey* (Besançon, 1912), p. 484; A. Aulard, *Recueil des actes du comité de salut public avec la correspondance officielle des représentants-en-mission et le registre du conseil exécutif provisoire* (26 vols., Paris, 1888–1923, cited hereafter as A.C.S.P.), vol. 12, p. 249, vol. 11, p. 685. For other complaints on this score see, for example, vol. 13, p. 607 (Niort), p. 226 (Meurthe et Moselle), vol. 15, p. 744 (Puy-de-Dôme).

[9] Hence the attempt by one *représentant* in Franche Comté, in his *arrêté* of September 1795, to make masters and directors of 'papeteries, forges, ateliers d'armes, usines quelconques' responsible for organizing the leisure days of their workers: Sauzay, *Histoire*, vol. 6, pp. 560–61. Cf. also the remarks in J. Leflon, *La crise revolutionnaire* (vol. 20 of *Histoire de l'église*, ed. A. Fliche and V. Martin, Paris, 1949), p. 117.

from respect for Sunday as a holy day, but sprang in part from that 'esprit de contrariété', which Revolutionary administrators were quite unable to overcome. As the mayor of a village in the Auxerre commented shortly after the Concordat:

> Or, un bon tiers des habitants ne veulent plus observer le dimanche. On reste au cabaret; on joue aux cartes pendant les messes et les vêpres; on fauche, on charroye . . . Mes concitoyens ont toujours tenu une conduite tout à fait opposée à tout ce que la loi prescrit. Pendant l'existence des jours de décadi tout le monde travaillait ce jour-là et célébrait religieusement le dimanche. Aujourd'hui que la décadi est supprimée, on ne veut plus reconnaître le dimanche.[10]

If there was a general refusal to observe the Revolutionary calendar, the policy promoting the use of new personal and place names was a yet more dismal failure. The records of the *état-civil* reveal that only sixty-two out of 593 children born at Poitiers during the year II received sound Republican names, and only twenty-six children born at Besançon in the same period, though some of the departmental administrators did adopt such names as Brutus, Fraternity, Endive and Brother Coriander; while a study of fifty-three towns and villages in the Midi, from Valence to Perpignan, suggests that the adoption of Republican names was rare, with the important exception of Montpellier, and that even here their use was extremely short lived.[11] The researches of Ann Debant show that in the department of the Gard some ninety-five communes, or about one quarter of the total number (a relatively high figure) changed their names during the course of the dechristianizing campaign, many following the arrival of the *représantant* Borie at Nîmes at the start of pluviôse year II. But twenty-seven of these communes simply replaced the word Saint in their name by Mont or Font (in the Lot Sen was often substituted for Saint), which hardly represented a whole-hearted commitment to principles of dechristianization. Only twenty-five communes, mainly the larger ones

---

[10] Cit. in H. Forestier, 'Le culte laïcal: un aspect spécifiquement auxerrois de la résistance des paroisses rurales à la déchristianisation', *Annales de Bourgogne*, xxiv (1952), pp. 106–7.

[11] R. Favreau (dir.), *Le diocèse de Poitiers* (Paris, 1988), p. 202; G. Gazier, 'Les prénoms révolutionnaires à Besançon en l'an II', *Mémoires de la société d'émulation du Doubs* (1923), p. 28; G. Cholvy, 'La révolution et la question religieuse: mutations et résistance culturelles', in *Religion, révolution, contre-révolution dans le Midi, 1789–1799*, Colloque International (Nîmes, 1989), p. 181, (cited hereafter as *Religion, révolution*).

with over 500 inhabitants, went in for a complete change of name and adopted a new, Republican, title. Moreover, the revision of place names in the department quickly began to generate administrative difficulties, and on 17 ventôse, at the very height of Borie's dechristianizing campaign, the Committee of Public Safety indicated that it wished to have the old and the new place names used alongside each other, 'afin d'éviter les entraves et les retards qui ont eu lieu jusqu'à présent'. Within a short space of time the old names alone had come back into usage, often without any formal deliberation on the matter by local officials, but simply as a matter of practice.[12]

Yet if those positive aspects of the dechristianizing campaign which sought to impose a Revolutionary culture by promoting a new calendar, new cults and new names achieved very little, the more negative aspects, which aimed for the destruction of the artefacts and edifices of the Catholic cult, achieved a greater degree of success. Driven on by the national emergency, which demanded precious metals to finance France's armies together with iron, copper and bronze to munition them, as well as by the urge to halt the administration of the sacraments by depriving the church of its consecrated vessels, the dechristianizers throughout France confiscated large quantities of metal plate, chalices, ciboria and candlesticks, as well as stripping churches of their altar rails, statues, books and clerical vestments, and seizing church bells, crosses, crucifixes and other 'external signs of worship'. The *représentant* Javogues reported to the Convention that he had collected more than 4,425 *marcs* of silver, a *marc* of gold and 649,643 *livres* in specie and a further 123,853 *livres* in *assignats* while in the Loire, much of it from churches. 3,300 kilos of silver and 276 tons of bronze were forwarded to Paris from churches in the diocese of Châlons; a great *autodafé* of wooden crosses and statues from the department of the Doubs on 20 prairial made a bonfire over 80 feet tall. In the Puy-de-Dôme, which experienced the attentions of Couthon, Maignet and Châteauneuf-Randon, amongst the most forceful proponents of dechristianization, metal weighing

---

[12] A. Debant, 'Changements de noms des communes du Gard en l'an II', in *Religion, révolution*, pp. 153–163, quote p. 158. Examples from the Lot can be found in A.D. Lot L.78. On the failure of the campaign to alter personal and place names in other regions see L. Perouas et al., *Léonard, Marie, Jean et les autres: les prénoms en Limousin depuis un millénaire* (Paris, 1984), pp. 133–45; P. Goujard, 'Sur la déchristianisation dans l'ouest', *Annales historiques de la révolution française*, 233 (1978), p. 438; M. Vovelle, *La révolution contre l'église*, pp. 69–72; and see the useful map in his *Religion et révolution, la déchristianisation de l'an II* (Paris, 1976), no. XVI, p. 160.

some 758,332 pounds from the churches of the department was collected, and a former curé could write in the year III that, 'Tous les clochers ont été mutilés ou renversés. Grand nombre d'églises paroissiales n'existent plus. On ne voit aucune marque extérieure de christianisme'.[13] In addition, the dechristianizers scored occasional propaganda successes, as at Besançon in March 1794, when members of the local *société* not only seized the 'Holy Shroud' (a local relic which had been exhibited annually to the faithful) but also proved conclusively that it was fraudulent.[14]

We should be careful not to exaggerate the extent of this anti-religious iconoclasm. Lengthy lists of crosses dismantled and precious metals collected were, after all, useful proofs of zeal, and the dechristianizers certainly had no incentive to underplay their achievements in this respect. In practice, the sheer organizational and logistical difficulties involved in the work of dechristianization played no small part in defeating their efforts. In the Lot an ambitious decree from *représentant* Bô began by ordering that bell towers be razed to the level of the rest of the building. Bô subsequently admitted that this was not always feasible and accepted that it was satisfactory merely to knock off the top of the steeple and replace any cross by some suitably Revolutionary symbol.[15] Where wholescale demolition of towers and churches was carried out this generally seems to have been done by civilian contractors interested in the salvage value of the stone. Even the removal of a large cross or bell from a church tower was a considerable undertaking, requiring ropes, ladders and a degree of expertise which members of the local *société* or *armée révolutionnaire* did not usually possess. The district of St. Hippolyte (Doubs) was obliged to hire a workman from Ornans to assist in August 1793: paid at the rate of 70 *livres* per cross he had earned 2,307 *livres* by December.[16] The going-rate for similar work around Châlons averaged 50 *livres*.[17] These extraordinarily

---

[13] C. Lucas, *The Structure of the Terror* (Oxford, 1973), p. 287; G. Clause (dir.), *Histoire du diocèse de Chalôns* (Paris, 1989), p. 132; J.-E. Laviron, *Annales de ce qui s'est passé de plus remarquable dans la ville de Besançon*, Bibliothèque Municipale de Besançon M.S. 1638, p. 42; Paillard, 'Fanatiques et patriotes', p. 396.

[14] Bibliothèque Municipale de Besançon, 241, 042, 'Procès-verbal de reconnaissance du prétendu suaire de Jésus'. The shroud was subsequently forwarded to the Convention, while copies of a pamphlet detailing the clerical fraud were widely circulated throughout the department: Sauzay, *Histoire*, vol. 6, p. 51.

[15] A.D. Lot L12, *arrêté* of 24 ventôse (14 March, 1794).

[16] Sauzay, *Histoire*, vol. 6, p. 494.

[17] Clause, *Histoire du diocèse de Chalôns*, p. 132.

high levels of pay reflected the difficulties of finding workmen able and prepared to tackle a job generally regarded as dangerous and sacrilegeous. The report from an official at Lanthenans was typical:

> Il avait proposé 60 livres à Lacour de l'Isle pour enlever [la croix] mais que celui-ci avait réfusé; qu'il avait adressé la même proposition à un couvreur de Mambouhans, mais que ce couvreur avait répondu qu'il ne voulait pas le faire, qu'il avait déjà enlevé d'autres croix, et qu'il s'en repentait.[18]

It was not altogether unsurprising, then, that *représentant* Bô, in a tacit acceptance of the limits of the possible, compromised and agreed that communes might retain a bell as a time-piece to make out the hours of the day, though its clapper had to be changed so as to distinguish the sound it gave out from that of the 'ecclesiastical' bell.[19]

Smaller ecclesiastical objects, floor-mounted crosses, crucifixes and statues were of course more vulnerable to the attentions of the members of the local *société* and *armée* though, as Mona Ozouf notes, a veneration for the dead often seems to have prevented them from extending their activities beyond the gates of the cemetery, where crosses grew 'like mushrooms after a storm'.[20] Even the most ardent dechristianizers could not be everywhere at once and the local officials and municipalities, upon whom the work of religious iconoclasm was devolved, often proved themselves very ineffective agents of dechristianization. As *représentant* Mallarmé complained from the Meuse and Moselle, 'les autorités elles-mêmes, ou faibles ou scélérates, s'étaient rendues l'organes des réclamations sacrilèges qui redemendaient le règne stupide et tyrranique de la théocratie et de l'encensoir'.[21] Here, as elsewhere, local councils used the excuse of bad weather, lack of workmen and confusion over the law to prevaricate endlessly.

The activities of the dechristianizers were equally thwarted, in whole or in part, by popular resistance, albeit of regionally varying intensity; an

---

[18] A.D. Doubs L2336, *agent* to *comité révolutionnaire* at Baume, December 1794.

[19] Above n. 15.

[20] M. Ozouf, *Festivals and the French Revolution* (London, 1988), p. 226. See too the comment from the commissioner of the Haut-Rhin: 'The graveyards of the rural cantons alone preserve some signs of religion on the tombs; veneration for the dead seemed to require this tolerance'.

[21] A.C.S.P., vol. 12, p. 738. Cf. also Lucas, *The Structure of the Terror*, p. 234.

aspect of the dechristianizing campaign which has not always received its due attention from historians.[22] Resistance took both passive and active forms. One local official ordered seven villagers from Vuillafans to assist with the removal of various *signes fanatiques*, but 'ayant attendu dans l'église depuis les 8 heures jusqu'à 10 heures, aucun des desdits ouvriers requis ne s'est présenté'.[23] Elsewhere workmen who presented themselves in a village were threatened, set upon and had their ladders stolen. Statues, pictures and sacred vessels were hidden by villagers, while objects of lesser value were left for the dechristianizers to take away. It was not so easy to hide a church bell (though it was just possible: gendarmes searching a village in the Yonne found one buried underground together with numerous church objects)[24] but handbells could be, and were, substituted instead. Villagers at Blanc (Indre) were unable to prevent the local *société* from holding meetings in the parish church, but they revenged themselves by mutilating the statue of Liberty which the *clubistes* had placed on the altar.[25] The inhabitants of Coulange-sur-Yonne almost succeeded in killing one member of a group of cavalrymen after an assault upon their crosses.[26] Elsewhere a veritable battle of the crosses developed around the crossroads, shrines and churches of France as villagers replaced overnight those lost during the day, while just as sedulously uprooting the tricolours and *arbres de liberté* which the dechristianizers left behind them.[27]

To what extent, and for how long, the dechristianizers succeeded in closing churches is less easy to establish. Barère's decree of 6 November effectively gave communes the right to do this, although one month later the Convention passed a further decree conferring religious freedom. Implementation of these laws in practice depended upon local circumstance, especially on the attitude of the *représentant*. Lejeune used the law on religious freedom to justify the closure of churches and removal of external signs of religion, arguing that Catholicism should not enjoy an advantage over other religion. Javogues ordered in December that all churches be converted into Temples of Reason or premises for the

---

[22] Plongeron, *Conscience religieuse*, pp. 118–19 and the pertinent comments in Vovelle, *La révolution contre l'église*, pp. 231–33 and pp. 230–55 generally.

[23] A.D. Doubs L1127, *procès-verbal* of commissioner.

[24] S. Desan, *The Revival of Religion during the French Revolution* (Michigan, 1988), pp. 257–8.

[25] A.C.S.P., vol. 11, p. 196.

[26] A.C.S.P., vol. 8, p. 237.

[27] Ozouf, *Festivals*, pp. 226–7.

clubs; whereas the violent and sanguinary ex-Oratorian Lebon gave a lower priority to the closure of churches than to the abdication and marriage of the clergy.[28] Once again there was some popular resistance. Guyardin wrote from Privas in March 1794 that, 'Il s'est formé dans des communes dont les églises étaient fermées depuis un, deux ou trois mois, des rassemblements qui sont portés en tumulte vers les officiers municipaux pour faire rouvrir les églises'.[29] But few of France's 40,000 or so churches were open for Easter communion in 1794; an uncertain number had anyway been closed down, sold off, demolished or converted into warehouses or factories long before this, and many, even if not badly damaged, were not to open again until 1795 or 1796.

There is however no doubt about the success of the dechristianizers' attack upon the constitutional church: the state had created it, and the state could destroy it. Unlike the attack upon the objects of the *culte* there was no popular resistance to this assault on the representative of the faith, just as there had been no popular uprising to prevent the loss of the refractory clergy earlier on. Threatened with death (occasionally), arrest, imprisonment, conscription or the loss of their income (more usually), perhaps 20,000 constitutional priests abdicated and handed over their letters of ordination. An unknown number of others simply ceased their clerical functions; and between 6,000 and 9,000 married. (It was surely a back-handed tribute to the success of the eighteenth-century French church in establishing clerical celibacy as a defining characteristic of the priesthood that marriage was taken as the ultimate proof of the rejection of clerical status). The constitutional church simply bled to death during the year II.[30]

To be sure, a few of these men sought to conduct a clandestine ministry after their abdication: a couple were denounced for doing so

[28] A.D. Doubs L523, *arrêté* of 1 messidor (19 June 1794); Lucas, *The Structure of the Terror*, p. 288; L. Jacob, *Joseph Lebon* (Paris, 1932), p. 155. For Albitte's defence of his interpretation of the decree on the *liberté des cultes*, cf. A.C.S.P., vol. 11, pp. 722–23.

[29] A.C.S.P., vol. 11, p. 684. For similar examples of resistance, albeit unsuccessful, in the Seine-et-Marne cf. vol. 8, pp. 424–5.

[30] On the numbers of abdications see P. de la Gorce, *Histoire religieuse de la révolution française* (5 vols., Paris, 1923–25), vol. 3, pp. 361–63; Vovelle, *Religion et révolution*, p. 19. For clerical marriages: J. Godel, *La reconstruction concordataire dans le diocèse de Grenoble après la révolution, 1802–1809* (Grenoble, 1968), p. 276. Grégoire, keen to minimize the number, puts it at 2,000, a figure repeated by Latreille: J. Leflon, *M. Emery. L'église d'ancien régime et la révolution* (2 vols., Paris, 1944–7), vol., 1, p. 388 and Latreille, *L'eglise catholique*, vol. 1, p. 165.

in the Doubs by midwives, traditional enemies of the clergy.[31] But the success of the dechristianizing campaign in this respect left most people in France without the services of a constitutional priest; indeed it left them without the services of a priest at all. The refractory clergy had emigrated in large numbers and, since August 1792, any non-juror found in France faced the guillotine or deportation to French Guiana. Some, it is true, stayed behind in hiding. One estimate puts their numbers at 400 in the Orne, but there were barely 100 in the Sarthe, hardly more than a dozen in the Aude, and only a handful existed in the Haut-Saône, Jura and Doubs.[32] A few endeavoured to make their way back into these frontier departments from their refuge in Switzerland, but they were pathetically ill-prepared and easily apprehended.[33] Elsewhere refractory clerics either were hunted down and reduced to a miserable fugitive existence, or they fled for their own safety during the year II, in face of the ruthless determination of the dechristianizers to rid France of what Albitte called 'la vermine sacerdotale'.[34]

The implications of the loss of a priesthood were profound and can hardly be overstressed. It meant the cessation of regular confession: indeed, for those people who doubted the power of a constitutional priest to deliver absolution and believed that confession to him was in itself a sin (common themes in the battle waged by the refractories against the juring clergy), the habit of confession had been broken well before the dechristianizing campaign. It meant too that there was no priest to baptize the new-born infant or to perform the last rites. Some people had ceased to have recourse to a priest to perform this function before the year II, not wishing to avail themselves of the services of a juror; in a few instances, constitutional priests had refused to perform the last rites. Raymond Francomie of Goujounac (Lot) complained to the local municipality in August 1792 that the priest had refused to bury his dead father on the grounds that the old man had not attended the priest's services, only to be told that he should dispose of his father himself, using his garden if

---

[31] A.D.Doubs L2884, *Vedette* newspaper, 2 messidor.

[32] R. and S. Pillorget, *Les messes clandestines en France entre 1793 et 1802* (Université d'Angers, Centre de Recherches d'Histoire Religieuse et d'Histoire des Idées, 1979), p. 156.

[33] One captured priest, for example, had decided that, 'je ne portasse point d'argent avec moi. Je serais par là entièrement sous la main de Providence pour tous mes besoins': cit. J. Panier, 'L'abbé Ann-Pierre Capon', *Mémoires de l'académie de Besançon* (1936), p. 128.

[34] A.C.S.P., vol. 10, p. 561.

necessary.[35] Yet such cases were rare and in general the constitutional priest was available at least as a long-stop to confess, baptize and bury the dead. All this was changed in the year II. Just as importantly, the dechristianizing campaign meant the ending of routine, regular public worship. Refractories, of course, had held clandestine masses from the summer of 1792 onwards and the few priests who remained in France in the year II endeavoured to continue doing so, albeit with increasing difficulty. These were perforce irregular, hole-in-the-corner affairs, conducted in woods and barns, available only to a very few, and conducted without the bells, processions and vestments which normally accompanied the ceremony. Finally it meant the definitive ending of any form of clerical instruction of the laity either through the Sunday sermon, at the end of mass, or in the catechism classes for the young which had been patchily maintained since 1791. The shortage of clerics after 1794 meant that in the worst case a whole cohort which came to seven or eight years of age in 1793 missed out on religious teaching and developed without the formal inculcation of a Catholic culture. Thus the bishop of Montpellier in 1807 found 'un grand nombre d'enfants, même d'un certain âge, qui ne savaient pas les vérités les plus essentielles . . . ni presque aucune prière'.[36]

As the bishop suggested, in the long-term the effects of all this could be significant. The *ancien régime* traditions of near universal, automatic religious practice, or what John McManners has referred to in a typically elegant phrase as 'the lethargical mystique of popular conformity, which made the *ancien régime* church appear all embracing and so powerful',[37] had been irrevocably shattered; and many who lost the habit of routine religious observance during the Revolution never regained it. Cardinal Consalvi, on his way to negotiate the Concordat, described the French as, 'indifférent dans sa plus grande partie: il est entièrement dans les villes, en partie dans les compagnes',[38] while Bishop Dupanloup, in a famous phrase, characterized the France of 1869 as 'une société déchristianisée'.[39] Such pessimistic assessments of religious detachment in the nineteenth century, are lent some support by the proxy indicators we have of gregarious

---

[35] A.D. Lot L7, *procès-verbal* of department, 9 August 1792.

[36] Cited in G. Cholvy and Y.-M. Hilaire, *Histoire religieuse de la France contemporaine* (3 vols., Toulouse, 1985–88), vol. 1, p. 44.

[37] McManners, *French Revolution and the Church*, p. 105.

[38] Cited in Cholvy and Hilaire, *Histoire religieuse*, vol. 1, p. 12.

[39] Cited in J. McManners, *Death and the Enlightenment* (Oxford, 1985), p. 440.

conformity in religious practice, such as the failure to respect the *temps clos* for marriages between Easter and Advent and the reduced numbers who attended Sunday mass and took the Easter communion. Only four-fifths of parishioners in the diocese of Soissons and two-thirds in the diocese of Tours performed the Easter duties during the First Empire, while in the diocese of Versailles in the mid 1830s only 16.6 per cent attended mass and a mere 6.5 per cent took Easter communion.[40] By mid-century baptism and marriage in church and a religious burial were pretty well universally established once more, with the important exception of Paris, but baptisms might be long delayed, and churchmen were insistent upon the general loss of the confessional habit.[41] To be sure, situating the effects of the Revolution in the *longue durée* of the reduction of religious fervour in France is fraught with difficulties and it would be wrong to blame the Revolution for everything. Matters were not helped in the early nineteenth century by the poor condition of the post-Concordat church, the shortage of priests (chronic in certain areas) and the continuing schism between refractories and the *petite église*. There were also new factors in the nineteenth century, not least of all social change and industrialization, making for a decline in religiosity.[42] Nevertheless, there seems little doubt that the 1790s, and the year II in particular, marked 'the end of a world in which obedience to religion went unquestioned and the advent of a world in which ever broader segments of the population drifted into religious indifference'.[43]

In coming to this overall assessment, we need of course to bear in mind that the dechristianizing campaign had soil of varying fertility on which to work. The various pieces of evidence for a reduction in

[40] R. Gibson, *A Social History of French Catholicism, 1789–1914* (London, 1989), pp. 160, 229 and table 6.5 on pp. 174–76. On marriage in the 'closed season' see the contributions in *Voies nouvelles pour l'histoire de la révolution française*, Commission d'histoire économique et sociale de la révolution française (Paris, 1978), pp. 59–112, esp. p. 77.

[41] Ibid., pp. 163–65. Cf. also Clause, *Diocèse de Chalôns*, pp. 152, 160–61; Plongeron, *Conscience religieuse*, p. 169; E. Sevrin, 'La pratique des sacrements et des observances au diocèse de Chartres sous l'épiscopat de Mgr. Clausel de Montals', *Revue d'histoire de l'église de France*, xxv (1939), pp 316–44. On delayed baptism: F. Charpin, *Pratique religieuse et formation d'une grande ville: Marseille 1806–1958* (Paris, 1964), ch. 5.

[42] Cholvy and Hilaire, *Histoire religieuse* vol I, pp. 13ff; R. Rémond, 'The Problem of dechristianization: The Present Position and Some Recent French Studies', *Concilium*, vii (1965), p. 79.

[43] F. Furet and M. Ozouf, *A Critical Dictionary of the French Revolution* (London, 1989), p. 21.

religious fervour in the four decades before 1789 – the decline in clerical vocations, the decline in testamentary evocations of saints, requests for masses and religious bequests, the spread of contraceptive practices and (ironically) the rise in illegitimacy rates, the dwindling proportion of religious books sold and so on – are open to interpretation. At Although the existence of such a decline is now generally accepted, it occurred in some areas rather than others. It is not possible to draw up a religious map of eighteenth-century France with the same precision as for the nineteenth and twentieth centuries, but areas of religious fervour, such as the extreme west, the east and Flanders, nevertheless stand in contrast to a relatively irreligious north and centre block, including Champagne, the western part of Burgundy, the Auvergne and Limousin and the area to the south-east of Paris. The Midi presented a more variegated pattern, while overall religious fervour was more marked in the countryside than in the towns of *ancien régime* France.[44] Nor was the dechristianizing campaign of uniform geographical intensity. It was most marked in those departments where the *représentant* was a committed dechristianizer, and where an *armée revolutionnaire* was active and regarded dechristianization as a chief concern: the Paris region, the Aisne, Yonne, Nièvre and Cher for example.[45] Even within a department the impact was localized. Much depended on the existence of a large and active *société populaire* in the vicinity, but generally it was the larger urban centres which were most severely affected. To endeavour to superimpose a map of the dechristianizing campaign onto a map of eighteenth-century religious practice in any detailed way is a task far outside the scope of this essay, even if it could be done given the present gaps in our knowledge. What does seem clear is that the impact of dechristianization was greatest in the larger urban centres and in those geographical regions where religious fervour was already weakest, such as the Limousin and parts of Burgundy. Conversely, it had least impact in those areas where religious attachment had proved resistant to erosion under the *ancien régime*. In this way Revolutionary dechristianization served to accentuate sharply pre-existing regional differences in levels of religious

---

[44] O. Hufton, 'The French Church', in W. Callaghan and D. Higgs (eds.), *Church and Society in Catholic Europe of the Eighteenth Century* (Cambridge, 1979), p. 25; J. Quéniart, *Les hommes, l'église et dieu dans la France du XVIIIe siècle* (Paris, 1978), pp. 218–21.

[45] Cobb, *Les armées révolutionnaires*, vol. 2, pp. 641–44, 666 ff; M. Reinhard, *Histoire de l'Ile-de-France et de Paris* (Toulouse, 1971), pp. 394ff.

practice and gave shape to the religious geography of nineteenth-century France.[46]

Revolutionary dechristianization had other, no less important, consequences. The absence of a clerical hierarchy during the 1790s, and in particular the virtual elimination of a priesthood in the year II, generated a need, and made room for, much greater lay activity in religious matters. Insofar as religious instruction of the young was carried on in 1793–94 and subsequently, for example, it was done in the home. Parents might read aloud to the children from a work of devotional literature, and a recitation of the rosary became a feature of the *veillées* those evening get-togethers in a particular cottage for family and neighbours which had caused such concern to the parish clergy before 1789 because of the dangerous opportunities they presented for liaisons between the sexes.[47] Printers responded to the demand for religious literature for domestic consumption and, especially in the post-Thermidorean period, produced a flood of brochures and pamphlets, run off on fragile paper and sold by itinerant hawkers. Evidence, from the Midi at least, suggests that standing alongside and perhaps supplanting the traditional catechisms and works of devotion was a literature which blended together folklore, myth and legend with stories of the saints, miracles and semi-magical remedies.[48] This type of literature reflected a popular approach to religion, characterized by a fondness for the cult of the saints, an attachment to local shrines and grottoes and a belief in the therapeutic qualities of religious rites and

[46] For the religious geography of nineteenth-century France see Cholvy and Hilaire, *Histoire religieuse* vol 1, ch. 9; F. Boulard and Y.-M. Hilaire, *Matériaux pour l'histoire religieuse du peuple français XIX-XXe siècles* (2 vols., Paris, 1982 and 1987); Boulard's famous map is reprinted in G. le Bras, *Etudes de sociologie religieuse* (2 vols., Paris), vol. 2, pp. 324–25. The differing regional impact of dechristianization and its relationship to existing levels of religious fervour can be traced in Vovelle, *Religion et révolution*, esp. the conclusion; his, 'Essai de cartographie de la déchristianisation sous la révolution française', *Annales du Midi*, lxxvci (1964), pp. 529–42; and notably his, *La révolution contre l'église*, 233–36, 262–66, and maps pp. 285, 287–89. Cf. also Goujard, 'Sur la déchristianisation', p. 448; T. Tackett, *Priest and Parish in Eighteenth-Century France* (Princeton, 1977), pp. 295–96.

[47] O. Hufton, 'The Reconstruction of a Church, 1796–1801', in G. Lewis and C. Lucas, (eds.), *Beyond the Terror: Essays in French Regional History, 1794–1815* (Cambridge, 1983), pp. 30, 32.

[48] R. Dartevelle, 'Stratégie missionaire et "rechristianisation" pendant le directoire', *Religion, révolution*, p. 142.

festivals, which the eighteenth-century clergy had struggled to suppress or reform.

The freedom from clerical tutelage during the 1790s permitted a reassertion of popular forms of religious practice. Indeed, to the resurrected pantheon of traditional thaumaturgic saints, such as Julien, Eloi and Fiacre, were added new ones. In the west, for instance, victims of Revolutionary violence, both *bleus* and *blancs*, received a popular canonization and their places of martyrdom became shrines. In the forest of La Guerche the *chêne de la vierge* where a young girl had been massacred in 1793 became a place of pilgrimage. The nearby grave of the *chouan* Houillot developed into a rendezvous for those wishing to be cured of a fever, though the most renowned place of pilgrimage in this area was the *tombe de la fille* in the forest of Teillay, where the daughter of a local patriot had been horrifically murdered (she lingered on for three days), a site which was credited with a wide range of thaumaturgic powers in respect of illness and female infertility.[49] A number of clerics in the late 1790s and early 1800s deplored what they quite properly regarded as this reversion to primitive pagan and superstitious practices. Even Revolutionary opponents of Catholicism noted with a mixture of bewilderment, contempt and glee this resurgence of rituals which the church had officially condemned. 'The follies of the carnival have reappeared with the mass', commented the Republican newspaper *L'Observateur* in 1800. 'They have perhaps never started so early, nor been so noisy . . . How is it possible to reconcile this attachment of some people to pagan institutions with their apparent zeal for a religion which has always outlawed them?'[50] The nineteenth-century church equally deplored the resurgence of gross and superstitious elements in popular religious practice. But it accepted that practice of this kind was better than no practice at all, and sought to arrive at an accommodation with it, albeit whilst attempting to put pilgrimages and processions once more under clerical tutelage, stripping out the most flagrantly abusive practices, and

[49] M. Lagrée, 'Piété populaire et révolution en Bretagne: l'exemple des canonisations spontanées (1793–1815)', *Voies nouvelles pour l'histoire de la révolution française* (Colloque Mathiez-Lefebvre, Paris, 1978), pp. 265–79; Desan *Revival*, pp. 281 ff; E. Audard, *Actes des martyrs et des confesseurs de la foi pendant la révolution* (2 vols., Tours, 1916–20). See also Cholvy and Hilaire, *Histoire religieuse* pp. 23 ff.

[50] Cited in Desan, *Revival*, p. 281. Interestingly, the incentive for the inhabitants of Montesquieu to reclaim their bell was the need for protection against 'un orage affreux mêlé de grêle': A.D. Lot L280, délibérations of canton of Maissac, 18 floréal IV.

promoting officially approved cults, of which the Marian devotion is the best known.[51]

However, the most striking example of the laicization of religion during the Revolution came not with the reassertion of popular practices of which the church disapproved, but in the novel development of a *culte laïque* in which laymen and women began to take over the functions of the priest. It is not so surprising that in the absence of a priesthood midwives should have baptized new-born infants: the authority to do so in respect of the sickly child on the verge of death had always been granted them by the eighteenth-century church. Much more remarkable was the initiative taken by the laity in holding services over which a priest would normally have presided. Laymen were to be found burying the dead, marrying couples and giving benedictions. Most remarkable of all was the holding of lay-led masses. Beginning during the general absence of a priesthood during the year II, assemblies were held at which prayers, psalms, the litany and the offices for the dead were recited, but these first fitful and rudimentary assemblies quickly took on a more developed form with the establishment of *messes blanches*, reasonable simulations of the mass at which a layman rather than a priest officiated. Once believed to have been isolated phenomenon, and restricted to areas of weak religious fervour,[52] these white masses are now known to have been widespread and numerous. They were found in areas of varying religious fervour, including Franche Comté and Alsace, the Lyonnais, the Aveyron and the Dordogne.[53] The lay person who officiated at these 'white masses' was frequently the schoolmaster (indeed the assemblies were referred to in the Ardèche as *messes de maître d'école*[54] or more infrequently the sacristan. This was hardly surprising, for both these individuals had been closely involved with the priest in the performance of his duties under the *ancien régime*. Since a frequent function of the schoolmaster was to second

---

[51] Gibson, *Social History*, ch. 5.

[52] La Gorce, *Histoire religieuse*, vol. 3, p. 427.

[53] In addition to works cited below, examples of white masses can be found in P. Pommerade, *La séparation de l'église et de l'état en Périgord* (Perigueux, 1976), p. 144; E. Bouchez, *Le clergé rémois pendant la révolution* (Paris, 1913), p. 548; P. Flament, 'Recherches sur le ministère clandestin', *Bulletin principal de la société historique et archéologique de l'Orne*, xc (1972), pp. 45–74., Examples of other types of lay-led services can be found in Desan, *Revival*, p. 124; A.D.Doubs L2637, *tribunal criminel*, trial of Linoir, ventôse VI.

[54] C. Jolivet, *La révolution dans l'Ardèche, 1788–1795* (Largentières, 1930), p. 533.

the *curé* during mass he was used to playing a prominent part in religious services and would probably know them off by heart. At the very least he was literate and could conduct a service using the necessary texts. Other laymen also featured as leaders of these 'white masses': at Préhy it was a roof thatcher who officiated; in the winter of 1794 two coal workers and a *cultivatuer*, a former royal official, François Angot led the worship at Rotours in Normandy; and there are very occasional references to women, as at Villars-sous-Chalamont where 'les chefs de ces rassemblements étaient notamment un ex-domestique des carmes, et une femme dite la Babet'.[55] These lay leaders appear to have come from the lower social ranks, rather than from the professional classes, in part perhaps because as lay ministers such people gained an authority and prestige from which they had been excluded by their social status under the *ancien régime*.

How far did the laity go in taking over the priest's functions during these 'white masses'? The question is not easy to answer, not least of all because official reports were often imprecise on the exact form of the *culte*. Thus the *représentant* Isoré wrote in February 1794 of 'une troupe de pédants, qu'on nomme *magisters* dans les campagnes; ces messieurs succèdent aux curés, et braillent tous les dimanches et fêtes catholiques dans les églises où ils rassemblent les habitants'.[56] Such evidence as there is suggests that the form of the mass was replicated as closely as possible: where possible it was held in church, bells were rung, with the lay minister singing the psalms, intoning the *Te Deum*, reciting the prayers from the *introit* to the benediction, and making all the priestly gestures. Some, like the schoolmaster at Ouanne, donned clerical garb.[57] It was rare, albeit not unknown, for a lay minister actually to consecrate the bread and the wine, though time might be left for the Host to be venerated, or some other ritual gesture substituted. At Doudeville (Seine Inférieure) an official from the commune who led the mass elevated a crucifix in place of the Host, whilst reciting the *O Salutaris*.[58] In short, as at Rotours where Angot recited the offices 'suivant le rit des prêtres catholiques romains, à l'exception de ce qu'il leur dit être réservé', only that part of the mass which

---

[55] Desan, *Revival*, p. 130; L. Duval, 'La messe de M. des Rotours', *Bulletin de la société historique et archéologique de l'Orne*, xxviii (1909), pp. 156–204; A.D. Doubs L226, commissionaire's report, 10 germinal.

[56] A.C.S.P., vol. 10 p. 647.

[57] Forestier, 'Le culte laïcal', p. 108.

[58] C. Ledré, *Le culte caché sous la révolution: les missions de l'abbé Linsolas* (Paris, 1949), p. 98; Desan, *Revival*, p. 124.

was most specifically reserved to the clergy was not generally performed by the lay minister.[59]

What was the significance of the holding of lay-led masses during the Revolution? On the one hand they represent a further instance of popular resistance to the dechristianizing campaign, and as such they clearly had their origins in the 'priest famine' of the year II. Yet they were not merely a response to the shortage of priests, but instead were a manifestation of a more profound laïcization of religion, as is evidenced by the fact that they continued to be held after the ending of the Terror and right through the period of the Directory, when priests were only intermittently scarce. They became especially frequent once again in the aftermath of the *coup* of fructidor in 1797, which initiated a period of draconian persecution of the clergy and reduced the numbers of available priests, although clerical numbers then were never reduced to the minimal levels of the year II. Priests could be sought out, albeit with some difficulty, but the *messes blanches* continued to take place.[60] Moreover they were conducted with a frequency and on a scale which in itself argues that they were more than a mere substitute for a scarce ecclesiastical personnel. One *commissaire* reported in September 1797 that they were attended by the majority of the inhabitants of his canton; in the nearby canton of L'Abergement they were held in every commune with the exception of two; such examples could be multiplied.[61]

The readiness of the laity to develop a cult in which the clergy was marginalized in this way becomes more easily comprehensible if we recognize that the Revolution not only deprived it of a priesthood, but also devalued the authority of the priest. One of the achievements of the eighteenth-century church had been the creation of a professional, united and uniform body of parish clergy. The Revolution undid much of that. Confronted by the oath to the Civil Constitution, the clergy revealed itself to be divided and in disarray: some priests swore the oath, and formed the constitutional church; others refused; a number retracted; many simply dithered. There followed a period of increasingly bitter rivalry between constitutional and non-juring clerics: each denounced the validity of the other's sacraments and even threatened damnation to the laity who received them. There were sordid and unedifying scenes as rival clerics

---

59 Duval, 'La messe de M. des Rotours', p. 198.

60 Hufton, 'The Reconstruction of a Church', pp. 48 ff. Desan, *Revival*, pp. 123.

61 A.D. Doubs L234, Jeanmaine's report vendémiaire VI; L226 report for brumaire VI.

hid church keys, barricaded themselves in the *presbytère*, stole each others' vestments, disrupted an opponent's services, occasionally came to blows, and squabbled endlessly over who was to maintain the parish register of births, marriages and deaths, with the result that in September 1792 the state gave this prestigious job to the municipalities, turned marriage into a civil contract and allowed divorce. A further series of oaths demanded of the clergy who remained in France produced yet more divisions in their ranks. A more serious blow to clerical prestige came with the dechristianizing campaign of the year II in which constitutional priests were humiliated and made to hand over their letters of ordination. They were sometimes obliged to marry or go through a buffoon ceremony of divorce from their breviaries whilst denouncing their calling and the Catholic religion as charlatanism and a sham. After thermidor, throughout the Directory and even following the Concordat in 1801, the accumulated hatred and mistrust which had developed between the rival clergies continued to manifest itself (despite some abortive attempts at reconciliation), often in the most violent fashion.[62] In these circumstances, it is not perhaps so surprising that many who held to their religious beliefs during the Revolution were nevertheless prepared to contemplate a cult in which the priest had a more restricted role than previously. As Peter Jones has suggested, 'By destroying the edifice of ecclesiastical authority the Revolution revealed the foundation of a quasi-autonomous lay religion'.[63]

The church itself was not wholly opposed to the holding of lay assemblies for certain purposes, and even encouraged them: Pope Pius VI himself granted an indulgence to laymen who prayed together in the half-hour before midday for the peace of France and of the church; Verdier, vicar-general in the diocese of Autun, encouraged lay assemblies in church for the recitation of prayers; and in the diocese of Lyon the Abbé Linsolas appointed *chefs de paroisse* to help assemble the faithful for prayer and to

[62] Cf. for example the tone taken against the constitutional clergy in the sermons of Maurice Augier, *professeur* of the seminary at Riez: Dartevelle, 'Stratégie missionaire', pp. 138–39. On this theme, and the damage done to the clergy by the dechristianizing campaign, Hufton, 'The Reconstruction of a Church', pp. 33, 45 ff.

[63] P.M. Jones, 'Quelques formes élémentaires de la vie religieuse dans la France rurale (fin XVIIIe et XIXe siècles)', *Annales E.S.C.*, 42 (1987), p. 95 (my trans.). Note too the perceptive comment by a member of Napoleon's *Conseil d'état*, 'The people would have preferred church bells without priests to priests without bells': A. Dansette, *A Religious History of Modern France* (2 vols., London, 1961), vol. 1, p. 114.

hear clerically-led clandestine services.[64] But the *messes blanches* went far beyond any of this and caused considerable disquiet amongst the clergy: in 1795 Viart, vicar-general of the *emigré* Bishop Cicé, reacted violently to what he called the 'mimicry of priests'. A priest in hiding in Franche-Comté complained of 'ces particuliers qui aiment faire M. le curé' and here the *messes blanches* were condemned as heresy. From the diocese of Lyon a correspondent of Bishop Marbeuf wrote: 'Il se forme parmi nous une espèce de culte dont je commence à craindre les suites. Ces laïcs jaloux de présider, de charmer par leurs chants semblent oublier la nécessité du ministre . . . J'ai déjà trouvé quelques-uns de ces chefs d'assemblées dans les églises à qui la tête a tourné. Ils veulent réformer, faire les curés . . . Le peuple s'accoutume à cet extérieur, à ces simulacres du culte; il s'accoutume à se passer de mitres.'[65]

Such fears about the displacement of the priest from his central position in the religious process and the long-term consequences of the development of a *culte laïque* proved to be not without foundation. 'White masses' continued to be celebrated after the signing of the Concordat and well into the nineteenth century. In the Marne, for instance, the prefect unsuccessfully intervened in an attempt to prohibit them in 1803 on the grounds that they drew more people than the parish priests. A threat of excommunication in the same year from Mgr. de la Tour-du-Pin, the bishop of Troyes, against laymen who wore surplices in church, sang the prayers of the mass, or performed any ecclesiastical function in the absence of a priest, was similarly without effect; lay cults persisted here until at least the late 1820s and possibly beyond.[66] Even in the Doubs, where religious fervour remained strong – the 300 strong village of Foucherans was overrun by 3,000 pilgrims early in the nineteenth century, who flocked to the *sanctuaire* of Saint-Maximin – the curé of Rognon could deplore the fact that 'some individuals here say that they get along very nicely without curés'.[67] Communities were prepared to use the threat of the reestablishment of a *culte laïque* in their dealings with the church hierarchy: the inhabitants

[64] Pillorget, 'Les messes clandestines', p. 157; Desan, *Revival*, p. 114.

[65] Desan, *Revival*, p. 153; A.D. Doubs L2617, intercepted letter, dated 18 February 1798; Ledré, *Le culte caché*, pp. 228–29.

[66] G. Clause, *Le département de la Marne sous le consulat et l'empire* (3 vols, Thèse d'Etat, Paris, 1974), vol. 2, pp. 561–63; H. Forestier, 'Le culte laïcal dans l'Yonne (1795–1828)', pp. 237–44, as cited in Desan, *Revival*, p. 169–97. See also C. Ledré, *Le Cardinal Cambacérès* (Paris, n.d.), p. 98 for their persistence in the diocese of Rouen.

[67] M. Rey (dir.), *Les diocèses de Besançon et de Sainte Claude* (Paris, 1977), p. 155.

of L'Hôpital, who in 1842 asked the bishop of Saint-Flour to approve the holding of routine religious services in their local chapel, posed the bishop a tricky problem, for the sub-text of their request was that if approval was not forthcoming they would stage the services themselves. Nor were such threats idle ones: one group of inhabitants in the Saint-Affrique district simply continued meeting in their church and holding 'white masses' after their parish was disestablished and their priest withdrawn; the inhabitants of Auxillac in the Lozère similarly resorted to the holding of lay assemblies after 1820 when their long-held hopes for separate parish status were frustrated.[68] Even so, we should not exaggerate the extent to which the *culte laïque* persisted after the Revolution. 'White masses' were a relatively infrequent phenomenon. But neither should we minimize the persistence of lay independence of a clerical hierarchy during the nineteenth century, of which the 'white mass' was but one manifestation, albeit the most striking. As we have already noted, this increased laicization is also to be seen in the continued attachment to popular forms of religious practice to the relative neglect of confession and absolution. It was similarly apparent in a reluctance to provide financial support for the clergy. When a project was floated in the diocese of Poitiers for parishes to provide supplementary funds for the support of their ministers a number refused outright, others paid up so reluctantly that the plan had to be abandoned after two years. An official report in 1830 on Franche Comté recommended that one way of restoring respect for the parish clergy was to make them entirely financially independent of their parishioners: 'Il est peu convenable, on pourrait dire même peu décent, que le ministre respectable de la religion se trouve forcé de solliciter, souvent sans succès et avec des humiliations, des secours qu'il devrait être en état d'accorder lui-même'.[69] There is little doubt that a laicization of religion must be numbered as one of the enduring effects of the Revolution.

One aspect of lay activity in religious matters during the 1790s which merits further consideration is the role played by women. A feature of the nineteenth century, which has frequently been remarked on by historians, was the marked feminization of religion. The major pilgrimages attracted far more women than men. Women were more assiduous in their attendance at

[68] Jones, 'Quelques formes élémentaires', pp. 96–97; and his 'Parish, Seigneurie and the Community of Inhabitants in Southern Central France', *Past and Present*, 91 (1981), p. 99.

[69] Favreau, *Poitiers*, p. 211; M. Pigallet, *Inventaire des documents . . . dans les archives du Doubs* (Paris, 1913), 1, p. 157.

mass, and took communion in greater numbers and more frequently than men; in 1805 the prefect at Rouen, for example, reported that one woman in four but only one man in fifty took the sacrament. And it was amongst the women's orders that growth was most spectacular. Four hundred female *congrégations* were created between 1800 and 1880, and nearly one quarter of a million women became novices in this period.[70] The reasons for this sexual dimorphism in religious matters are complex and as yet only partly understood, although it is clear that it relates in part to developments in the nineteenth century. For instance, the increasing interest which the nineteenth-century clergy took in contraceptive practices and, in particular, their censuring of males who practised *coitus interruptus*, led to many men abandoning not just confession and communion but religious practice altogether in disgust at what they regarded as a prurient and unjustified intrusion into their private lives.[71] Yet the roots of this gender dichotomy in religious matters extend back into the eighteenth century and even before. During the *ancien régime* women were already beginning to dominate the membership of the devotional confraternities; the decline in monastic recruitment was much less pronounced with regard to the female orders than it was amongst their male counterparts. There is also evidence that rural women were more likely to give money to the church and to charity than men and it appears that women bucked the general trend with regard to the drop in the purchase of religious books in the late eighteenth century. An experienced and much respected cleric, the Abbé Pochard, noted in his manual of advice for confessors, published in 1772, that 'Les personnes de l'autre sexe viennent plus facilement au confessional que les hommes,' thus confirming that gender differences with regard to the uptake of the sacraments were not confined to the nineteenth century.[72]

---

[70] J.P. Chaline, *les bourgeois de Rouen: une élite urbaine au XIXe siècle* (Paris, 1982), p. 261; C. Langlois, *Le catholicisme au féminin: les congrégations françaises à supérieure générale au XIXe siècle* (Paris, 1984).

[71] Gibson, *A Social History*, pp. 185–86.

[72] See, for example, L. Pérouas, 'La diffusion de la confrérie du Rosaire au XVIIe siècle', *Mémoires de la société des sciences naturelles et archéologiques de la Creuse*, 38 (1975), pp. 442–43; P. Hoffman, *Church and Community in the Diocese of Lyon, 1500–1789* (Yale, 1984), p. 126; K. Norberg, *Rich and Poor in Grenoble, 1600–1814* (London, 1985), pp. 250–52; P. Chaunu, *La mort à Paris aux XVIe, XVIIe et XVIIIe siècles* (Paris, 1978), pp. 333–36, 434; J. Pochard, *Méthode pour la direction des âmes dans le tribunal de la pénitence et pour le bon gouvernement des paroisses* (2 vols., Besançon, 1784), vol. 1, p. 139 for quote.

However, it was during the Revolution that this sexual dimorphism emerged with particular clarity; developments then set the agenda for the nineteenth century. Women were notably involved in the disputes over the clerical oath-taking in 1790–91, and in the subsequent disturbances which frequently surrounded the installation of an *intru* in the parish, intervening mainly, but not exclusively, on the side of the jurors.[73] They were in the forefront of resistance to the dechristianizers during the year II, defending crosses, calvaries, shrines, bells and church ornaments with great vigour.[74] In the Haute-Loire women, including some former *Soeurs de St. Joseph du Puy*, undertook burials of the dead at midnight, even threatening relatives in order to get hold of the body, thus ensuring that even at the height of Revolutionary dechristianization some religious rituals were maintained whatever might have been the wishes of the deceased. When, in a ceremony at Le Puy, the *représentant* Albitte sought to have the local *béates* swear a civic oath they refused *en bloc* and, in a display of female collective defiance, all the women in the crowd lifted up their skirts at a pre-arranged signal, the sight of their exposed backsides bringing about the representative's total discomfiture.[75] In the aftermath of the year II women were also prominent in the movement to reestablish a church. In the Yonne and elsewhere women were almost invariably the dominant figures in religious riots, which often had the reopening of a church as their aim; women were frequently responsible for pulling priests from hiding and obliging them to say mass; and there were numerous instances of women ringing bells to summon other women to join them in prayers and hymns.[76]

It is easier to recognize than to account for this marked gender differentiation in religious matters during the Revolution.[77] On the one hand

[73] See, for example, T. Tackett, *Religion, Revolution and Regional Culture in Eighteenth-Century France: The Ecclesiastical Oath of 1791* (Princeton, 1986), pp. 172–77; R. Dupuy, 'Les femmes et la contre-révolution dans l'ouest', *Bulletin d'histoire économique et sociale de la révolution française* (1979–80), pp. 61–70.

[74] Vovelle, *La révolution contre l'église*, pp. 239 ff. has some good examples of female resistance, and his *Religion et révolution*, pp. 280–82.

[75] I am grateful to Professor Olwen Hufton for the details on Le Puy.

[76] Desan, *Revival*, esp. pp. 257–58, 295–98; Hufton, 'The Reconstruction of a Church', *passim.*; her, 'Women in Revolution, 1789–1796', *Past and Present*, 53 (1971), pp. 107–8; H. Daniel-Rops, *L'église des révolutions* (Paris, 1960), p. 93.

[77] Nineteenth-century historiography tended to be dismissive of the role of women in resisting dechristianization, ascribing their actions to a hysterical and gullible temperament; J. Michelet, *Les femmes de la révolution* (Paris, 1854); his *Du prêtre, de la femme, de la famille* (Paris, 1845); Aulard, *Le culte de la raison*.

one may point to the breakdown of clerical leadership and authority which presented women with the opportunity to develop a religious role which had already been growing under the *ancien régime*, the more especially so since much religious activity during the year II had of necessity to be carried on within the home, rather than in public, and this was traditionally the woman's sphere. One may point also to the fact that the Revolutionary authorities dealt less severely with former members of the female religious orders than with the men, tacitly acquiescing when some continued their work as nurses and teachers. The authorities were also uncertain of how, or even whether, Revolutionary religious legislation on the regular orders should be applied to *béates*, *beguines* and *congrégannistes* who, since they were not cloistered, wore no veil and swore no perpetual vows, were not easily classified as regulars. In practice this permitted the continued existence in the community during the 1790s of women with a strong religious commitment, who had manifested robust independence and a capacity for individual initiative during the *ancien régime*, and who were prepared, like the *béates* and *Soeurs de St. Joseph* at Le Puy, actively to oppose the dechristianizers of the year II.[78]

The particular roles and techniques of resistance to authority which had traditionally been accorded to women during the *ancien régime* were also transferred to the situation of the Revolution. Just as they had done during *ancien régime* bread riots, for example, the women of St. Vincent Lespinasse positioned themselves in the front ranks of rioters, and filled their aprons with cinders and ashes, which on this occasion were used to blind Laurent Catusse and his servants when they attempted to take possession of the newly-purchased *presbytère*.[79] Elsewhere too Revolutionary officials were subjected to verbal and sexual harassment of a type which would have been instantly familiar to their *ancien régime* counterparts. The belief that women were, in some circumstances, less culpable for their actions, a belief which had certainly been pervasive in the eighteenth century, was also transferred to the circumstances of the Revolution, not only permitting women greater leeway than men during riotous assemblies but subsequently allowing them to escape punishment

[78] On the women's orders in the eighteenth century see 0. Hufton and F. Tallett, 'Communities of Women, the Religious Life and Public Service in Eighteenth-Century France', in M. Boxer and J. Quataert, *Connecting Spheres: Women in the Western World, 1500 to the Present* (Oxford, 1987), pp. 75–85.

[79] A.D. Lot L242, *arrêté* from canton of Moissac, 10 primaire V. A similar instance from Ribérac (Dordogne) in Hufton, 'The Reconstruction of a Church', p. 41.

altogether, or at least to receive more lenient treatment than men.[80] Thus, when a mixed group of men and women assembled at the church of St. Pierre in 1793 to prevent the municipal officers removing its sacred objects, it was the women who provided the most energetic opposition, one *vigneron* who was there calling out to the others to, 'Let the women do as they wish. They are in a state to kill them [the officials]'. While women of the Tourcy, charged early in 1795 with breaking down church doors, urged that, 'We are only women; they don't do anything to women'.[81]

Under the *ancien régime* the leniency displayed towards women involved in grain riots hinged upon the belief that in some circumstances they had a moral authority to take collective action in order to secure bread for their families. During the Revolution it centred upon the belief that women were more hysterical and easily led than men, consequently lacking responsibility for their actions. This pervasive conception of women as weak and malleable was shared by Catholic villagers and the Revolutionary authorities alike, but official rhetoric was extreme in its condemnation of their foolishness and propensity to be deceived by the lies of the clergy. 'Remember,' one officer in an *armée revolutionnaire* told his men, 'it is fanaticism and superstition which we will be fighting against; lying priests whose dogma is falsehood . . . whose empire is founded upon the credulity of women. These are the enemy'.[82] *Représentants* throughout France spoke of 'l'imbécilité' and 'la sottise des femmes', who were 'fanatisées par leurs prêtres'. This sort of rhetoric probably reflected long-established male fears about the power which the clergy was supposed to have over their wives, fears which found peculiarly trenchant expression in the circumstances of the Revolution when priests became hate-figures. Rhetoric of this kind also, of course, allowed committed Revolutionaries to dismiss the continuing manifestations of a Catholicism, which they had proved unable to suppress, as being of no importance. Hearing that it was only women who assembled in a local chapel to recite the rosary, one *représentant* commented merely that, 'Elles se lasseront de cette ridicule pratique et dans peu, elles y renonceront tout à fait', and took no further action.[83] This type of discourse, whilst it acknowledged the

---

[80] An order on 28 germinal II in the Haute-Loire for the imprisonment of *béates* was an unusual piece of specifically anti-female legislation, and was directed only against this particular group of women: Vovelle, *La révolution contre l'eglise*, pp. 247–48.

[81] Desan, *Revival*, pp. 306–7, 309.

[82] Cited in Cobb, *Les armées révolutionnaires*, vol. 2, p. 450.

[83] A.C.S.P. vol. 10, p. 449.

sexual dimorphism in religious matters which had come about during the Revolution, equally helped to reinforce it: religion was viewed increasingly as being part of the female sphere. The language of the nineteenth century subsequently confirmed this gender differentiation in religious matters. Churchmen were obliged to pay tribute to the predominant part women had played in sustaining religion during the Revolution, and continued to allocate them a special role in religious matters, while Republicans, of whom Michelet and Ferry are but the two best-known examples, continued to point to the intellectual and temperamental inferiority of women which made them subject to a malign clerical influence.[84]

A final point which helps to explain the growing sexual dimorphism in religious matters in the 1790s was the fact that religion offered women virtually their only opportunity for autonomous activity during the Revolution. Whereas men found new and expanding areas for *sociabilité* and political activity in the taverns, in the clubs, in the *sociétés populaires* and committees, women were largely excluded from such institutions. Efforts to found women's clubs met with only limited success, their activities being anyway restricted to issues deemed suitable for women such as price fixation and support for the war effort.[85] Women in general were simply expected to support their men: to stand in the bread queues for hours, to prepare the evening meal and knit socks for the boys at the front and bear more sons who would defend the Revolution. Religion was one area of life which women could, and did, make their own.

Clearly, the developments with which this essay has been concerned – the decline in levels of religious observance, the emergence of more sharply defined geographical patterns of observance, the laicization of religion and its feminization – were not the product of the year II alone, but, properly speaking, of the Revolutionary experience as a whole. Yet the campaign of dechristianization played the pivotal role in these developments, not least of all because of the success of its attack upon the clergy. In the long term the campaign bequeathed one further legacy to France, for it above all was responsible for establishing in the minds of many Catholics the notion that the Revolution was directed against them and their faith.

[84] On nineteenth-century clerical attitudes see Gibson, *A Social History*, esp. pp. 186–87: for those of Republicans see the essay by J. McMillan in this volume. esp. pp. 55–6.

[85] H. Perrin, 'Le club des femmes à Besançon', *Annales révolutionnaires*, ix (1917), pp. 629–53, x (1918), pp. 37–63, 505–32, 645–72; M. Cerati, *Le club des citoyens républicaines révolutionnaires* (Paris, 1966), pp. 172–74.

Quite how profound and enduring this legacy of bitterness and mistrust between supporters of the Revolution and supporters of the church was to be can be gauged by the hostility with which large numbers of Catholics responded to the bicentenary celebrations of the Revolution. As one of the women who, with her seven children, was amongst the 10,000 celebrants at a mass held at Paris in August 1989 as an atonement for the crimes of the Revolution was to put it:

Mes enfants ont parfaitement compris qu'il était nécessaire de réparer publiquement les crimes qui ont été commis sous la Terreur. Bien sûr, ils ont appris leur histoire de France à l'école. Mais, avec leur père, nous leur avons expliqué ce que les professeurs ne disent jamais: que la révolution était avant tout dirigée contre les catholiques.[86]

---

[86] *Le Figaro*, 16 August 1989.

2

Negotiating the Divide: Women, Philanthropy and the 'Public Sphere' in Nineteenth-Century France[1]

Hazel Mills

In 1840 Clement Villecourt, bishop of La Rochelle, visited a school run by nuns for daughters of the town's *notables*. He addressed the pupils on the subject 'Portrait de la femme forte'. Paradoxically, in an institution staffed by nuns, Villecourt's *femme forte* was quintessentially a mother: 'une mère . . . des plus heureux enfants'. Amiable, prudent and diligent, especially in the running of her household; simple and modest in her dress, she devoted herself to her home and family. On her feet from the appearance of the first rays of the rising sun, she was constantly busy, bringing order and cleanliness throughout. Characterized above all by her piety and chastity, she was also solicitous for others, and compassionate to the poor. She spoke very little.[2] By thus presenting herself, Villecourt argued in this and other

[1] I should like to thank the British Academy and Fitzwilliam College, Cambridge for financial assistance towards the costs of the research upon which this article is based. Stefan Collini, Andrew Freeman, Ralph Gibson and Colin Jones have provided advice and encouragement in formulating and presenting these ideas, and I would also like to acknowledge the extremely helpful response given to earlier versions of this paper by the members of the Cambridge Historical Society, and Gonville and Caius College History Society. My gratitude and greatest intellectual debt is owed to Olwen Hufton, source of the initial and continuing inspiration.

[2] J.P. Migne, *Collection intégrale et universelle des orateurs sacrés* (99 vols., Paris, 1844–66), vol. 82, col. 1366–69. Cited hereafter as Migne, *Collection*.

sermons, a married woman revealed that she had triumphed over 'toutes les imperfections de la nature' and could be designated 'virtuous'. However, hers was a specifically female kind of *vertu*: 'On n'a pas une vertu turbulente, bruyante, menacente; mais une vertu indulgente, complaisante, pacifique'.[3]

The bishop's sermon falls within a series of texts he wrote in the 1830s and 1840s on different aspects of a woman's condition and role in society.[4] It is also part of a wider body of literature produced by the French Catholic church in the early and middle decades of the nineteenth century on the same subject and on related issues. These texts range from curial pronouncements and encyclicals to episcopal letters and the sermons written and delivered by rural clergy; from theological treatises to confessional and devotional handbooks advising the clergy and laity respectively.[5]

By the middle decades of the nineteenth century in France, the dominant cultural models of 'woman' and 'man', although in many ways replete with contradictions and tensions, were apparently unambiguous in one respect. 'Man' was depicted as having the virtues and 'nature' which qualified him for activity rhetorically located in the 'public' domain. In necessary comparison, *le sexe* was, we are frequently reminded, represented as possessing the virtues and nature appropriate for duties which were quintessentially 'private'.[6] To paraphrase Michelle Perrot, men had 'power'; women had 'powers'.[7]

This essay will seek to demonstrate that these dominant images of masculinity and feminity require very careful analysis: that each had many possible 'faces', and that lurking within representations of a woman's nature as essentially qualifying her for private responsibilities and domestic duties was a powerful sub-text stressing her latent moral superiority. This

[3] Villecourt, 'Allocution aux Dames de Travail (1842)', *ibid.*, col. 1375.

[4] See collected sermons of Villecourt, *ibid.*, *passim*.

[5] This article is based on material in the Migne collection; on printed and M.S. sermons deposited in the Bibliothèque Nationale, Paris; in the Archives Nationale, Paris; and on material from diocesan and civil archives in the diocese of Besançon.

[6] On this theme, see S. Michaud, *Muse et Madonne: visages de la femme, de la révolution française aux apparitions de Lourdes* (Paris, 1985); J.B. Landes, *Women and the Public Sphere in the Age of the French Revolution* (London, 1988); M.H. Darrow, 'French Noblewomen and the New Domesticity, 1750–1850', *Feminist Studies*, 5:1 (1979), pp. 41–65; B. Smith, *Ladies of the Leisure Class: The Bourgeoises of Northern France in the Nineteenth Century* (Princeton, 1981); R. Deniel, *Une image de la famille et de la societé sous la restauration* (Paris, 1965)

[7] M. Perrot, 'Women, Power and History: The Case of Nineteenth-Century France', S. Reynolds (ed.), *Women, State and Revolution: Essays on Power and Gender in Europe since 1789* (Brighton, 1986), pp. 44–59.

language of moral powers was available to legitimate some types of female activity beyond the home – activity in many ways 'political' in its remit and consequences if not rhetorically acknowledged as such by most (male) contemporaries.

It is, of course, important to acknowledge that at any one time there is no single dominant discourse on gender difference, but rather a number of competing languages, proposed and used by various constituencies, influencing each other's construction and informing the manner in which each is encountered. This essay will focus upon the language used by the Catholic church in France in the first two-thirds of the nineteenth century to represent women, their differences from men, and their social roles. It will do this in the belief that this vocabulary and idiom reached a particularly wide audience, and was displayed within an extensive and varied body of texts which has not been closely studied for this purpose before. Moreover, it has been frequently commented upon by both contemporary and historical observers that French women manifested a particular attachment to the restored Catholic church during the nineteenth century.[8] In investigating this claimed phenomenon, it would seem particularly helpful to examine whether the nineteenth-century church disseminated a particular vision of the religious woman, and if so, how that was constructed. The material available for such an investigation in some respects reflects regional and local circumstances – religious, economic and political. In others it transcends provincial particularism. Women were addressed as *femmes françaises* and the services they had rendered Catholicism in its 'recent history' were frequently outlined and praised. Some possible causes, consequences and contexts of this rhetoric are the subject of what follows.

First, the essay will outline the conceptions and images of female nature and the forms of female virtue that are found in Catholic literature, indicating continuities with the conceptions and images dominant in the eighteenth century, but emphasizing those ideals which only became prominent in the early nineteenth. From there it will explore the ways in which these conceptions were related to, and embodied in, the various forms of female Catholic *association* that so strikingly flourished in this period, before concluding with a few more general reflections about what these

---

[8] For a good recent survey of this phenomenon and a guide to the literature see R. Gibson, *A Social History of French Catholicism, 1789–1914* (London, 1989), pp. 180 ff.

developments meant for the possibilities available to women in French society in this period. A revision of two common polarities in histories of nineteenth-century French society will thus be suggested: that between the figures of the 'public man' and the 'private woman', and also that between the virgin nun and her secular sister.

Three further points should be made clear at the outset. The first is that although this analysis is concerned with both changes in the linguistic or rhetorical representations of female identity – changes in images – *and* with changes in the actual social and political forms taken by female association, explanatory priority is not assigned to either dimension. Secondly, some of the fundamental tensions in the representation of female nature which are discussed here were by no means unique to French Catholicism in this period, but have in different forms a long history in the Christian tradition.[9] Finally, although the literature drawn on for the present reconstruction of those images includes books and other material intended for a national audience and circulated throughout France, as well as sermons drawn from across her dioceses, my own archival research has chiefly concentrated on the diocese of Besançon, in the east of France, and some of my findings may reflect local peculiarities.[10]

For most of the eighteenth century, the language used by the Catholic church to describe virtue and sin in women and men depicted woman's nature as less perfect than man's, less resilient to temptation, easily and frequently corrupted by 'worldly' concerns. It was commonly clearly implied that Eve bore more of the blame for the Fall than Adam. Women were warned:

> Vous descendez de cette première Eve; vous avez herité d'elle son sexe, sa faute et ses peines. La femme a été la porte par où le diable est entré au monde;

[9] See U. Ranke, *Eunuchs for Heaven: The Catholic Church and Sexuality* (London, 1990); L. Roper, *The Holy Household: Women and Morals in Reformation Augsburg* (Oxford, 1989); P. Brown, *The Body and Society: Men, Women and Sexual Renunciation in Early Christianity* (New York, 1988); R. Ruether, *Religion and Sexism: Images of Women in the Jewish and Christian Tradition* (New York, 1974); M. Warner, *Alone of All Her Sex: The Myth and Cult of the Virgin Mary* (London, 1976).

[10] This essay is taken from a larger study, 'Women and Catholicism in Provincial France, 1800–1850' (D. Phil., Oxford, in preparation). The religious history of the diocese of Besançon was particularly characterized, in the early and mid-nineteenth century by three linked phenomenon: Ultramontanism, support for Lamennaisian ideas; and an early attachment to, and role in, the dissemination of Liguorian moral theology.

elle a donné le fruit défendu, elle a été la première prévaricatrice de la loi de Dieu. La femme a porté au pêche celui que Satan n'osait seulement aborder; elle a ruiné l'homme, qui était l'image de Dieu; elle a obligé le Fils de Dieu à mourir honteusement en croix. [11]

Since Eve, (and hence intrinsic to the natures of all subsequent women), women were subordinate to men. Paradoxically this subordination of women could be presented at the same time as a punishment for the sins of Eve, hence the sins of all women, and also as the 'natural' state of all women, including the pre-Fall first woman. [12]

More a prey to their 'passions', women were ever-likely to cause sin in men. [13] The sins of the unrepentant Magdalene were implicitly of a sexual nature but more generally those of a *femme du monde*; characterized by a love of self, laziness, indolence, vanity, pride and love of 'worldly pleasures'. [14] This 'worldly woman' was, moreover, 'like many women', while a virtuous and 'pure' woman was rare and hard to recognize. [15] The latter was, crucially, almost always a virgin. Reliable female virtue was explicitly linked to virginity and a denial of sexuality, and virginity was clearly delineated as a 'higher' state than marriage:

[11] Etienne Bertal (late seventeenth-century preacher), 'De la beauté', Migne, *Collection*, vol. 38, col. 274.

[12] See for example, Julien Loriot (1633–1715), 'Des devoirs des femmes à l'egard de leurs maris', *ibid.*, col. 1016–1027; Père Daniel de Paris, (Capuchin missionary, early 1700s), 'Devoirs des femmes envers leurs maris', *ibid.*, vol. 48, col. 706–717: 'Il est vrai que si l'état d'innocence eût duré toujours, elle lui aurait aussi soumise; mais cette soumission n'eût que dans la joie, parce que l'empire du mari aurait été doux et plein d'une tendre amitié' (col. 711).

[13] This is particularly marked in sermons on the popular eighteenth-century theme, 'De l'impurité'. Women were depicted as the source of 'impure thoughts' in men, leading to the 'degeneration' of the latter.

[14] See, for example, Dom Jérôme (d. 1721), 'Sur les crimes d'une femme du monde dans la Madéleine pécheresse', Migne, *Collection*, vol. 30, col. 587. Similarly, the Jesuit François Bretonneau (1660–1741), in 'Sur la pénitence de Madéleine', listed her sins as love of self, indolence, a passion for 'les commodités de la vie', and a love of pleasure, games and 'the world': *ibid.*, vol. 40, col. 600. Joachim de la Chetardie (d. 1714) reminded his audience that in the Apocalypse Saint John selected the figure of a woman as a symbol of lust and depravity; that depravity 'par sa mollesse, change les hommes même en quelque chose bien au-dessous de la femme, puisqu'il les met au rang des effeminées'. In contrast, through their great religious faith he argued that some female saints 'deviennent des hommes'. See 'Sur la Madéleine', *ibid.*, vol. 35, col. 778.

[15] De la Tour (1700–1780), 'Sur la direction des femmes', *ibid.*, vol. 62, col. 445–61: 'Le sexe est faible . . . fragile, irresolu, léger, peu instruit' (col. 457).

Il n'y a rien que Dieu aime tant que la virginité: c'est la plus ancienne de toutes les virtues; elle est plus ancienne que le mariage . . . Les vierges ont plus de disposition à la vertu, elles se tournent au bien et à la règle de la religion avec plus de promptitude.[16]

Thus, in this dominant voice, woman as a potentially virtuous individual was separated from woman as a participant in actions beyond the 'home', or as a sexual being, certainly as a willing participant, or initiator of sexual acts. Only by those separations could the former be constructed in the language then available. Moreover, the 'whole' woman was the virginal woman: praise was frequently given to the Virgin Mary's *integrité virginale*.[17] Within the descriptions and representation of the Mother of God, the juxtaposition of female virtue and a complete denial of sexuality received its most detailed articulation. Mary was *entirely* pure;[18] her body was *completely* subdued.[19] All the virtues of this 'ultimate in female goodness' sprang from her virginity.

Alongside this general representation of virginity as the only reliable path to, and indication of, female virtue – followed by so few – lay frequent and detailed praise for the nun:

Une mère de famille, quelque renoncement qu'elle ait fait du monde, est encore obligée d'y penser souvent, au lieu qu'une vierge peut se maintenir sante de corps et d'esprit, vivant dans un sainte loisir, ou elle ne pense qu'à Dieu seul.

---

[16] Masson (early eighteenth-century Oratorian), 'Sur Sainte Marthe', *ibid.*, vol. 13, col. 1188.

[17] Claude de Marolles, (1712–92), 'Eloge de la Sainte Vierge', *ibid.*, vol. 64, col. 153.

[18] On the figure of the Virgin Mary there are hundreds of sermons from the eighteenth century within Migne alone. For some particularly representatives texts see the forty sermons on the theme of the Virgin by Le Jeune, vol. 4, *passim*; Anselme (1651–1737), 'De la conception de la Vierge Marie', *ibid*, vol. 20, col. 61–74; the eight sermons of Edme-Bernard Bourrée (d. 1722) on the Virgin, *ibid.*, vol. 39; those of Jean-Baptiste Massillon (d. 1742), *ibid.*, vol. 42; Martin Pallu, (d. 1742), 'Pour la jour de la visitation', *ibid.*, vol. 46, col. 795; Edme Mongin (d. 1746), 'Pour l'assomption', *ibid.*, vol. 46, col. 1072–1080; and Sebastien Dutreil (mid-eighteenth century), 'Sermon sur les grandeurs de la Vierge', *ibid.*, vol. 47, col. 1391.

[19] 'Son corps était entièrement soumis à l'esprit, son esprit à la raison, sa raison et sa volonté à la volonté de Dieu, et la partie inférieure de son âme à la supérieure . . . Elle n'avait point de rébellion dans sa chair, point de passion en l'appétit irascible, point de révolte dans le concupiscible, point de mélange d'imperfections dans ses vertus', Le Jeune, 'Des vertus de la vierge', *ibid.*, vol. 4, col. 118–124.

Une femme mariée ne peut être sans une infinité d'inquiètudes pour les choses de la terre; une vierge peut s'occuper que de l'éternité. Une femme mariée n'est à elle-même qu'à moitié, elle est partagée entre Jésus-Christ et un homme mortel . . . mais une vierge est toute à Jésus-Christ.[20]

It was argued that only the coming of Christianity had permitted virtuous women to sanctify their lives by *la plus grande gloire* – virginity – which represented a victory over 'les infirmités de la nature . . . malgré la faiblesse naturelle de ce sexe'.[21] However, there were competing images of the most appropriate channeling of this virtue – through the cloister, or through activity beyond the convent walls. Across the eighteenth century the former, older vision remained extremely powerful: the figure of the contemplative nun was the paradigm of earthly female virtue, at least in the eyes and voice of the clerical hierarchy.[22]

While all people were enjoined to be pious, attend church and take part in the sacraments, little *specific* attention was directed to lay women in these areas. In sermons on the duties of parents and the stewardship of the home, the language of titles, of *Les parents*, *Les pères et les mères* and *Maîtres et maîtresses* in the body of sermons quickly became simply *pères* and *maîtres*.[23]

---

[20] Père Loriot, (d. 1715) 'Sur la virginité', *ibid.*, vol. 31, col. 129–130.

[21] Molinier, 'Sur les vierges et la virginité', *ibid.*, vol. 44, col. 759.

[22] The Counter-Reformation, while stimulating a female religious life with a clearly defined practical and social role *beyond* the convent, also manifested continuing clerical hostility towards female autonomy and the idea of women working and moving freely within the wider community, even if engaged in charity. Enclosure, a rule, and strict vows eased this anxiety. The Ursulines, the *Filles de Notre Dame de Charité*, and the Visitandines, despite their original orientation beyond the cloister, eventually became enclosed orders, their teaching and nursing activities vastly restrictly. For a concise and stimulating introduction to the female religious orders of the seventeenth and eighteenth centuries see O. Hufton and F. Tallett, 'Communities of Women, the Religious Life, and Public Service in Eighteenth-Century France', M.J. Boxer and J.H. Quataert (eds.), *Connecting Spheres: Women in the Western World, 1500 to the Present* (Oxford 1987), pp. 75–85. See also C. Jones, 'Sisters of Charity and the Ailing Poor', *Social History of Medicine*, 19 (1989), pp. 339–48; M. de Chantal Gueudré, *Histoire de l'ordre des Ursulines en France*, (2 vols ., Paris, 1957–60); R. Devos, *Vie religieuse féminine et société. Les Visitandines d'Annecy aux XVIIe et XVIIIe siècles* (Annecy, 1973).

[23] See, for example, Charles Perrin, (d. 1767), 'Sur l'éducation des enfants', Migne, *Collection* vol. 53, col. 1171; Daniel de Paris, 'Devoirs des pères et mères envers leurs enfants', *ibid.*, vol. 48, col. 665–66, & 671; Dom Jérôme, 'Devoirs envers les domestiques', *ibid.*, vol. 30, col. 302; Julien Loriet, 'Des devoirs des maîtres à l'égard de leurs serviteurs', *ibid.*, vol. 36, col. 1128; Ballet, 'Les devoirs des maîtres et maîtresses envers leurs domestiques', *ibid.*, vol. 49, col. 368.

This was not mere shorthand: fathers and masters were clearly positioned as founts of authority, decision-making, and ultimate sanction. There was little delineation of a separate positive role for mothers and housewives. Women in the home were to be above all obedient, diligent and silent.

In other sorts of eighteenth-century religious texts, particularly the sermons of rural priests and the handbooks of confraternities, lay women were encouraged to engage in some activities beyond the home, in the 'public domain'. Membership of a confraternity, or charitable work was a means of developing and displaying piety.[24] Women were nevertheless warned in sermons of the common sin of attending church or a confraternity out of vanity and a wish to display false piety.[25] Even the most apparently virtuous woman was not to be trusted. For always directly juxtaposed with the image of the virtuous virgin was that of her worldly vice-ridden counterpart. In the language used to describe figures like the Virgin Mary and the repentant Magdalene, the implications of exceptionality and unattainability were intrinsic to the finished image. Similarly, in texts on the use of the confessional and on the direction of men, great stress was laid on the supreme difficulties of fully controlling female 'passions'. All women were to be strictly and effectively supervised and rigorously investigated in the confessional. Priests were warned to beware even nuns, and they were cautioned 'En général, il y a moins de risque à courir, et plus de bien à faire, en confessant les hommes'.[26]

Towards the end of the eighteenth century and into the nineteenth, alongside this continuing rhetoric of gender difference and greater, possibly innate, female corruptibility, a language by which the non-virginal, yet virtuous woman could be described was beginning to be more easily discernible in Catholic texts. This is to be seen indirectly in sermons on charity and on marriage, but is most clearly visible in material on the Virgin Mary and on correct female behaviour. Two common threads occur across

---

[24] As well as sermon material, this encouragement is to be found in the handbooks, and devotional tracts of eighteenth-century female confraternities. See for example, 'Règlement des Dames de Charité de Besançon' (eighteenth century), A.D. Doubs, M.S. 158, 'Règlement de l'Association pour les Dames de Charité d'Arbois', (1760s), A.M. Arbois, Q. 248: *Dames de Charité*; and 'Statutes de la Confraternité de Ste. Barbe à Conflans, 1705', A.D. Haute Saône, 34.J.6.

[25] See, for example, François de Toulouse (*c.* 1700), 'Sermon sur les Confréries du Saint-Sacrement', Migne, *Collection*, vol. 11, col. 780.

[26] Joseph Pochard, *Méthode pour la direction des âmes dans le tribunal de la pénitence, et pour le bon gouvernement des paroisses* (2 vols., Besançon, 1783), vol. 1, p. 143.

these texts. The first is the value ascribed to 'piety' in saving women from their own 'natures' – a piety manifest through daily behaviour and religious worship, humility, docility, gentleness, modesty and, above all, chastity. The second, through this growing focus on chastity alongside virginity, was the increased space permitted for the virtuous non-virgin.

During the first half of the nineteenth century the nature of woman, and the social roles to which that nature directed her, became more common as the stated focus of an enquiry. In the 1830s, 40s and 50s unprecedented numbers of devotional handbooks and manuals, in addition to sermons, were produced by clerics to advise women of their responsibilities and the proper discharge of their duties.[27] The focus was on the domestic arena. Authors were largely, but not exclusively concerned with women as wives and mothers. Yet in the attention which was also given to the areas where women could legitimately operate beyond the home, in the so-called 'public' domain, the fundamental tenets of the overall image were curiously challenged and their inconsistencies further revealed.

The juxtaposition of female vice and female virtue necessarily continued from the earlier period, together with the description of woman as less perfect than man. Yet in the first half of the nineteenth century it was more common, for example, to depict Eve *and* Adam as sharing the blame for the Fall than had been the case earlier.[28] Similarly, while the Virgin Mary remained 'a woman apart', greater stress was nevertheless laid on her humanity, on her status as a wife and above all a *mother*. 'Marie n'est pas seulement Fille et Epouse d'un Dieu, mais aussi Mère d'un Dieu: voici son privilège le plus singulière, son titre le plus incommunicable, le comble de sa gloire.'[29] Attention was frequently directed to the Virgin's preference for the

[27] See, for example, Jauffret, Evêque de Metz, *Des services que les femmes peuvent rendre à la religion: ouvrage suivi de la vie des dames françaises les plus illustres en ce genre dans le XVIII siècle* (Paris, 1801); Abbé Frédéric-Edouard Chassay, *Bibliothèque d'une femme chrétienne* (Paris 1849–53), 7 vols: 'La pureté du coeur'; 'Manuel d'une femme chrétienne'; La femme chrétienne et le monde'; 'Influence des femmes dans le monde'; 'Les devoirs des femmes dans la famille'; Les difficultés de la vie de famille'; 'Epreuves du mariage'.

[28] For example, Claude Tailland (1798–1854; missionary and parish priest in the diocese of Autun), 'Sur l'homme', Migne, *Collection*, vol. 80 cols. 725–26; Jean-Baptiste Boudot, (1765–1850), 'Discours sur les grandeurs de Marie', *ibid* vol. 79, col. 826: 'un homme et une femme avaient perdu le genre humaine'; Mercier (1791–1850, missionary and parish priest), 'De l'influence salutaire ou pernicieuse que la femme exerce dans la société', *ibid.*, vol. 87, cols. 1137–72 (six sermons): 'Eve . . . présente le fruit à Adam qui devait arrêter ou consommer notre perte' (col. 1141).

[29] Mercier, 'Sur les primitives grandeurs de Marie', *ibid.*, col. 582.

spiritual and the pious. Women were advised they could imitate either her *pureté corporelle* or her *virginité intérieure et spirituelle*. From this 'spiritual virginity' sprang charity, faith and chastity.[30] The Virgin Mary thus on one level became more accessible as exemplar to lay women:

> Dans la reine et la grande dame, elle y est; car Marie était noble et fille des rois: dans la femme du peuple, qui gagne son pain de chaque jour et celui de ses enfants du travail de ses mains, elle y est; car Marie fut pauvre, et pour vivre travailla comme les pauvres; dans la petite fille, elle y est; dans la jeune vierge, elle y est; dans l'épouse, elle y est; dans la mère, elle y est; dans la veuve, elle y est. Marie, Marie toujours, Marie partout'.[31]

However, one key Catholic text, apparently contradicting the greater 'accessibility' in the nineteenth century of the potent image of the mother of God cannot be ignored. The declaration by Pius IX in 1854 that the Immaculate Conception of the Virgin Mary would henceforth have the status of dogma has been interpreted in a number of ways. It is possible that it represented a final successful coup for dualism – for the combination of the aesthetic and the more 'life-affirming' strands within Catholicism.[32] Alternatively it may have reflected the final abdication by the Papacy in favour of populism and 'the people's cults', in the particular political and social circumstances faced by the Catholic church in this period.[33] Each of these explanations undoubtedly has value. However, *Ineffabilis Deus*, as Kristeva suggests, may also represent an attempt by the (masculine) hierarchy of the Catholic church to regain control both of the 'maternal', one of the most powerful constructs within the 'symbolic economy' of the contemporary imagination, and of a certain set of activities and developments taking place contemporaneously in religion and society.[34]

---

[30] Mercier, 'Caractères de la femme modèle', *ibid.*, cols. 1142–46.

[31] J. Gaume, *Histoire de la société domestique, chez tous les peuples anciens et modernes; ou l'influence du christianisme sur la famille* (Paris, 1844), p. 229. Gaume was born in the Doubs and held ecclesiastical positions in the diocese of Nevers, Reims and Montauban. A further example of the construction of the Virgin Mary as an exemplar accessible to ordinary women is found in André Charvaz (1793–1855, priest in the diocese of Haute Savoie, from 1833, bishop of Pignerol), 'Discours sur l'immaculée conception de la Sainte Vierge', Migne, *Collection*, vol. 80, col. 792; and in the sermons of the late eighteenth-century parish priest of Flangebouche in the diocese of Besançon, Bergier, *ibid.*, vol. 69, cols. 809–64.

[32] This is the interpretation offered in M. Warner, *Alone of All Her Sex*, p. 236.

[33] See T. Kselman, *Miracles, Magic and Prophesy in Nineteenth-Century France*, (New York, 1983).

[34] J. Kristeva, 'Stabat Mater', in T. Moi (ed.), *The Kristeva Reader* (Oxford, 1986), pp. 160–86.

Nonetheless, despite the proclamation of the new official status of the Immaculate Conception, or perhaps because of it, the nineteenth-century Catholic church above all praised Mary's maternity, and through that the role of every mother. Motherhood became a means to female virtue that challenged the previous hegemony of virginity. As *une réparatrice* Mary the *mother* of God was 'une modèle à laquelle toutes les femmes devront ressembler et s'unir'.[35] Like virginity, motherhood was frequently described as a 'vocation'.[36] Through chaste motherhood a woman could overcome her weaker nature,[37] and achieve a state beloved of God:

> Elles furent grandes sans doute les faveurs accordées par le Ciel au Coeur de Marie, mais grande aussi fut sa reconnaissance. Quand il s'agit de former le coeur d'une Mère, Dieu, mes frères, y donner tous ses soins; car le coeur d'une Mère, c'est le chef d'oeuvre du Créateur.[38]

Moreover, it was argued that motherhood was particularly protected by Catholicism in its denunciation of divorce and its recognition of the 'dignity' and the 'grandeur' of a woman's role in the family and hence society.[39] If she practised the virtues, broadly speaking, of piety, self-denial, devotion to her children, diligence in all tasks, modesty, humility, chastity, silence and charity, a woman, though not a nun, could thus be called a *femme forte*. Constant vigilance, of course, was still required to ensure she had overcome 'all the imperfections of her nature'. For there were, it was frequently stated, two types of *femme forte* – '1' une forte selon le monde, et l'autre selon Dieu'.[40]

[35] Gaume, *Histoire*, p. 225.

[36] Jauffret, *Services*, p. 11.

[37] Mercier, 'Suite de l'influence salutaire ou pernicieuse que la femme exerce dans la famille et la société', Migne, *Collection*, vol. 87, cols. 1158–63.

[38] Frederic Doucet (1806–38), 'Instruction sur le très-Sainte Coeur de Marie', *ibid.*, vol. 74, col. 985.

[39] Gaume, *Histoire, passim*. According to Gaume Catholicism had a 'sollicitude toute particulière pour la femme'.

[40] Mercier, 'Suite de l'influence. . .', Migne, *Collection*, vol. 87, col. 1153. Considerable attention continued to be given to the *ease* with which a woman's virtue could be corrupted and to the destruction that could result if female 'power' was misdirected. The 'natural' woman was the sexually chaste mother. If she acted in a 'worldly' fashion she could still easily be described as 'unnatural'. See, for example, Chassasy, *La femme chrétienne dans ses rapports avec la monde*, pp. 15, 45–46. Alternatively such a woman, even if she had children, was not a true mother: 'Je viens vous dire, de la part de Jésus-Christ, qui si vous préférez les usages du monde à l'éducation de vos enfants, et les plaisirs à la joie qu'éprouve une mère dans la société de ses enfants, vous n'êtes pas encore mères, vous ne savez pas même ce que c'est une mère.' Mercier, 'Mission des mères', Migne, *Collection*, vol. 87, col. 1166.

Even while this was constantly acknowledged, the detail given to lay, non-virginal female virtue grew. It was to be measured in the care and success with which a woman ran her home, assisted her husband and brought up her children as good Catholics and loyal citizens:

O mères! Vous êtes les instruments vivants, les chefs visibles d'un pouvoir spirituel et redoutable. Votre pensée, en devenant la pensée de chaque génération, se mêle à la vie universelle, et pour ainsi parler, à la respiration même de l'humanité. Pour n'oublier jamais quelle est votre responsabilité, n'oubliez jamais quelle est votre puissance: car, si les hommes font les lois, les femmes font les moeurs, qui ont plus d'influence encore que les lois sur les destinées de monde.[41]

Lay female virtue was also to be seen in a woman's devotion to religion, her attendance at church, and her charity and care for the poor.[42] A virtuous non-virgin in all likelihood attended a confraternity,[43] and spent as much time as she could spare engaged in 'good works' beyond the home. Women were encouraged to visit the houses of the poor, prisons and 'houses of reform'; to direct themselves to the moral regeneration of prostitutes and the assistance of the work of the regular orders. 'Les femmes peuvent contribuer bien plus qu'elles ne s'imaginent à rendre universelle cette resurrection de la charité des anciens temps.'[44]

[41] Donnet (Archbishop of Bordeaux) 'Instruction pastoral sur l'éducation de famille, Carême 1845', Migne, *Collection*, vol. 81, col. 64.

[42] For example, Mercier, 'Mission des mères, *ibid.*, vol. 87, cols. 1163–72; Chassay, *Bibliothèque d'une femme chrétienne*.

[43] See, for example, Rendu (Bishop of Annecy) 'Mandement sur les confréries, Carême 1845', Migne, *Collection*, vol. 85, cols. 131–145; Le Courter (Vicar-General of Angers) 'Trois oeuvres oratoires', *ibid.*, vol. 86, cols. 9–16; Pierre Faudet (1798–1855), curé in Paris, 'Trois instructions', *ibid.*, cols. 647–663. See also the large number of printed and M.S. Confraternity *règlements* and *statuts* in central and Bisontin archives. For example A.N. F19 6424; A.N. F19 6424; and 'Règlemens et statuts de la Confrérie de Notre-Dame du Mont', (Besançon, 1827); 'Règlement des Dames de Charité de Besançon', (*c.* 1825); 'Prières en l'honneur de Ste. Anne et statuts de la conférence établie sous son invocation' (Besançon, 1863), all located in Archiepiscopal Archives, Besançon.

[44] Chassay, *La femme chrétienne*, p. 99. Cf. also Jauffret, *Services*, pp. 52–58. Mercier encouraged women to direct their maternal powers to 'les classes obscures et laborieuses': see his 'Influence salutaire ou pernicieuse . . .', Migne, *Collection*, col. 1150, and more generally 1156–57. See also Legns-Duval (1765–1850), 'Sur l'oeuvre des fille répentis', *ibid.*, vol. 73, col. 561. Similar encouragement is to be found in the handbooks, statutes and devotional works of nineteenth-century confraternities.

As well as the 'governement de l'intérieure',[45] women were thus directed to religious and philanthropic activity: 'il y a des choses que les femmes font infiniment mieux que les hommes quand il s'agit de charité'.[46] Occasional comments, and some clerical suspicions about greater female than male attendance at church,[47] gave way to frequent acknowledgment of, and eulogies to, women's piety:

Deux camps, deux étendards sont au foyer. Les pères et les fils combattent la plupart sous les bannières de l'indifférence et du sensualisme; les mères et les filles, restées fidèles au Christianisme, dévorent en silence leurs larmes et leurs douleurs'.[48]

While for a man achieving faith might be a slow and difficult process if he felt, wrongly, that he had to come to that state through the exercise of 'sa raison', for a woman, 'sa foi est plutot un instinct'.[49]

In this literature mention was frequently made of the 'recent services' that women had made to the Catholic religion and the French church. Women, it was reported, had remained faithful to the church 'même en face des échafauds':[50] they had provided in their hearts a sanctuary for religion in its hour of greatest need and worked thereafter for the rechristianization of France. In this fashion, and sometimes more explicitly, mention was often made of the Revolution of 1789–99, which in its most radical phase had pursued a policy of dechristianization, removing from the church its material base and eventually outlawing its personnel, rites and rituals. Although this policy met enormous resistance in provincial France, it had been women above all, certainly from 1796 onwards, who had queued outside boarded-up churches just as they had outside bakers' shops; hidden priests from the authorities; and run clandestine masses and religious ceremonies. In many areas they had reconstructed a Catholic church from the base up before its official reestablishment by Napoleon in the Condordat of 1801.[51] In

[45] Chassay, *Epreuves du mariage*, p. xiii.
[46] Chassay, *Le femme chrétienne*, p. 295.
[47] For example, Pochard, *Méthode*, vol. 1, p. 149.
[48] Gaume, *Histoire*, p. vii.
[49] Guillaume-Laurent Angebault (bishop of Angers) 'Mandement sur ce que les femmes ont fait pour la religion', Migne, *Collection*, vol. 84, col. 454.
[50] André Charvaz (bishop of Pignerol), 'Discours sur l'immaculée conception de la Sainte Vierge', 1833, *ibid.*, vol. 81, col. 1263.
[51] O. Hufton, 'The Reconstruction of a Church, 1796–1801', C. Lucas and G. Lewis (eds.), *Beyond the Terror* (Oxford, 1985).

their nineteenth-century rhetoric many Catholic churchmen appear to have acknowledged this and to have tried to accommodate both it, and its consequences, in their representation of women's value and roles in society.

In confessional literature priests were now reminded of the benefits that could accrue from the greater ease with which women attended their confessors in comparison with many of their menfolk. At the same time a less rigorous moral theology concerned with the use of the confessional and the regulation of behaviour, associated with the writings newly translated into French of Alphonse di Liguori, was adopted in preference to the previously dominant Augustinian and Jansenist model.[52] Alongside, and perhaps related to efforts to defend and extend regular Catholic practice, women were being described as agents of the church in the difficult times it faced. In the 1850s Angebault, bishop of Angers, argued that a wife and mother was a veritable 'priest of the home'. She had, moreover, the power to fill churches and to save whole societies:

> Au sein de la famille, c'est la femme qui, par sa piété douce et tendre, convie à chaque instant au retour vers Dieu ceux qui s'éloignent de Lui. Toujours fidèle à son culte, toujours embrassée d'amour divin, au milieu d'indifférence de nos sociétés, c'est elle . . . qui remplit nos temples, qui visite les lieux saintes, et qui ne laisse point sans voix ce cantique auguste, cette harmonie de prières que la terre doit au Créateur . . . C'est par la femme que les sociétés se corrompent ou s'améliorent. En France, au temps de nos malheurs, elles seules ont conservé le depot sacré: leur foi surnagea dans ce déluge universel. Malheur à une nation ou les femmes seraient sans croyances; tout serait perdu sans retour et il faudrait désespérer de l'avenir.[53]

In the middle decades of the nineteenth century, in the Catholic imagination, the virtuous *femme forte* could be one of two broad categories of women. Firstly she could be a nun: virginal and married to Christ (an ambiguous sexual status which contributed to her social and symbolic position in the community). This was, moreover, an image in which the role of nun beyond the cloister had finally overtaken that of the purely contemplative.

---

[52] J. Gawber, 'Le ralliement du clergé français à la moral Liguorienne', *Analecta gregoriana*, 193 (1973); J. Stengers, 'Les pratiques anticonceptionnelles dans le mariage au XIXe et au XXe siècle: problèmes humains et attitudes religieuses', *Revue belge de philologie*, 49:2 (1971), pp. 403–81.

[53] Angebault, *op.cit.*, Migne, *Collection*, vol. 84, cols. 457–59.

This imagined individual was empowered by her traditional and ambiguous status, but also by her service to the community and to the poor.[54]

Alternatively the *femme forte* could be a lay woman, married and a mother, virtuous through her maternal tasks, her selflessness and chastity. She too, however, served the church and drew virtue from the services women in France's recent past had already given. Lay woman and nun were linked by the figure of the virgin mother of God. Thus, like the nun, the lay woman could be *forte* through her association with other women. First, she was encouraged to associate in lay societies devoted to similar tasks to those of a regular congregation. Secondly, she derived empowering virtue through her shared gender status with the virgin nun and her association with some of the tasks undertaken by female congregations. Finally, lay women were *forte* through their association with women in the recent past in the imagination of the Catholic hierarchy. Collectively women had defended Catholicism during the Revolution and would, it was proclaimed, continue to do so. The place of the lay woman in the contemporary religious imagination was subtly different from that of her eighteenth-century predecessors.

One of the most dynamic sectors of the French Catholic church throughout the nineteenth century, but especially during its first seventy-five years, was the female congregation.[55] Despite considerable problems in successfully reconstructing reliable statistics for the entire century,[56] it is possible to be confident that there was, across its course, a sustained increase in the numbers of both female religious houses or establishments and their personnel. From 1808, when Claude Langlois has estimated that there were at least 12,300 nuns and 1,600 novices in France, (a figure which represented about one-third of the female personnel of the church in 1789), the number of women living in religious communities grew to around 27,000 in 1825: 31,000 in 1831; 66,000 in 1850; 90,000 in 1861; 127,000 in 1878 and 128,000 in 1901. The number of establishments in which these women lived, Langlois calculates, grew from 2,057 in 1808 to 12,006 in 1861; 20,460 in 1878 (of which 16,500 were schools); and 16,172 in 1901. This increase was constant across the century, but strongest in the period 1808–31 (from the 1808 base at a rate of 4.1 per cent per annum in personnel) and weakest

54 See pp. 45–46 below.

55 See the magisterial study by Claude Langlois, *Le catholicisme au féminin: les congrégations français à supèrieure generale au XIXe siècle* (Paris 1984).

56 C. Langlois, 'Les effectifs des congrégations féminines au XIXe siècle: de l'enquête statistique à l'histoire quantitative', *Revue d'histoire de l'église de France*, 60 (1974), pp. 44–53.

from 1861–78 (2.3 per annum).[57] These general figures, however, need to be treated with some caution. Langlois himself acknowledges that individual diocesan studies have tended to show both the likely underestimation of figures essentially based on periodic departmental surveys undertaken in response to a request from Paris and the different pace and rhythm of the phenomenon in different regions. The records housed at the local level for the diocese of Besançon indicate that the Parisian figures are sometimes an underestimate of the totals of nuns and establishments in that region at least for the first half of the century.[58] The figures, certainly for 1808 and 1825, beg the question of what the recorders were classifying as a congregation.[59]

It is further significant to note that while on the eve of the French Revolution the male personnel of the church outnumbered the female by at least two to one, across the nineteenth century that sexual disparity in vocation was reversed. In 1830 there were around 45,000 male clergy, compared to around 31,000 nuns. By 1861, while the figure for nuns had increased to approximately 90,000, that for the male clergy had reached only 75,000, and in 1878 there were only around 80,000 men in religious orders and the secular clergy, compared to 125,000 nuns. Thus, in 1831 women comprised 41 per cent of the personnel of the French Catholic church; in 1861, 54.5 per cent; and in 1878, 58 per cent. This phenomenon has rightly been identified as a 'feminization' of the personnel of the church across the course of the nineteenth century.[60]

The reasons for this remarkable increase in the number of nuns in France in the nineteenth century are undoubtedly very complex and defy brief analysis. A number of factors can, however, be high-lighted.[61] The first is the political context in which this development occurred. Alongside the cloister-bound, contemplative female religious life, grouping the daughters of the wealthy and titled, it has already been shown that there had arisen since the Counter-Reformation an alternative type of female order more

[57] *Ibid.* pp. 50–56.

[58] A.D. Doubs 38.V.1–5; A.D. Jura 7.V.1–10; A.D. Haute Saône 2.V.8, 4.V.1; A.M. Besançon, R.1:1, 1:2, 1.25; A.A. Besançon, *Fonds congréganistes*.

[59] Langlois, 'Les effectifs . . .', pp. 54–55. In the returns for the Jura (1808) a pious association in St. Claude is listed alongside congregations: A.N.F.19 6336.

[60] Langlois, 'Les effectifs . . .', pp. 62–63.

[61] See Langlois, *Le catholicisme au féminin*, esp. pp. 627–648; C. Jones, 'Sisters of Charity', pp. 339–48; and particularly C. Langlois, 'Le catholicisme au féminin', *A.S.S.R.*, 57 (1984), pp. 29–54.

directed to wide-ranging charity beyond the convent. This newer model was favoured by the politics of the Revolution and Napoleon's Empire, while the older, contemplative form, stripped of its property, was increasingly marginalized. During the first half of the nineteenth century France thus witnessed the emerging dominance of highly organized, action-oriented female orders, which found favour with a wide variety of political regimes. Moreover, the phenomenon of female association per se, and the female religious order were not politically suspect in this period in the way that their male equivalents were. Female congregations were subject to only very loose civil supervision at least up until the 1870s and their authorization was much less problematic for most nineteenth-century French administrations than that of male orders.[62]

The vitality of the female congregation in this period may also have been linked to rates of female celibacy in the population at large. Whilst not an inconsiderable figure throughout the nineteenth century, this was a category that remained relatively stable over the era as a whole at around 12 per cent of the adult population.[63] There were certain regional discrepancies between male and female celibacy due to higher migration among men than women, as for instance in the west. This is an area that requires further investigation, together with the wider question of available female employment. What is certainly marked is that with their four different 'ranks' of sister, and their lower dowries, the congregations of the nineteenth century were open to women from a very wide range of social backgrounds, including increasingly the daughters of urban artisans and peasant farmers.[64]

What must be stressed, however, is the remarkable adaptability of this form of female congregation in the nineteenth century. In particular it proved very successful at penetrating the emergent educational and health-care professions and institutions of the early and mid century. Seen by the wider community and the civil authorities as professionally competent in these spheres, and alone able to respond to the increased demand for female teachers and nurses, these communities, like their less numerous *ancien régime* counterparts, soon provided fundamental public services.[65] At least

[62] Langlois, 'Le catholicisme au féminin', passim.

[63] R. Pressat & L.C. Chasteland, 'La nuptialité des générations françaises pendant un siècle', *Population*, (1962), pp. 215–40; L. Henry, 'Schema de nuptialité: déséquilibré des sexes et celibat', *Population*, (1969) pp. 457–86.

[64] Langlois, *Le catholicisme au féminin*, pp. 563–626.

[65] Jones, 'Sisters of Charity'; Langlois, 'Le catholicisme au féminin'.

in part for this reason they enjoyed remarkable popularity. At the same time, they also developed a private sector in each of their activities, especially in the field of female education. Often profits from these private schools or *pensions* were channelled back to the schools catering for the children of the less well-off.[66] In the three departments originally in the concordataire diocese of Besançon, there were at least sixty-nine communities of nuns by 1850 (scattered more densely in the traditionally religious and mountainous Jura, less in the 'irreligious' lowlands of the Haute Saône), living in groups ranging from two or three individuals to more than 100 in a *maison mère* in Besançon itself. They belonged to at least twenty different congregations and orders, the largest single number being attached to the Besançon mother-house of a local congregation, the *Soeurs de Charité de St. Vincent de Paul*. In addition there were twelve communities of semi-independent *soeurs hospitalières*, staffing the region's hospitals and occasionally running attached schools.[67]

This form of the female religious order not only benefited from a changing political and social environment, it also drew on the rich heritage of the position of the nun in the religious and popular imagination, to stretch the potential limitations of that vision of female purity and virtue in a changed environment. Although visible in alternative versions of the cloistered ideal since the sixteenth century, the active female religious life was fully permitted within the Catholic imagination only in the nineteenth century, when it also won unequivocal, and increasingly necessary, secular support.[68]

The vibrant and dynamic female congregation was not the only form of female Catholic association in the nineteenth century. In certain regions of France there were groups of lay women approximating in some of their activities and patterns of association to communities of nuns. This is an area as yet under-investigated and hence early conclusions are necessarily tentative. It includes, for instance, the *Tiers Ordres* of Brittany and Touraine, active in the prerevolutionary era, but particularly active in the early and mid nineteenth century, often reappearing as early

---

[66] In Besançon the *Soeurs de la Sainte Famille* (formed around 1799), from 1803 or possibly earlier, ran a *pension* and also a class for poorer girls who paid no, or low fees, according to means. Several poor girls were nominated and funded through the school by the *Dames de Charité* (see pp. 48–9 below): A.N.F.19.6295; A.D. Doubs 38.V.1–3; A.M. Besançon R.1.2, R.1.25; A.A. Besançon, *Fonds congréganistes – Sainte Famille*.)

[67] As n. 58 above.

[68] Langlois, *Le catholicisme au féminin*, p. 627.

as 1797. Engaged in wide-ranging pastoral activity, especially teaching the catechism to young children, *Tiers Ordres* grouped widows and spinsters, who sometimes took a vow of chastity but did not live communally, although they attended retreats. In this region at least these were clearly a popular choice of association for women who did not want, or were unable, to cut themselves off completely from their community, parish or family.[69]

Similarly the *béates* of the Haute Loire, lay women who either singly or in pairs gave religious instruction and taught the skill of lace-making to young girls in the villages and hamlets of a region, whilst forming neither a congregation nor a *Tiers Ordre*, were nevertheless active assistants to the priest in the life of the parish. Having their origins in this region in the seventeenth century, in the early nineteenth they appear particularly numerous. In some cases they seem to have run small *salles d'asile* for the indigent and destitute; they were labelled 'vicaires en leurs petits secteurs' by the Prefect in 1863.[70]

A third, broader category of non-congregational female Catholic association in this period is the confraternity, or lay religious association. Our habitual image of this institution is of a form of association on the decline during the eighteenth century from its medieval and Counter-Reformation heyday, or at least of one in the process of changing into various secular alternatives focused more around occupational solidarity and mutual aid than explicitly religious activities.[71] Although during the Revolution confraternities were proscribed, from 1797 or 1798 certainly in some regions, these lay religious associations, particularly those grouping only women, started to reappear, or indeed appear for the first time.

It is impossible to provide an estimate of the total number of female confraternities in France in the first half of the nineteenth century. Parisian sources indicate a potentially widespread phenomenon although

[69] C. Langlois and P. Wagret, *Structures religieuses et célibat féminin au XIXe siècle* (Lyon, 1972).

[70] A. Rivet, 'Des ministres laiques au XIXe siècle? Les béates de la Haute Loire', *Revue d'histoire de l'église de France*, 64 (1978) pp. 27–38.

[71] See for example, G. Le Bras, 'Esquisse d'une histoire des confréries', *Revue d'histoire de droit français et étranger*, (1940–1), pp. 310–63; and 'Les confréries chrétiennes: aperçus historiques, problèmes et propositions', *Annuaire de l'école pratique des hautes études, section des sciences religieuses*, (1941), pp. 92–98; M. Agulhon, *Pénitents et franc-maçons de l'ancienne Provence*, (2e éd. Paris, 1984).

casual references in civil reports can seldom be traced far.[72] Certainly in the diocese of Besançon surprisingly rich material exists in local archives documenting the reappearance and activities of dozens of female confraternities from *c.* 1797 to 1850.

These fall into three broad categories. In the rural environment parochial associations focused around the altar of a particular church or chapel were the most common form of female confraternity. These frequently prove to be reformed *ancien régime* confraternities: groupings, moreover, which during the eighteenth century had enjoyed a membership of both sexes but which after the Revolution were immediately, or quickly became, solely female in composition.[73]

The second type of female confraternity had no pre-Revolutionary antecedents in this diocese. It grouped women along occupational lines, and its best documented and most striking example is a confraternity of domestic servants, which formed in 1787 or 1788. Probably spontaneous in origin, it was quickly appropriated by a particularly active cleric and attached to one of the parish churches of Besançon. It flourished throughout the first half of the century, reaching a peak of over 300 members by the 1860s. It also spawned a number of 'daughter societies', initially in nearby towns within the diocese, thereafter beyond its borders.[74]

The final category is the best documented of the three. Charitable societies which grouped between twenty and sixty bourgeois women in

[72] See A. N. F19 6296 and 6424–27. For example in 1800 the Minister of the Interior annotated a report on charitable establishments in the Jura. He noted the existence in the town of Gigny of a 'Conférence des dames et filles établie dans laditte église' of which few further sources have been discovered to date: A.N. F15 1431, Report of 22 October 1800.

[73] Reports from rural parish priests to the civil and diocesan authorities abound with references to such associations, generally referred to by the title *Conférence des femmes* or *Conférence des filles.* See for example A.D. Doubs, 2.V.1, letter from curé of Morteau to Sub-Prefect, Yr.12;2.V.2, report from Sub-Prefect on Conference in Landresse, 1808; A.D. Haute-Saône, 24.J.12. 'Registre de la Confrérie de l'immaculée conception de ville de Gonflans'. An example of a previously mixed confraternity becoming exclusively female in membership is provided by the *Confrérie de Nôtre-Dame de Mont Carmel* at St. Julien, and the *Confrérie de Saint Sacrement de l'Autel* in the commune of Colombier: A.D. Haute-Saône 34.J.127–78, 'catalogue de la Confrérie de Notre-Dame de Mont Carmel': and 34.J.35. 'Registre de la confrérie de Saint Sacrament de l'Autel'.

[74] A.D. Doubs, 38.V.5, especially 'Rapport de maire de Besançon sur la Société des Filles de Service', 13 thermidor Yr 11; A.A. Besançon, *Fonds congréganistes*, 'Archiconfrérie de l'Assomption'; and *Notes de M. l'Abbé Busson.*

at least sixteen different towns in the diocese, these were most often titled *Dames de Charité*.[75] Many had pre-Revolutionary antecedents but several were new foundations. They engaged in far-ranging charitable activity, often being directly associated with the work of a particular regular female congregation. Thus the *Dames de Charité* of Besançon contributed to the funds of, and sponsored children through, the schools run by the *Soeurs de la Sainte Famille*.[76] Similarly, in Arbois in the Jura, a remarkable group of women, once again called the *Dames de Charité*, met fortnightly, initially in opposition to the parish priest. They not only provided bread and soup to the town's poor throughout the nineteenth century, but acquired a house and funded the establishment of a school for girls; bought a field and sold straw to the town prison; and ran a small part of a vineyard at a profit, which they reinvested in the work of the organisation.[77]

In each of these cases the membership of the confraternities clearly mirrored the communities in which they were found and also in some senses reflected and permitted their development. As the economic and social context in which they occurred changed, there was an apparent fragmentation of earlier parochially defined groups into a larger number of associations organized along occupational and class lines. Similarly a given group's image and rhetoric, seen in its handouts, minutes and devotional literature, gradually altered over time to mirror and shape a changing language of female responsibilities and potential. All the confraternities, at least initially, directed themselves towards broadly 'religious' ends. Indeed

[75] Evidence has been found for the existence of such associations in Arbois, Bletterans, Desnes, Dole, Lons-le-Saunier, Morez, Orgelet, Poligny, St. Claude, Sellières and Vernatois in the Jura; Besançon, Montbéliard and Vercel in the Doubs; and Grey and Vesoul in the Haute-Saône. There is evidence that this list is far from complete. The first lay grouping with the title *Dames de Charité* was established by Vincent de Paul in the early seventeenth century at Chatillon-les-Dombes where he was curé. On this aspect of de Paul's work see C. Jones, 'Sisters of Charity', pp. 343–44; I. Druhen *De l'indulgence et de la bienfaisance dans la ville de Besançon* (Besançon, 1860), pp. 347–49.

[76] See n. 66 above. Sometimes there could be rivalry between a regular congregation and a charitable confraternity about the extent of the latter's authority. Such a dispute appears to have severed relations between the *Filles de Charité* and the *Dames de Charité* in Besançon: see F. Trochu, *Sainte Jeanne-Antide Thouret* (Besançon, 1933), pp. 208–12; A.A. Besançon, *Fonds congréganistes-Thouret*.

[77] A.M. Arbois Q. 248: *Dames de Charité*, especially 'Livre contenant règlements, délibérations, rendus et comptes, des réunions de l'Association des Dames de Charité' and 'règlements et statuts de l'établissement de l'ermitage à Arbois'.

those involved in charity would not necessarily have perceived the stark divide between these two types of activity that the twentieth-century observer might be tempted to draw.

In assessing why these patterns of association were so popular among women it is important to acknowledge that different women joined different sorts of confraternity. All, however, provided some degree of mutual aid, material and psychological, for this world and the next. Considerable attention was given, especially in the rural and occupational groupings, to observing the death of a *consoeur*, to the funeral ritual and to the provision of requiem masses.[78] All confraternities also afforded the opportunity to socialize and to meet other women of the same social class or occupation. Within the bourgeoisie and provincial elite, so thoroughly represented in the charitable associations, this performed a vital function, especially as that social group reformed or accommodated the changes to its constituency wrought by the Revolution. Similarly, over time, these societies could assist with the need to interpellate to the local elite new members who had moved either geographically or socially so as to recognize, even permit their 'new' social standing. Links between landed, noble wealth, local government, commerce, banking, and the military were facilitated in confraternities. In one example at least it is clear that families linked in this manner also experienced considerable intermarriage.[79]

These patterns of association contributed to the establishment of a member's identity. That contribution to identity was multi-faceted: geographic, social, occupational, and gendered. Key rituals and activities bound the confraternity together and gave its members a position within the wider community. With the dispensing of charity, this was further achieved by the relationship to the constructed community of the recipients: the deserving poor; a school; but increasingly more precisely defined groups such as pregnant women, poor girls and prisoners.

For some women the confraternity, like the regular congregation, also permitted a real involvement with formal structures of local government. In their charitable activity they often cooperated, or came into conflict with, the local *bureau de bienfaisance*; they were thus permitted, or acquired a

[78] To be seen in *statuts* and *règlements* of all the groups discussed.

[79] This is to be seen in links within the membership of the *Dames de Charité* of St. Claude, traced through notarial records of wills registered and heirs of estates. See A.N. F19 6336, membership list, 1808, and A.D. Jura Q. p. 6864.

'political' role in the wider community.[80] This was particularly the case in matters relating to the poor, to children, to other women and to the regulation of morals. This can be seen to be a domestication of politics, an exporting of the powers and responsibilities of the housewife beyond the confines of the home. It can also be viewed as a negotiation of the dominant, yet internally contradictory, contemporary language of separate spheres of activity for the two sexes: the public being a priori a male sphere, the private the domain of women.

This could have been a conscious strategy on the part of the women involved, a means to an end in a society which in all other respects denied such involvement; it may have been unconscious, or only partially acknowledged. The power which women thus acquired derived most particularly from the legitimacy of the structure of the female confraternity and of female philanthropy. This in turn derived from both dominant rhetorical models of female virtue and the close similarity in the activities involved with those undertaken by the uncloistered nun. Its articulation by the Catholic church was also informed by that institution's recent history, and by the perception of the tasks facing the Catholic religion in the new century. This necessarily introduces the complex arenas of 'autonomy' and control. The evidence suggests that the church did not narrowly create this pattern of female religiosity and association, either by its rhetoric or actions. Rather, it could be argued, certain of its institutions were permitted to change and develop over time in ways which in part reflected a shifting base of 'demand'. This tacit bargain, whereby women acquired and retained a space of piety and function on their own terms provided that it was within a very broad definition accorded by the church, was also informed by both national and local politics. In particular groups of women often had to negotiate a very difficult path, in the clerical as well as civil imagination, between 'piety' and *fanatisme*.[81]

Increasingly dominant rhetorical divisions into appropriate male and female behaviour could be and were negotiated by some women in this period, who thus found release from the restrictions of purely 'private' responsibilities and passive virtues. Yet at the same time these

[80] For example the *Dames de Charité* of Besançon were in frequent conflict in the 1820s with the *Bureau de bienfaisance* over control of bequests made to the former. See A.D. Doubs, 38.V.4 and A.M. Besançon Q.2.5.

[81] In reports of female religious activity it was common, especially regarding attendance at missions or collective activity in the public spaces of the community, and particularly in civil records, to describe women's behaviour as 'fanatical'.

boundaries and divisions were reinforced. Ultimately the language and idiom of nineteenth-century French Catholicism was restrictive of female action and self-perception at least as much as it allowed or facilitated agency. It permitted women an involvement in community regulation, in the 'public sphere', but only in certain ways, and above all in ways generally not rhetorically acknowledged as such. By and large the available contradictions within the representation of types of female virtue only empowered certain women in this particular manner.

Thus in return for her virginity, poverty and nominal obedience to the male hierarchy of the church, the nun achieved a prominent, valued status in the public spaces of the community. By 1850 she dominated primary education and hospital nursing in France. In addition, for certain groups of bourgeois women, the images of femininity and female virtue propagated by the French Catholic church, when laid alongside their economic and social status, offered an access to legitimate public and political activity. Provided certain moral codes were clearly observed, some lay women were thus able to act in similar spheres, even alongside and in cooperation with the brides of Christ, whilst knowing the joys and travails of earthly marriage and material comfort.

The empowerment permitted by the images and idiom of French Catholicism to lay women lower down the social hierarchy was neither so far-reaching nor so implicitly political. The unavoidable economic and social constraints to active philanthropy and leisured sociability for women who spent most of their waking hours working in the family home, the field, the factory or the house of their bourgeois counterparts, meant that for them Catholic association provided legitimate but limited opportunities to socialize, occasional psychological or material aid and support and increased access to a model of virtue or strength through the traditional channels of quiet, passive endurance. Yet it also served to restate and reinforce their particular position in society and status in the local community, as well as their particularly feminine obligation to accept this, if they wished to remain within the ranks of the virtuous. It threw them into, or contributed to, a troubled, client-patroness relationship with other women and constrained moral and sexual choices as tightly, if not more tightly, than ever.

Even for the nun and the member of the middle-class charitable association it is arguable that in the long run the role that Catholic discourse played in the construction of female virtue and thus female opportunity limited as well as liberated the activities and apparent choices of women. The pattern of the emergence of the female 'professions' of the nurse and the primary school-teacher in France in the second half of the nineteenth century and beyond is relevant here. Similarly it is worth noting that the French suffrage movements in the period after 1850 faced greater difficulty in recruiting middle-class women to their cause, than did broader, less explicitly 'political' feminist groups whose aims were directed as much to moral reform and wide-ranging philanthropy as to particular civil and political aims.[82] The particular parameters of an emerging female political identity in France in the latter half of the nineteenth century – the ways and manner in which groups of women came to see themselves, as well as be seen, as having a political role or duty in society – seem to be crucially predicated upon earlier, essentially religious patterns of female association and its associated discourse of the means to female virtue. Certainly, in one case at least, a direct continuity of membership and structure can be traced from an explicitly religious charitable confraternity in the late eighteenth century, grouping widows and spinsters with considerable property and the wives and daughters of a town's commercial, landed and business elite, to that of a mid twentieth-century secular, philanthropic and vaguely political association joined among others by their female descendants.[83]

The belief of men, particularly those with power, that the Catholic church exercized a powerful influence over women (a belief which even if not sincerely held was nevertheless sufficiently plausible to convince or propitiate), was used to defend the continued denial of the vote

[82] See S.C. Hause and A.R. Kenny, *Women's Suffrage and Social Politics in the French Third Republic* (Princeton, 1984); P.K. Bidelman, *Pariahs Stand Up! The Founding of the Liberal Feminist Movement in France, 1858–1889* (Westport, 1982); C. Moses, *French Feminism in the Nineteenth Century* (Albany, 1984). In 1889 and 1900 two international congresses of female charities and institutions were held in France. Following the latter occasion discussions with the organizers of a separate congress on the rights and conditions of women resulted in the formation of the *Conseil National des Femmes Françaises*, an offshoot of which eventually directed itself to obtaining the vote for women. Suffrage, when sought, was thus seen by many feminists as a means to wider goals of social reform at least as much as an end in itself.

[83] Namely the *Dames de Charité d'Arbois*. The links between local and national philanthropic groups, between confraternities and lay societies, between Catholic and Protestant patterns of activity and politicization require further study. I am indebted to Brian Fitzpatrick for bringing to my attention an early example of organized female philanthropy apparently crossing another 'divide': the *Association des Dames des Deux Cultes* at Sauve in the Gard, apparently founded in 1841, which distributed material help to households where there were sick, elderly and impoverished people: A.D. Gard 6M.772, Prefectoral report 1861.

to French women right up to 1944.[84] This belief, while undoubtedly informed by deep anticlericalism and class bias, surely spoke at least as much to profound and particular assumptions about sexual difference – to the difference between *la femme forte* and *l'homme fort*: between the strong, virtuous philanthropic woman, and the powerful, wise, political man.

3

Religion and Gender in Modern France: Some Reflections

James F. McMillan

We might usefully begin by considering two celebrated anticlerical texts. In 1845 Jules Michelet wrote: 'Our wives and daughters are raised, governed *by our enemies. Enemies of the modern spirit* of liberty and of the future . . . *our enemies*, I repeat, in a more direct sense, being naturally envious of marriage and family life'. The enemies were, of course, the Catholic clergy, and Michelet affirmed, 'The direction, the government of women, is the vital point of ecclesiastical power, which they will defend to the death'.[1] In 1870, in a famous speech at the *salle Molière* in Paris, Jules Ferry stated, 'Equality of education is unity reconstituted in the family'. He went on: 'Today there is a barrier between woman and man, between wife and husband, which makes many marriages, while outwardly harmonious, result in the most profound differences of opinions, of tastes, of feelings: but then there is no longer a real marriage, for real marriage, gentlemen, is the marriage of souls'. His conclusion was unambiguous: '. . . you must choose, citizens, either woman must belong to science or she must belong to the church'.[2]

Michelet and Ferry, it need hardly be said, were neither isolated nor marginal voices in nineteenth-century France. On the contrary,

[1] J. Michelet, *Du Prêtre, de la femme, de la famille* (Paris, 1845), avant-propos.
[2] J. Ferry, *De l'égalité de l'éducation: conférence populaire faite à la salle Molière, 10 avril 1870.*

they were two of the most prominent representatives of a Republican political culture which by the third quarter of the century had established its ascendancy in the country. Their views on the 'woman question' are entirely characteristic of a Republican discourse in which women were represented as specially subject to clerical influence, through their schooling, attendance at mass and, perhaps most sinister of all, via the confessional. The result was that families were dangerously divided between enlightened, rational, progressive and anticlerical husbands, and pious, *pratiquantes*, religiously-oriented wives.

The discourse had other practical consequences. One was that women were denied the vote until 1944. Throughout the seventy-year history of the Third Republic, the enfranchisement of women was opposed by the champions of 'universal' suffrage on the grounds that to allow women to vote was to benefit the 'clerical party' and therefore to endanger the Republic itself. While prime minister, Georges Clemenceau produced a pamphlet in 1907 in which he claimed that, 'if the right to vote were given to women tomorrow, France would all of a sudden jump backwards into the Middle Ages',[3] Alexandre Bérard, *rapporteur* to the Senate of a suffrage bill which was passed by the Chamber of Deputies in 1919 only to be thrown out by the Senate in 1922, prepared a fourteen point anti-feminist tract which, *inter alia*, alleged that 'the "Catholic mentality" of the majority of French women, combined with the hostility of the Church towards the Republic and liberty, mean that women's suffrage would lead to clerical reaction'.[4] Because of their alleged religious sympathies, French women were refused the right to citizenship in a democratic regime which prided itself on its progressive politics.

The idea that women were more religious than men has not been confined to nineteenth-and early twentieth-century anticlerical Republican propagandists. Modern historians, too, have been persuaded of its essential truth. Bonnie Smith, for instance, in her influential study of bourgeois women in the department of the Nord, contrasts her pious female subjects with their rational, secular-minded menfolk. Catholicism, she affirms, was at odds with 'the modern world' and consequently 'lost the allegiance of

---

[3] G. Clemenceau, *La 'justice' du sexe fort* (Paris, 1907).

[4] *Journal Officiel, Sénat, documents*, 3 October 1919. Quoted and translated by S.C. Hause and A.R. Kenney, *Women's Suffrage and Social Politics in the French Third Republic* (Princeton, 1984), p. 238.

many men'. For politicians, businessmen and intellectuals, 'doctrinaire Catholicism' was 'politically reactionary, hostile to economic progress and fraught with superstition'. Women, on the other hand, retained a traditional and theocratic outlook, ultimately because of the mysteriousness of the functioning of their own bodies:

> The mathematical explanation of life proposed by modern science appeared as patent fatuity to the visibly bleeding, swelling, pained women of the nineteenth century. They preferred theology and the pre-Copernican vision of the universe, for reproduction predisposed them to a religious world view.[5]

Biology was religious destiny.

Historians of French Catholicism have likewise spoken of a 'feminization' of the Catholic religion in the course of the nineteenth century. In his impressive doctoral thesis, Claude Langlois has documented the massive expansion in female religious orders which took place between 1800 and 1880, with around 400 new orders founded and some 200,000 women entering the religious life.[6] In the matter of religious practice, women consistently loom larger than men in any statistics of attendance at mass or the making of Easter Duties. 'Sexual dimorphism' appears to be one of the truisms established by French *sociologie religieuse*.[7] A number of historians have tried to account for this *féminisation de la pratique* by pointing to a clerical strategy which consciously promoted an 'ultramontane' piety which was emotional, sentimental and anti-intellectual, so as to have greater appeal to its primarily female adherents. Devotion to Mary, the Sacred Heart, pilgrimages at both local and national level and, generally speaking, a more openly festive and demonstrative religion have been represented as more attractive to women than to men, as the nineteenth-century clergy took to replacing the more austere and

---

[5] B. Smith, *Ladies of the Leisure Class: The Bourgeoises of Northern France in the Nineteenth Century* (Princeton, 1981), pp. 95–96 and chapter 5 generally. Historians who have given Smith's these wider currency include R. Gibson, *A Social History of French Catholicism, 1789–1914* (London, 1989) and J. Rendall, *The Origins of Modern Feminism: Women in Britain, France and the United States, 1780–1860* (London, 1985).

[6] C. Langlois, *Le catholicisme au féminin: les congrégations françaises à supérieure générale au XIXe siècle* (Paris, 1984).

[7] On *sociologie religieuse*, see F. Boulard, *An Introduction to French Religious Sociology: Pioneer Work in France* (London, 1960) and G. Le Bras, *Etudes de sociologie religieuse* (2 vols., Paris, 1955–56).

Jansenistical Catholicism of the eighteenth century with a religion of love.[8]

Insofar as modern historians have turned their attention to the question of the relationship between religion and gender (and the field is still grossly under-researched), their work has tended to endorse the claims of contemporary Republicans and anticlericals that nineteenth-century French Catholicism was overwhelmingly a religion for women. Indeed anticlerical discourse is sometimes cited as evidence for the veracity of the proposition. The remainder of this essay will take issue with this now 'orthodox' view. It has no aspirations to being a definitive study of the subject, but it will suggest ways in which the received wisdom may be in need of revision or qualification. Without denying the variations in patterns of religious practice according to gender which are now familiar to all students in the field, it challenges the thesis that gender provides the key to religious belief and practice, and rejects the enormously condescending view that what allegedly made Catholicism unattractive to men – its non-scientific doctrines, superstitious cults and sentimental piety – were precisely what made it attractive to women.

In the first instance such a view rests on unproven and highly dubious assumptions about the attitudes and outlook of nineteenth-century French men. For men, too, adhered to Catholicism, and there is little to suggest that their faith was of a qualitatively different kind from that of women. Most obviously Catholicism was staffed by a male clergy: for some men, therefore, the appeal of religion was sufficiently strong to encourage a life-long dedication to its service. Historians may argue about the genuineness of vocations and the mixture of motives that produced a clerical calling (though the curé of Ars would appear to be a more representative figure than Stendhal's Julien Sorel);[9] what is not in contention is the gender of priests. Furthermore, even if it is allowed that the clergy are a special breed of men, set apart by their seminary education and training, we might usefully remind ourselves that among the faithful were not only pious women but prominent lay men: Montalembert, Falloux, Ozanam, Veuillot, Keller, de Mun, Harmel, Sangnier, Piou to cite but some of the

---

[8] Cf. Gibson, *Social History* and G. Cholvy and Y.-M. Hilaire *Histoire religieuse de la France contemporaine* (3 vols., Toulouse, 1985–88), vol. 1.

[9] Gibson, *Social History*: and A. Gough, *Paris and Rome: The Gallican Church and the Ultramontane Campaign, 1848–1853.* (Oxford, 1986), are good on the training and outlook of the clergy.

best known names. A history of nineteenth-century French Catholicism which left out the men of *L'Avenir* and *L'Univers*, the *parti clérical* of the Second Empire and the *Ralliement*, the Society of Saint Vincent de Paul and the *Oeuvre des cercles*, the A.C.J.F. and the *Sillon*, would make strange reading. Again one need hardly labour the point, but we are dealing here with *men* – liberal Catholics, social Catholics, ultramontanes, *ralliés* – who were not necessarily the least rational or feeble-minded of their sex. One might love them or hate them, but their gender is hardly in question.

Nor can it seriously be maintained that nineteenth-century males deserve to be regarded as rational, progressive and 'modern', while nineteenth-century females remained pious, reactionary and retrograde. The contemporary anticlericals who made such claims can hardly be regarded as unbiased witnesses. Historicans are expected to be critical of their sources, and in this instance, when the discourse of the anticlericals is deconstructed, one might be left wondering whether they had any monopoly on modernity or rationality. Take the case of Michelet, who makes a particularly poor apologist for the rational, enlightened, nineteenth-century male. Though profoundly anti-Catholic, like many other Romantics he was not anti-religious. His concerns were deeply spiritual and moral. He explicitly described his desire to talk to women about 'things that touch the heart and moral life, eternal things – religion, the soul, God'.[10]

As regards women, Michelet was obsessed with their 'otherness' and with gender difference. He had a morbid, possibly perverse, fascination with female physiology, and notably with menstruation, which he described as a 'wound': '. . . for fifteen or twenty days out of twenty-eight (one could say almost perpetually) woman is not only ill but wounded'.[11] His view of woman, ostensibly based on medical and scientific data, in reality reflected his own fantasies about female nature. The woman he celebrated was a *femme imaginaire* who was morally superior to men and who, ideally, should be placed on a domestic pedestal:

[10] Michelet, *Du prêtre*, avant-propos.

[11] J. Michelet, *L'Amour* (Paris, 1859). For a discussion of these views, see L. Jordonova, *Sexual Visions: Images of Gender in Science and Medicine between the Eighteenth and Twentieth Centuries* (Hemel Hempstead, 1989) and T. Moreau, *Le sang de l'histoire: Michelet, l'histoire et l'idée de la femme au XIXe siècle* (Paris, 1982).

Man must nourish woman. Both spiritually and materially, he must nourish her who in turn nourishes him with her love, with her milk, and with her blood.[12]

Or again:

They shape us – this is a superior type of work. To be loved, to give birth, then to give moral birth, to raise man up (this barbarous time does not yet understand this), this is the business of woman.[13]

Whatever else he was – and he was many other things – Michelet was a sexist, a patriarch and an apologist for the doctrine of separate spheres. What outraged him was that priests should usurp the place that properly belonged to husbands. It was the latter who alone had the right to control their wives. It is certainly hard to see him as a 'feminist' or an 'enlightened' commentator on the 'woman question'. If, as many others have rightly pointed out, churchmen were strong apologists for the ideal of *la femme au foyer*, so too was Michelet. And, of course, famously, as a writer and historian, Michelet was noted for the opposite of scientific detachment – his prose was emotional, passionate, over-wrought. He was anything but 'rational' man.

Jules Ferry, on the other hand, was a leading representative of that first generation of Third Republican politicians who had been marked by the spirit of rationalism and positivism. Self-consciously an heir of the *philosophes*, he was one of the staunchest champions of the new, 'modern', society which had supposedly issued from the French Revolution. It would, however, be idle to pretend that Ferry's *monde moderne* meant the contemporary, actual, society of the 1870s and 1880s. Rather, it was an ideological construct, an ideal society and polity which he hoped to see come into existence as the result of a successful struggle against a different conception of society in which Christianity was accorded a leading ideological role. Ferry's aim, as he candidly acknowledged, was 'to organize humanity without God or without kings'.[14] His claims to be a spokesman for *the* 'modern world' need not be accepted at face value. In practice, Ferry's modern world was a conservative, sexist, bourgeois democracy, a liberal capitalist state, a modern society in no need of

---

[12] J. Michelet, *Du prêtre*, avant-propos.

[13] Ibid.

[14] On Ferry's political and moral ideas, see P. Chevallier, *La séparation de l'église et de l'école: Jules Ferry et Léon XIII* (Paris, 1981).

further transformation in the direction which the French Left wished to take it. As social Catholics, among others, were not slow to point out, the Third Republic which supposedly embodied modernity permitted offensively high levels of social inequality and social injustice. It was a long way from being the kind of model state which would give it the right to castigate its enemies as 'irrational' or 'anti-modern'. Ferry and his ilk stood for one version of what the modern world might look like. Many people – Socialists as well as Catholics – did not like what they saw.

In short, to identify nineteenth-century anticlericals as the embodiment of a rational/progressive/modern world view is to replicate the value judgements of a prejudiced nineteenth-century rhetoric. How 'modern', for example, was Emile Combes? In venting his private resentments against the church which had rejected him and in instigating what can only be described as a persecution of the religious orders, he cuts a poor figure as an 'enlightened' statesman. His bigotry and intolerance, on the other hand, might well be considered *very* modern, since the twentieth century was to set new standards in such matters. Arguments about the essential rationality and modernity of nineteenth-century Frenchmen appear all the most implausible when one remembers that there were powerful intellectual currents at both ends of the century – Romanticism in the first half, the 'revolt' against reason towards the end – which made anti-rationalism a respectable attitude of mind. Catholicism was a notable beneficiary, as the spectacular 'conversions' of prominent literary figures attest. Chateaubriand wept and believed, while the likes of Bloy, Claudel, Péguy and Huysmans had little time for the achievements of the 'scientific' spirit. On the other hand, practising Catholics could be numbered among those who contributed to the advances in science which indubitably took place in the age.[15]

Because men did not practise the Catholic religion to the same extent as women, it does not necessarily follow that they were inevitably or invariably hostile to it. A study of the Nièvre at the beginning of the twentieth century reveals that, despite the prevalence of 'seasonal conformity' and low levels of male church attendance, men 'accepted even with a secret satisfaction that their wives practised, and that their children made their first communion: and they almost always firmly insisted on their

[15] H.S. Paul, 'In Quest of Kerygma: Catholic Intellectual Life in Nineteenth Century France', *American Historical Review*, lxxv (1969), pp. 387–423.

being baptised'.[16] In the middle of the nineteenth century, it seems that the wealthier peasant farmers of the Beauce, while harbouring misgivings about the hold which clerics might be able to establish over their wives, approved of feminine religious devotion as a guarantor of marital fidelity. Religion might be likewise useful in persuading young people to obey their parents and domestics to respect their masters.[17] Gérard Cholvy makes similar observations about the Midi:

> Masculine anticlericalism is most often in no way prejudicial to feminine attitudes. Nowhere are the two sociabilities so different. The man of the Midi, who refrains from entering a church, sees his wife and young children go without displeasure.[18]

If the thesis which views gender as the key to nineteenth-century religious attitudes misrepresents the attitudes of many men, it is still more misleading as regards the religious beliefs and practices of French women. Though not stated in so many words, what is being contended is that, because of their intellectual inferiority (or 'pre-Copernican outlook'), allied to their bodily weaknesses, women were peculiarly gullible and susceptible to the mawkish charms of an Ultramontane piety peddled by priests who had the express intention of duping their female flocks. The condescension is staggering, as is the presumption to be able to identify the sources of a gender-specific, feminine, religiosity. It is by no means evident that, say, the cult of the Virgin appealed exclusively to women: its leading votary in the nineteenth century was Pope Pius IX, while male Catholics like Montalembert also devoted themselves to the cult of the saints. By the same token, anticlericalism was by no means a male preserve. Maria Deraismes, pioneer feminist, and Maria Vérone, first female Freemason in France, and many of the other leading lights of 'mainstream' bourgeois feminism, shared the anticlerical prejudices of the Republican politicians whom they endeavoured to cultivate. The women of the Commune, led by the 'Red Virgin' Louise Michel, were as rabidly anticlerical as male *communards*. It would be a mistake to assume that all French females – or even simply all middle-class females – were models of Christian virtue. If it serves no other purpose, this

---

[16] Quoted in G. Dupeux, *French Society, 1789–1970* (London, 1976), p. 186.

[17] C. Marcilhacy, *Le diocèse d'Orléans au milieu du XIXe siècle* (Paris, 1964), p. 215.

[18] Cholvy and Hilaire, *Histoire religieuse*, vol. 1, p. 256.

essay hopes to dispel some of the more extravagantly reductionist notions which have passed for explanations of femine piety and religious practice.

In the absence of systematic research into the religious sensibilities of both sexes in a nineteenth-century French context, statements about the religious motivations of women must, of course, remain speculative and tentative. Yet it may be assumed that, as in the case of men, and varying enormously from individual to individual, religious behaviour was a manifestation of both sacred and secular impulses. The latter need not be restricted to defective education and menstruation. For instance, in the case of the substantial numbers of women who elected to dedicate themselves to the religious life, along with an authentic desire to serve Christ and the church, many may have been fired by an ambition (by no means incompatible with their religious vocation) to have a career. The vast majority of nineteenth-century nuns, unlike their predecessors in the Middle Ages, were not confined to closed orders and convents, but carried out a range of jobs in schools and hospitals. They were, effectively, professional women at a time when professional opportunities, especially for middle-class women, were severely curtailed. Theirs was not a retreat from the world but an engagement with it. The founders of new orders acquired status and power. Nor should one underestimate the attractions of escaping the dangers of childbirth and the gynaecological problems to which many nineteenth-century women were subject as a result of sexual activity (venereal infection being the worst, but by no means the only hazard).[19] Equally, for lay women, the church may have offered an outlet not just for their spirituality but also for their sociability. Going to church and becoming involved in church-related activities were legitimate and respectable things for women to do, whereas men had different patterns of sociability (which frequently involved bars, drinking and membership of all-male clubs and *cercles*). In consorting with the clergy, women were not necessarily subjecting themselves to clerical brainwashing but seeking a sympathetic ear to discuss their worries and anxieties. The confessor-penitent relationship which excited the outrage and jealousies of Michelet and other anticlericals looks a lot healthier and more innocent when considered from a female vantage point, as Theodore Zeldin observed some years ago.[20]

[19] T. Zeldin, *France, 1848–1945* (2 vols., Oxford, 1973–77), vol. 2, p. 867.
[20] Ibid., p. 993

As a pointer to the direction which future research might take, I would suggest that historians concern themselves less with the degree to which French women were allegedly subjected to clerical manipulation and more with the positive ways in which they related to Catholic Christianity in order to find meaning and fulfilment in their lives. Religious commitment allowed women first of all to express their piety, but sometimes also to discover possibilities for social and political action. Take, for instance, the case of the *Ligue Patriotique des Françaises*, an organization founded in 1902 to combat the anticlerical onslaught on the religious orders unleashed by *le petit père* Combes. Ostensibly an apolitical and purely religious society, the *Ligue* considered its primary task to be the rechristianization of France. It organised an *oeuvre des retraites* for the creation of spiritual elites within its ranks and expected local group leaders to sanctify themselves for their task by attendance at special masses. Yet, at the same time, the *Ligue* was drawn not only into the wider sphere of social Catholicism but also into the political arena proper, developing links with the Catholic *ralliés* led by Jacques Piou in the *Action Libérale Populaire*. By the end of the First World War, the *Ligue's* leadership had become converts to the cause of women's suffrage. Given the size of its membership – by 1914 it had 585,000 members and by 1932 one-and-a-half million – the *Ligue Patriotique des Françaises* therefore developed into a powerful voice for votes for women.[21] It is more than time that the importance of this organization was recognized by historians of French feminism as well as by historians of the religious history of France.

Similarly, in the field of social Catholicism in the late nineteenth and early twentieth centuries, women were active at every level of the movement. Distinctive feminine initiatives like the *cercle* of Jeanne Chenu, *L'Action Sociale de la Femme*, the settlement movement of Mlle. Gahéry and Mercédès Le Fer de la Motte, or the development of female Catholic trade unions were attempts to realize the principles expounded by Pope Leo XIII in his encyclical *Rerum Novarum* (1891). Although *Rerum Novarum* was a deeply conservative document, inspired by fear of the spread of Socialism and prescribing a limited, family-based social role for women, the practical achievements of female Social Catholicism, while further promoting a degree of rechristianization, subverted as much as

---

[21] J.F. McMillan, 'Women, Religion and Politics: The Case of the Ligue Patriotique des Françaises', in *Proceedings of the Annual Meeting of the Western Society for French History*, 15 (Flagstaff, Arizona 1988), ed. W. Roosen, pp. 355–64.

implemented its doctrines by creating new careers for women as social workers and opening them up to political militancy.[22]

There is also the example of Christian feminism itself. This is an area which has received little attention from historians. Yet, as one pioneering article began by pointing out, 'The Catholic women's suffrage movement converted more women to suffragism than all other feminist groups combined'.[23] Christian feminists, headed by Marie Maugeret, were active in France from the 1890s, insisting that the pursuit of women's rights and adherence to the Catholic religion were not incompatible. From the outset Maugeret was in favour of campaigning for the vote, but recognized that at the turn of the century this demand was too radical for most of her membership. Nevertheless she succeeded in pushing through a resolution in favour of women's suffrage at the third *Congrès Jeanne d'Arc* in 1906, having argued the *ralliement* line that 'in order to clean up a house, it is first necessary to enter it'. Wider acceptance of the suffragist position among Catholic women had to wait until the time of the First World War, but thereafter it took off in a big way. It may indeed have become too successful for its own good, allowing anticlerical Radical politicians to oppose their cause on the grounds cited at the beginning of this essay. Once again, however, we are looking at an instance of how political commitment could be seen as an extension of religious conviction. The pull of Christianity was not always towards domesticity and subordination.

Gender, in short, would appear *not* to be the single most important factor governing religious belief and practice in modern France. To the extent that secular influences can be invoked, it is more helpful to turn to the influence of geography. The religious map of France is well established and it shows that, in dechristianized areas, though the religious practice of women may have been higher than that of men, it was still very low.[24] Thus in Chartres around 1900 only 1.5 per cent of men and 15 per cent of women made their Easter duties, while in the Yonne, on the eve of the First World War, the

[22] J.F. McMillan, 'Women and Social Catholicism in Late Nineteenth and Early Twentieth-Century France', in *The Church and Women: Studies in Church History*, xxvii (Oxford, 1990).

[23] S. Hause and A. Kenney, 'The Development of the Catholic Women's Suffrage Movement in France, 1896–1922', *Catholic Historical Review*, 68 (1981), pp. 11–30.

[24] The map may be studied in Boulard, *An Introduction*, or in Gibson, *Social History*. See also F.A. Isambert and J.P. Terrenoire, (eds.), *Atlas de la pratique religieuse des catholiques en France* (Paris, 1980) and F. Boulard, et al. *Matériaux pour l'histoire religieuse du peuple française, XIX–XXe siècles*, (2 vols., Paris, 1982–87).

comparable figures were 2.6 per cent and 16.8 per cent. By contrast, in Nantes at the turn of the century, 95.7 per cent of the women and 82.4 per cent of the men fulfilled their Easter obligations.[25] It is always possible that the explanation for the difference is that the women of Chartres and the women of the Yonne were more modern and less 'pre-Copernican' than the women (and indeed the men) of Nantes – but it seems unlikely.

[25] Figures taken from Gibson, *Social History*, pp. 174–76.

4

The Catholic Church and the Business Community in Nineteenth-Century France[1]

Colin Heywood

What did the French bougeoisie make of religion? Maurice Colrat, president of the *Société pour la Défense des Classes Moyennes*, hesitated when confronting this question during the 1900s, as well he might when addressing the followers of Frédéric Le Play. He then ventured to suggest that the bourgeoisie could best be described as faithful Catholics and passionate anticlericals:

> We are nearly all Voltairians in the café, that is to say sceptics and scoffers, but come one of those great events in life, before the white dress of a first communicant or the black cloth of mourning, we return to the idealism of our fathers, vanquished by the eternal need to establish an indestructible link between the generations: a *religion*.

The speaker concluded, amidst general applause, that 'our religion is a modest one, to which we, the sons of Voltaire and Jean-Jacques, like to give a twist of incredulity'.[2] Such an ambivalent attitude

---

[1] The author would like to thank Ralph Gibson, Olena Heywood and Roger Price for their comments on an earlier draft of this chapter.

[2] 'Du rôle social des classes moyennes', in *Les classes moyennes dans le commerce et l'industrie: XXIXe congrès de la société internationale d'économie sociale et des unions de la paix sociale, fondées par F. Le Play* (Paris, 1910), p. 30.

to religion gives a hint of the tensions that would mar relations between the Catholic church and the business community throughout the nineteenth century. This essay will argue that in principle the two sides had much to offer each other, but that in practice differences of outlook all too often divided them. As a framework for analysis, it will consider three common assumptions. None of these, in our view, can give more than a partial insight into the subject. First, one can hardly avoid the 'Weber thesis' that Catholics were generally less successful in business than Protestants, since it continues to cast its spell on historians. Second, there is the widely-held Marxian view that religion was the 'opiate of the people'. Here the church is held to have served the interests of the bourgeoisie in its struggle with the working class. Finally, contradicting the previous approach, there is stress in some of the literature on the *conflict* between church and bourgeoisie.

Catholics and Protestants in Business

A curious paradox emerges from the literature in this area. On the one hand, the old idea that there was a link between Protestantism and the rise of capitalism has frequently been refuted by specialists. Indeed, it might be said that the whole debate around the 'Weber thesis' has gone dead in recent years. On the other hand, many historical works treat the thesis as if it were a self-evident truth.[3] Why should this be? To begin with, we must return briefly to the original formulation of the argument in 1905: Max Weber's *The Protestant Ethic and the Spirit of Capitalism*. Three points are worth bearing in mind. First, Weber proceeded from an idealist, as opposed to a materialist, conception of history. The subject matter of the book was the 'influence of certain religious ideas on the development of an economic spirit, or the ethos of an economic system'.[4] Second, Weber relied on the sociological method of constructing abstract ideal

---

[3] H.M. Robertson, *Aspects of the Rise of Economic Individualism: A Criticism of Max Weber and his School* (Cambridge, 1935); R.W. Green, *Protestantism and Capitalism: The Weber Thesis and its Critics* (Boston, 1959); K. Samuelsson, *Religion and Economic Action*, trans. E.G. French, (London, 1961).

[4] *The Protestant Ethic and the Spirit of Capitalism*, trans. Talcott Parsons. (London, 1930), p. 26. See also M. Weber, *General Economic History* (London, 1927), pp. 352–69.

types. The ideal type of capitalist entrepreneur, according to Weber, 'avoids ostentation and unnecessary expenditure', and has certain ascetic tendencies, obtaining 'nothing out of his wealth, for himself, except the irrational sense of having done his job well'.[5] Third, Weber felt that in the modern world capitalists were no longer driven by the spirit of religious asceticism – though this did not prevent him from asserting that Protestants were more enterprising than Catholics around 1900.[6]

That some religious codes are more compatible with economic growth than others has not been denied by economists. W.A. Lewis noted that, 'If a religion lays stress upon material values, upon work, upon thrift and productive investment, upon honesty in commercial relations, upon experimentation and risk bearing, and upon equality of opportunity', then it will be helpful to growth. Conversely, in so far as it is hostile to these values, it will tend to inhibit growth.[7] In the case of nineteenth-century France, there is no doubt that many members of the Catholic church deeply resented the spread of industrial capitalism and its values.[8] The majority of bishops and parish priests probably followed Pius IX in his notorious denunciation of 'progress, liberalism and recent civilization' during the Syllabus of 1864.[9] Among the laity there emerged a formidable line of 'intransigent' Catholics, running from de Maistre and Bonald at the beginning of the century to Veuillot and Blanc de Saint-Bonnet after 1848. They were vehement in their critique of the modern economic order. The vicomte de Bonald, for example, considered the love of money the worst of passions, and the spread of market relations a social disaster. In similar vein, Louis Veuillot of *L'Univers* made no effort to conceal his contempt for the bourgeoisie

[5] *Protestant Ethic*, p. 71.

[6] *Ibid.*, pp. 35–42, 72, 174–83. For further details, consult A. Giddens, *Capitalism and Modern Social Theory* (Cambridge, 1971), pp. 119–32, 205–23.

[7] W.A. Lewis, *The Theory of Economic Growth* (London, 1955), p. 105. See also B. Higgins, *Economic Development* (London, 1958), pp. 163–66.

[8] For useful surveys on the attitude of the Catholic church to capitalism at various periods in history, see: W. Sombart, *The Quintessence of Capitalism*, trans. M. Epstein, (New York, 1967), ch. 18; Robertson, *Economic Individualism, passim*; A. Fanfani, *Catholicism, Protestantism and Capitalism* (London, 1938), ch. 5.

[9] See, for example, A. Latreille and R. Rémond, *Histoire du catholicisme en France*, vol. 3, *La période contemporaine* (Paris, 1962), p. 371; J. Gadille, *La pensée et l'action politiques des évêques français au début de la IIIe république, 1870–83* (Paris, 1967), *passim*; R. Gibson, *A Social History of French Catholicism, 1789–1914* (London, 1989), ch. 3.

and its economic liberalism.[10] Even the 'social' Catholics, that small wing of the church that took a progressive line on the plight of the working class, were no less inclined to condemn the 'burning thirst for wealth', the 'cupidity' and even the 'usury' of industrialists.[11] In sum, although not all Catholics were so out of sympathy with the modern world, the major themes emerging from the discourse of leading church figures were scarcely favourable to capitalist enterprise. They yearned for spiritual values rather than materialism; spurned the present for the medieval past; harked back to a corporative society in place of individualism; preferred agriculture to industry and domestic workshops to factories. Whether French businessmen ever paid much attention to this barrage of criticism is another matter. Let it merely be noted here that during the 1940s and 1950s, when discussion of entrepreneurial weakness was much in vogue, Catholicism was often accused of contributing to an unfavourable intellectual climate for economic growth.[12]

That Protestants were closer than Catholics to the ideal type of capitalist entrepreneur has also been argued by a number of authors concerned with nineteenth-century Europe.[13] In the French case, Georges Duveau appears to have been the most influential supporter of the Weber thesis. His famous work on working-class life during the Second Empire, a source of inspiration for many a historian of the post-war generation, was keen to emphasize

[10] D.K. Cohen, 'The Vicomte de Bonald's Critique of Industrialism', *Journal of Modern History*, xli (1969), pp. 475–84; L. Epsztein, *L'économie et la morale aux debuts du capitalisme industriel en France et en Grande-Bretagne* (Paris, 1966), pp. 106–9; J.-M. Mayeur, 'Catholicisme intransigeant, catholicisme social, démocratie chrétienne', *Annales E.S.C*, xxvii (1972), 483–99; A. Gough, *Paris and Rome: The Gallican Church and the Ultramontane Campaign, 1848–1853* (Oxford, 1986), pp. 80–102.

[11] J.-B. Duroselle, *Les débuts du catholicisme social en France, 1822–70* (Paris, 1951), *passim*; P. Droulers, *Action pastorale et problèmes sociaux sous la monarchie de juillet chez Mgr d'Astros* (Paris, 1954), pp. 1–6; his, 'Des évêques parlent de la question ouvrière en France avant 1848', *Revue d'action populaire*, (1961), 442–60; Mayeur, 'Catholicisme', 484, 490–94.

[12] J.E. Sawyer, 'The Entrepreneur and the Social Order: France and the United States', in W. Miller (ed.), *Men in Business* (Cambridge, 1952), pp. 7–22; S. Hoffman, 'Paradoxes of the French Political Community', and J. Pitts, 'Continuity and change in Bourgeois France', both in S. Hoffman et al., *France: Change and Tradition* (London, 1963), pp. 1–117 and 235–304.

[13] Weber, *Protestant Ethic*, pp. 35–40; D. Jeremy (ed.), *Business and Religion in Britain* (Aldershot, 1988), pp. 15–18.

the links between Protestantism and industrialism.[14] He asserted that Protestantism encouraged both asceticism and individualism, thereby creating a favourable climate for capitalist development. Unfortunately, he concluded, these Protestant characteristics were very unFrench! More recently Jean-Pierre Chaline has in his turn highlighted the prominent role of Protestant families in the economic life of nineteenth-century Rouen. Chaline depicts the native bourgeoisie of the town persisting with the *ancien régime* tradition of using business as a stepping stone to land or office, while outsiders from England and the Rhineland injected much-needed technical competence and a spirit of enterprise. The career of Henri Barbet is perhaps instructive from this point of view. Born into a flourishing Protestant family from Rouen, he was responsible for running its calico-printing works under the Restoration. The lure of politics and landed wealth proved too strong and, doubtless as a symptom of his declining commitment to industry, he converted to Catholicism. Guaranteed access to high society with his new religious allegiance, he liquidated his business interests around 1848, and moved on to 'des états plus nobles et plus estimés'.[15]

Despite the weight of this kind of evidence, recent work by economic historians at least has tended to reject the Weber thesis. Two lines of attack can be discerned. The first substitutes a materialist interpretation for Weber's idealistic one. Instead of religious ideas influencing the economy, it is more a question of economic forces influencing religion. This line of argument assumes that where underlying conditions in a region were favourable to trade and industry, a new breed of entrepreneurs would emerge. These men would develop their own scale of values, revolving around material progress, hard work, honesty, thrift and so on. They were not easy for any of the churches to assimilate, given that the guiding principles of Christianity since the Reformations have been the renunciation of this world and the quest for eternal salvation. Nonetheless both Catholic and Protestant clergy were inclined to make some concessions in their teaching to the changing environment created by capitalism.[16] Successful businessmen could therefore be expected to emerge from both religious camps.

[14] G. Duveau, *La vie ouvrière en France sous le second empire* (Paris, 1946), p. 129.

[15] J.-P. Chaline, *Les bourgeois de Rouen: une élite urbaine au XIXe siècle* (Paris, 1982), pp. 57–61, 97–108, 372.

[16] B. Groethuysen, *The Bourgeois: Catholicism versus Capitalism in Eighteenth-Century France*, trans. M. Ilford (London, 1968), *passim*; Robertson, *Economic Individualism*, *passim*.

A number of historians have played down the role of confessional differences among entrepreneurs in nineteenth-century France, asserting that differences *within* the Catholic camp were as important as those between Catholics and Protestants. The classic case of a dynamic group of Catholic businessmen has always been the textile *patronat* of the Nord, who yielded nothing to their *alsacien* rivals in a single-minded dedication to business.[17] Some at least were fervent in their religious faith, and all were convinced of the benefits of free competition. Thus Alfred Motte, a dyer from Roubaix, was perfectly clear on the way forward against his rivals: 'God, who has made all things well . . . only assures a leading position for those who apply themselves the most to good work'.[18] The south-east provides further examples of entrepreneurial Catholics, including the silk merchants of Lyon and the famous Montgolfier family of Annonay.[19] Also there was Albert de Broglie, the dominant figure in the Saint-Gobain glass-works during the 1860s. He was apparently influenced by the ideals of the medieval military orders. It might be thought that the prospects for an industrialist who saw himself as an aristocratic 'fighting-monk', dedicated to service and honour, would not be very good in the modern world. But then again, if early Japanese entrepreneurs could apply themselves to business as modern Samurai . . .[20] In the final analysis though, it has to be admitted that devoutly Catholic businessmen were thin on the ground in France. There is also some difficulty in proving that their Catholic faith was in any way linked to the dynamism of individual entrepreneurs, even in the Nord. David Landes had to admit failure when he tried to 'find something in the Catholicism of Roubaix-Tourcoing that would resemble the Protestant ethic of Weber'.[21]

This paves the way for a second type of reaction against Weber. Instead of debating whether it was religious ideas that influenced business or vice-versa, some historians deny that a connection existed. In the words

[17] C. Fohlen, *L'industrie textile au temps du second empire* (Paris, 1956), pp. 69–78; J. Lambert Dansette, *Quelques familles du patronat textile de Lille-Armentières, 1789–1914* (Lille, 1954), *passim*.

[18] L. Bergeron, *Les capitalistes en France, 1780–1914* (Paris, 1978), p. 192.

[19] *Ibid.*, pp. 179–80.

[20] J.-P Daviet, *Un destin international: la compagnie de Saint-Gobain de 1830 à 1939* (Paris, 1988), p. 68.

[21] D. Landes, 'Religion and Enterprise: The Case of the French Textile Industry' in E. Carter, R. Forster and J.N. Moody (eds.), *Enterprise and Entrepreneurs in Nineteenth and Twentieth-Century France* (Baltimore, 1976), pp. 41–86 (p. 66).

of Samuelsson, business values cut across religious creeds – or went over or around them.[22] Entrepreneurs could be seen to compartmentalize their economic and their religious activities, as those in the Nord interviewed by David Landes in the 1970s claimed to do. Alternatively, they can be depicted as essentially secular creatures, preoccupied with life in a material world.[23] All the evidence from the local studies indicates that the latter was very much the case for the majority of businessmen in nineteenth-century France, as Weber himself was well aware.[24] On a slightly different tack, one can challenge Weber's assumption that the 'ideal type' of capitalist was an austere, puritan type of character. At all periods of capitalist development there were undoubtedly entrepreneurs with a taste for large-scale speculation. One thinks of a long list of capitalist dynasties launched during the Revolutionary and Napoleonic periods by the fabulous profits to be made from military supplies. No less impressive was the opulent lifestyle of, say, the great Parisian bankers or *nouveau riche* owners of the *grands magasins*.[25]

Thus neither the idealist conception of history nor the specific 'ideal type' posited by Max Weber stand up well to close examination in the context of modern France. The consensus among historians today is that religious belief was not a significant influence on French economic development.[26] Most surveys of the French economy or of entrepreneurship in fact ignore the Catholic dimension altogether.[27] Given a predominantly materialist perspective, the fact that Catholic representatives of the old economic order were calling hellfire and damnation on the bourgeoisie was of no great significance for overall growth. Most entrepreneurs were either too detached from the church to be influenced, or sufficiently flexible in their faith to be able to combine Catholicism with money-making.

[22] Samuelsson, *Religion*, p. 152.

[23] *Ibid.*, p. 26.

[24] See below, pp. 83–85.

[25] Samuelsson, *Religion*, pp. 81–87; L. Bergeron, *Banquiers, negoçiants et manufacturiers parisiens du directoire à l'empire* (Paris, 1978), *passim*; his, *Les capitalistes*, pp. 52–53.

[26] C.P. Kindleberger, *Economic Growth in France and Britain, 1851–1950* (Cambridge, Mass., 1964), pp. 94–97; G. Palmade, *French Capitalism in the Nineteenth Century*, trans. G.M. Holmes, (Newton Abbot, 1972), pp. 220–22; Bergeron, *Les capitalistes*, p. 199.

[27] For example, C. Fohlen, 'Entrepreneurship and Management in France in the Nineteenth Century', in P. Mathias and M.M. Postan (eds.), *The Cambridge Economic History of Europe*, vol. 7, *The Industrial Economies: Capital, Labour and Enterprise*, part 1 (Cambridge, 1978), pp. 347–81; F. Caron, *An Economic History of Modern France*, trans. B. Bray, (London, 1979).

Indeed, the recent trend among economic historians to suggest that the French economy performed quite creditably in the nineteenth century casts supposedly 'Catholic' cultural values in a new light. A pattern of industrialization which allowed some preference for work on the land and for skilled labour deployed in small workshops can now be presented as part of a successful adaptation to prevailing economic circumstances.[28]

It should now be clear why the Weber thesis has had such a good run in the French literature. On the one hand, it appears to hold good because French Catholicism in its nineteenth-century form was generally hostile to the 'materialism', 'rationalism' and 'liberalism' of the new capitalist elite. For as long as French economic development was considered 'retarded', its Catholic cultural traditions were a prime candidate for being considered a source of weakness in the Weberian mould. On the other hand, the success of the thesis may be attributed to the immense prestige of certain Lutheran and Calvinist business groups. Outstanding in this respect were the Protestant families of the *haute banque* in Paris and the cotton manufacturers of Alsace, not to mention 'Anglo-Saxon' rivals abroad. Their exceptional dynamism naturally impressed contemporaries, and at first sight it appears to confirm the Weber thesis.[29] Yet, like other successful minorities, they probably flourished for reasons that were not essentially religious, such as the bracing experience of persecution, a tendency to mutual support and exclusion from certain elite positions.[30] Religious faith would then have to be seen less as the driving force behind individual entrepreneurs, and more as a cohesive influence for the group. The limelight given to these Protestant entrepreneurs should not be allowed to blind us to the achievements of avowedly Catholic employers, such as those in the Nord and the Lyonnais, or of 'dechristianized' employers, notably those in the Paris region.

[28] Recent surveys include: R. Roehl, 'French Industrialization: A Reconsideration', *Explorations in Economic History*, xiii (1976), 233–81; P.K. O'Brien and C. Keyder, *Economic Growth in Britain and France, 1780–1914* (London, 1978); R. Cameron and C. Freedeman, 'French Economic Growth: A Radical Revision', *Social Science History*, vii (1983), 3–30; J.-C. Asselain, *Histoire économique de la France du XVIIIe siècle à nos jours*, vol. 1, *De l'ancien régime à la première guerre mondiale* (Paris, 1984).

[29] Bergeron, *Banquiers*, chs. 2 and 3; P.N. Stearns, 'British Industry through the Eyes of French Industrialists, 1820–48', *Journal of Modern History*, xxxvii (1965), 50–61.

[30] Lewis, *Economic Growth*, pp. 104–5.

The Catholic Church and the Social Order

No less attractive than the Weber thesis, in its own way, is the suggestion that the churches of nineteenth-century Europe acted as bastions of the social order. Depicting priests as 'gendarmes in cassocks' and the good works of Christians as contributions to the class struggle always makes good sport for historians. This type of interpretation can be given theoretical support by reference to the Marxist theory of historical materialism, and in particular to its development in the hands of Antonio Gramsci. The theory contends that in a capitalist society the ruling bourgeoisie will inevitably seek to defend the existing economic order. The threat to capitalism comes from a collectivist mode of production, represented in the political sphere by the proletarian movement. During the course of the struggle between the 'two great classes' of the nineteenth century, the bourgeoisie wields its economic and physical power to repress opposition from the proletariat. But it will also rely on an intellectual elite to assert its 'hegemony': that is to say, its cultural and moral ascendancy over the working class.[31] In the words of Karl Marx, 'The government is represented by the instruments of repression, the organs of authority, the army, the police, the officials, the judges, the ministers, the *priests*'.[32] However, it is not only Marxists who have presented the social role of the church along these lines. Numerous sociologists and historians have subscribed to the vaguer notion of 'social control'. Again there is the suggestion that the social order is maintained as much by persuasion as by coercion.[33] This section will examine the extent to which business interests in nineteenth-century France looked to the church for support in politics and in the management of labour. Two key questions need to be kept in mind. First, how far were capitalists and members of the Catholic church in fact willing to cooperate in such a pact? Second, did they have any success in manipulating the working class?

[31] J. McLeish, *The Theory of Social Change* (London, 1969); A. Smith, *Social Change, Social Theory and Historical Processes* (London, 1976), ch. 6; J. Joll, *Gramsci* (Glasgow, 1977), pp. 8, 76–87; R. Simon, *Gramsci's Political Thought* (London, 1982), pp. 21–28.

[32] 'The Class Struggles in France: 1848 to 1850', in *Surveys from Exile*, ed. D. Fernbach, (Harmondsworth, 1973), pp. 35–142 (p. 113).

[33] A.P. Donajgrodzki (ed.), *Social Control in Nineteenth Century Britain* (London, 1977). Also useful are F.M.L. Thompson, 'Social Control in Victorian Britain', *Economic History Review*, 2nd ser., xxxiv (1981), 189–208; and G. Stedman Jones, 'Class Expressions vs. Social Control', *History Workshop*, iv (1978), 163–70.

To begin with, the briefest of surveys will reveal that there was never any concerted effort by the business community to harness the spiritual power of the church in national politics.[34] What stands out is the variety of options taken over the course of the century. The first was to support Catholic Ultraroyalism. In the aftermath of the Revolution, an alliance between the Bourbon monarchy and the Catholic church, the two bastions of the *ancien régime*, might appear the surest basis for stability. Ultraroyalism was of course more associated with the interests of the landed aristocracy than with those of business. Interestingly, Gramsci considered priests as defenders of the old feudal order rather than of capitalism – and French priests in the nineteenth century probably fulfilled this role better than any other. Nonetheless, isolated groups of businessmen evidently considered the hierarchical, corporative type of society idealized by the Ultras as favourable to their business interests. One can cite merchants in Marseilles and other Royalist strongholds in the south under the Restoration; big ironmasters like the De Wendels in the Moselle or Benoist d'Azy in the Nièvre; some of the textile *patronat* of the Nord; and the silk magnates of Lyon.[35]

A second option, appearing after 1830, was the more cynical Orleanist approach, associated with the world of high finance, and the upper reaches of commerce and industry. The Orleanists were characteristically sceptical in religious matters themselves, but willing to see the masses 'moralized' by the church. For example, the Guizot law of 1833 demanded that 'moral and religious instruction should hold the front rank' at all levels of elementary schooling, in order to 'penetrate' the souls of pupils with those sentiments and principles which safeguard good order and inspire the fear and love of God'.[36] Subsequently, as Marx gleefully noted, the Revolutionary upheaval that brought down Louis Philippe provoked an undignified stampede by businessmen into the Bonapartist camp, and they were quickly joined by much

[34] This section relies on R. Rémond, *The Right Wing in France* (Philadelphia, 1966); his, *L'anticléricalisme en France de 1815 à nos jours* (Paris, 1976); R. Magraw, *France, 1815–1914: The Bourgeois Century* (London, 1983).

[35] A.-J. Tudesq, *Les grands notables en France, 1840–1849* (2 vols., Paris, 1964), vol. 1, p. 194; Bergeron, *Les capitalistes*, pp. 178–80.

[36] M. Gontard, *Les écoles primaires de la France bourgeoise, 1833–1875* (Toulouse, 1957), p. 7. See also M. Crubellier, *Histoire culturelle de la France* (Paris, 1974), pp. 104–5; Chaline, *Bourgeois de Rouen*, pp. 267–68.

of the clergy.[37] The Falloux law of 1850 was a sure indicator of the renewed desire to use religious teaching in the schools as a buttress for the social order. The Abbé Mayzonnier summed up the general feeling at the period by asserting: 'We must moralize the working class, it is the gangrenous part of our society today: all responsible men rightly proclaim this . . . Religion alone has the secret.'[38]

A further option was to give up on the church altogether, and rely instead on popular anticlericalism to mobilize support. According to the well-known thesis of Sanford Elwitt, after 1870 the industrial bourgeoisie turned to democratic Republicanism as a way of establishing its ideological and political hegemony. The emphasis was now on democratic, egalitarian and secular values. 'Sentiments of civic dignity' would replace 'Sentiments of Christian humility' in the schools; the answer to the class struggle would be the solidarity of capital and labour, and the common citizenship of all Frenchmen.[39] Of course one can always point out that the new Republican morality taught in the schools was merely a laicized form of the morality traditionally taught by the church.[40] By the 1890s, a softening of attitudes to the Republic among the church hierarchy permitted a new conservative alliance between moderate Catholics (many of them businessmen) and opportunist Republicans.[41] This development should not be allowed to obscure the virulent anticlericalism of the smaller businessmen, particularly in a 'dechristianized' area like Paris.[42]

[37] Karl Marx, 'The Eighteenth Brumaire of Louis Bonaparte', in *Surveys from Exile*, pp. 146–249 (pp. 221–25).

[38] E. Levasseur, *Histoire des classes ouvrières et de l'industrie en France de 1789 à 1870* (2 vols., New York, 1969 (1904)), vol. 2, p. 666. For an excellent local illustration of this point, see P. Pierrard, *La vie ouvrière à Lille sous le second empire* (Paris, 1965), ch. 9.

[39] S. Elwitt, *The Making of the Third Republic: Class and Politics in France, 1868–1884* (Baton Rouge, 1975).

[40] J.-M. Mayeur and M. Rebérioux, *The Third Republic from its Origins to the Great War, 1871–1914* (Cambridge, 1984), p. 102; F. Braudel and E. Labrousse (eds.), *Histoire économique et sociale de la France*, vol. 3, *L'avènement de 1'ère industrielle, 1789–années 1880*, part 2, (Paris, 1976), p. 921.

[41] D. Shapiro, 'The Ralliement in the Politics of the 1890s', in D. Shapiro (ed.), *The Right in France, 1890–1919* (London, 1962), pp. 13–48; A. Sedgwick, *The Ralliement in French Politics, 1890–1898* (Cambridge, Mass., 1965), *passim*; H. Lebovics *The Alliance of Iron and Wheat in the Third French Republic, 1860–1914: Origins of the New Conservatism* (Baton Rouge, 1988), *passim*.

[42] See, for example, Gibson, *French Catholicism*, p. 210.

One might conclude that there was indeed some basis for an alliance between Catholics and businessmen. Louis Bergeron notes that capitalists were attached to the simplest of political credos: a horror of disorder.[43] Any regime that let the mob loose on the streets or threatened property was anathema. A Catholic church that had been devastated by the Revolution was bound to agree wholeheartedly. Hence both groups tended to support the Right, and could agree on the need to 'moralize' the lower orders. However, matters were complicated by the fact that France in the nineteenth century was never a purely capitalist society; a number of modes of production overlapped.[44] Hence the church could be involved simultaneously in movements as diverse as Catholic Ultraroyalism, Liberal Catholicism and Christian Socialism. Political alliances never coalesced purely and simply along confessional or socio-economic lines. The bourgeoisie, however narrowly defined, always divided on ideological issues. Businessmen could not agree on the nature of the regime they wanted, nor on religious issues. Catholics faced Protestants, 'clericals' came into conflict with 'anticlericals'.

A more direct relationship between entrepreneurs and the church was to be found at the local level: paternalism was another possible strategy for ensuring bourgeois hegemony. The middle of the nineteenth century was the high point for paternalist regimes in industry, until a less accommodating political and social environment gradually emerged under the Third Republic.[45] Ideally the employer would care for his workers like a good father; in return he would receive unquestioning obedience. If all went according to plan, labour turnover could be reduced, productivity improved and social tensions reduced. Where the churches could be brought in to this system was through their traditions of pastoral care and their campaigns against such 'impious' doctrines as Socialism or radical Republicanism. In all cases some kind of balance had to be struck between the philanthropic impulse to provide benefits for employees,

[43] *Les capitalistes*, pp. 167–68.

[44] See N. Poulantzas, *Political Power and Social Classes* (London, 1973), p. 229.

[45] P.N. Stearns, *Paths to Authority* (Urbana, Ill., 1978) *passim*; Bergeron, *Les capitalistes*, pp. 147–63. For general surveys, see J.-M. Mayeur, 'Les églises dans la société', in Mayeur (ed.), *L'histoire religieuse de la France, 19e–20e siècle* (Paris, 1975), pp. 109–42; R. Price, *A Social History of Nineteenth-Century France* (London, 1987), pp. 261–306; Gibson, *French Catholicism*, pp. 195–212; C. Heywood, 'The Catholic Church and the Formation of the Industrial Labour Force in Nineteenth-Century France: An Interpretative Essay', *European History Quarterly*, xix (1989), 509–33.

and the necessity in a capitalist system to make a profit.[46] The various approaches tried in French industry can be placed on a spectrum according to these two criteria.

In splendid isolation at the philanthropic end was Léon Harmel and his *usine chrétienne* at Val-des-Bois. A handful of other industrialists attempted to follow his example, but never quite managed to reproduce the chemistry.[47] A variant on the 'Christian factory' was to be found towards the end of the century in the Nord, centralized around the *Confrérie Notre-Dame de l'Usine*. Here the inspiration was no less Catholic than the original, but the welfare element was more narrowly conceived, and the *patrons* maintained a firm grip on the organization: Harmel described them as 'little Louis XIVs in their factories and their towns'. In varying degrees the spinner Philibert Vrau and like-minded colleagues suppressed work on Sundays, separated the two sexes, put up crucifixes and introduced nuns into their mills to encourage 'decency, obedience, charity and prayer'. Similar forms of organization have come to light in other regions, notably in the Tarn and in Saint Chamond.[48]

Closer to the mainstreams of French capitalism was the paternalist regime in a number of large-scale enterprises, where the Catholic influence was less pervasive than in the 'Christian factory'. Augustin Cochin was prominent in this milieu, working to promote socially-responsible policies among Catholic employers. For example, under the Second Empire he persuaded the *Compagnie du Chemin de Fer d'Orléans* to provide various services, including free medicine, a canteen supervised by the Sisters of Saint-Vincent-de-Paul, a mutual aid society and evening classes. In 1855 he also managed to secure a regulation on Sunday observance, which required company offices, workshops and stores to

---

[46] See R.H. Campbell, 'A Critique of the Christian Businessman and his Paternalism', in Jeremy, *Business and Religion*, pp. 27–46.

[47] H. Rollet, *L'action sociale des catholiques en France, 1871–1901* (Paris, 1947), pp. 227–35; A. Dansette, *Histoire religieuse de la France contemporaine* (Paris, 1965), pp. 496–509; P. Pierrard, *L'église et les ouvriers en France, 1840–1940* (Paris, 1984), pp. 343–53.

[48] Lecanuet, *L'église de France sous la troisième république*, vol. 2, *Pontificat de Léon XIII, 1878–1894* (Paris, 1910), pp. 431–32; R. Talmy, *Une forme hybride du catholicisme social en France: l'association catholique des patrons du Nord, 1848–1895* (Lille, 1962), *passim*; J. Faury, *Cléricalisme et anticléricalisme dans le Tarn, 1848–1900* (Toulouse, 1980), pp. 315–48; E. Accampo, *Industrialization, Family Life, and Class Relations: Saint Chamond, 1815–1914* (Berkeley, Calif., 1989), pp. 167–74.

close on the Sabbath.[49] The big mining and metallurgical companies were also well known for encouraging the activities of the clergy in their communities. Employers with 'theocratic' tendencies have been noted in the Pas-de-Calais, in Lorraine, at Carmaux, the Grand-Combe and Décazeville.[50] Then there were the 'convent-workshops' of the silk industry.[51] These varied in character. Some, like the Providences of the Lyon area, were charitable organizations, aiming to provide an apprenticeship and some means of support for orphaned girls. Others, run by private enterprise, must be placed firmly at the profit-orientated end of the spectrum, for they relied on a ruthless exploitation of female labour. Located in the mountainous regions of southern France, they employed approximately 50,000 young women during the 1850s in the preparation of silk fibres. Special religious orders were introduced to supervise the girls lodging in the mills, and in some cases the nuns were trained to act as overseers in the workshops.

Paternalist regimes in industry, buttressed to a greater or lesser extent by the Catholic church, could function effectively in nineteenth-century France. Val-des-Bois under Léon Harmel served for thirty years as a Mecca for 'social' Catholics: a sublime source of inspiration, even if impossible to emulate. In Lille the Vrau mill could boast 110 operatives with twenty-five years of service in the firm at the turn of the century, and a record of harmonious labour relations. In Saint Chamond the moralizing efforts of Catholic braid manufacturers were generally held to have been rewarded with a tranquil labour force. Jujurieux, first of the silk mills to set up a *couvent-atelier*, lasted for sixty-one years without a strike. Even hostile observers of the system in these mills had to admit that the nuns fostered discipline, cleanliness and education among the young women workers in

[49] Duroselle, *Les débuts*, pp. 649–51. See also Daviet, *Saint-Gobain*, pp. 143, 207.

[50] A.N. C 3018, Enquête sur la situation des classes ouvrières, 1872–75 (Pas-de-Calais); Y.-M. Hilaire, 'Remarques sur la pratique religieuse dans le bassin houiller du Pas-de-Calais dans la deuxième moitié du XIXe siècle', in L. Trénard (ed.), *Charbon et sciences humaines* (Paris, 1966), pp. 265–79; D. Reid, *The Miners of Décazeville* (Cambridge, Mass., 1985), pp. 20–21.

[51] Louis Reybaud, *Etudes sur le régime des manufactures: conditions des ouvriers en soie* (Paris, 1859), pp. 197–204; Dominique Vanoli, 'Les ouvrières enfermées: les couvents soyeux', *Les révoltes logiques*, ii (1976), 13–39; Heywood, 'Church and Labour', 516–20; Y. Turin, *Femmes et religieuses au XIXe siècle* (Paris, 1989). I am grateful to Ralph Gibson for providing me with the final reference.

the Midi.[52] The atmosphere in the mining communities was more turbulent and the underlying problems of recruiting and holding labour more acute. Nonetheless, Donald Reid can conclude that in Décazeville at mid century, 'aided by the State and the church, the Houillères et Fonderies had little trouble establishing hegemony in the Basin'.[53]

Such achievements should not distract our attention from the drawbacks to the system. It could be marred by strained relations between industrialists and the clergy. In the Pas-de-Calais, for example, coal owners resisted any clerical activity that threatened to stir up the 'social question' (the plight of the workers).[54] Similarly, in Lorraine, the great iron masters occasionally fell out with a priest judged to be identifying himself too closely with the interests of the workers.[55] Above all, the scope for introducing Catholic paternalism was limited by widespread indifference or even outright hostility to the church among large sections of the French population. In order to work it required highly selective conditions. The 'neo-feudal' environment of a company town like Décazeville, or an isolated rural site like Val-des-Bois, was better than the 'contaminated' atmosphere of a big city like Lille. Women (and very young women at that) proved more suitable than men, as in the *moulinages de soie* and some of the northern mills, because of a certain 'feminization' of Catholicism. And of course Catholics had to be taken to the exclusion of non-believers. This confined the system to relatively *dévot* areas like Flanders and parts of the south, or to firms hiring labour from a Catholic rural area, such as the *Société des Mines de Carmaux* and its coal miners from the *Ségalas tarnais* and the *Aveyronnais*.

No precise figures can be given, but the large majority of employers were probably opposed to involving the church in their affairs. Whatever the 'social control' model might suggest, they preferred a more down-to-earth

[52] Talmy, *Patrons du Nord*, p. 73; Accampo, *Saint Chamond*, p. 173; Vanoli, 'Couvents soyeux', 27–36; Frédéric Monnier, *De l'organisation du travail manuel des jeunes filles: les internats industriels* (Paris, 1869), p. 39.

[53] Reid, *Décazeville*, p. 21. On labour problems in the mines, see Rolande Trempé, *Les mineurs de Carmaux, 1848–1914* (2 vols., Paris, 1971), vol. 1, pp. 147–253; Marcel Gillet, *Les charbonnages du nord de la France au XIXe siècle* (Paris, 1973), pp. 324–30; O. Hardy-Hémery, *De la croissance à la désindustrialisation: un siècle dans le Valenciennois* (Paris, 1984), pp. 31–37.

[54] Hilaire, 'Remarques', p. 271.

[55] J.-M. Moine, *Les barons du fer: les maîtres de forges en Lorraine* (Nancy, 1989), pp. 315–25.

approach to management, relying on wage incentives, detailed workshop regulations and the threat of dismissal.[56] Even in the Nord only a minority of mill owners were prepared to try the 'Christian' path to paternalism: the original *Association Catholique des Patrons du Nord* was only thirty-six in number.[57] Large-scale enterprises might rely heavily on such devices as company housing to control labour, which did not necessarily involve the church, and even a pious family like the Schneiders could entrust their schools at Le Creusot to lay teachers.[58] For the smaller workshops, so common in metalworking, textiles, clothing and the Parisian luxury trades, welfare schemes were too expensive to contemplate. Workers for their part often considered the intrusion of the church a violation of their civil liberties. Witness the offensives against the regime at Monceau-les-Mines and against Notre-Dame de l'Usine towards the end of the century. Similarly coalminers at Carmaux and in the Nord and Pas-de-Calais fields were notable for their Socialist and anticlerical stance under the Third Republic.[59] Not surprisingly the whole paternalist edifice slowly crumbled around the turn of the century under pressure from a new climate in the church, political offensives from the Left and evolution in management methods. Once again, the simplistic notion that the church acted hand-in-glove with capitalist interests requires extensive qualification.[60]

[56] B. Mottez, *Systèmes de salaire et politique patronales* (Paris, 1966), *passim*; A. Melucci, 'Action patronale, pouvoir, organisation: règlements d'usine et contrôle de la main-d'oeuvre au XIXe siècle', *Le mouvement social*, xcvii (1976), 139–59; M. Perrot, 'The Three Ages of Industrial Discipline', in J.M. Merriman (ed.), *Consciousness and Class Experience in Nineteenth-Century Europe* (New York, 1979), pp. 149–68.

[57] Talmy, *Patrons du Nord*, p. 42; B. Smith, *Ladies of the Leisure Class* (Princeton, 1981), ch. 2.

[58] L. Murard and P. Zylberman (eds.), *Le petit travailleur infatigable ou le prolétaire régénéré: villes-usines, habitat et intimités au 19e siècle*, special issue of *Recherches*, xxv (1976); Moine, *Barons du fer*, pp. 325–29; F. Courtois, 'Les écoles du Creusot, 1787–1882', *Mémoires de la société éduenne*, xxi (1893) pp. 129–57.

[59] C. Willard, 'Les attaques contre Notre-Dame de l'Usine', and J. Bruhat, 'Anticléricalisme et mouvement ouvrier en France avant 1914', both in F. Bédarida and J. Maitron (eds.), *Christianisme et monde ouvrière* (Paris, 1975), pp. 245–50 and 79–115; Trempé, *Les mineurs*, vol. 2, pp. 834–57; Pierrard, *L'église*, pp. 353–54; Faury, *Cléricalisme*, pp. 429–30; Y.-M. Hilaire, 'Les ouvriers de la région du Nord devant l'église catholique, XIXe et XXe siècles', *Cahiers du mouvement social*, i (1975), pp. 228–30.

[60] For the same conclusion, see Gibson, *French Catholicism*, pp. 207–12.

The Catholic Church and the Business Community

Church against Bourgeoisie

Eglise contre bourgeoisie: this was the deliberately 'provocative' title for a book chosen by Emile Poulat. To justify it he argued that the common emphasis in the literature on *collusion* between the church and the middle classes risked distracting attention from the numerous *conflicts* separating the two sides.[61] So far in this essay we have provided evidence that would support either case. Is it not possible to draw up a more precise balance sheet? There was certainly a widespread feeling among contemporaries that the activities of the industrial bourgeoisie were little short of disastrous for the church. Factory owners were accused of defying the authority of the clergy; of preventing their employees attenting mass by insisting on Sunday work; and of creating a new class of materially and spiritually impoverished 'barbarians'. Under the Restoration, for example, the dean at Aubigny (Pas-de-Calais) found himself embroiled with the manager of a local cotton mill. He complained that his opponent, a retired army officer, was hostile to the clergy and preferred to stop work on Monday instead of Sunday. In the same vein Mgr. d'Astros of Toulouse fulminated against employers carried away by the 'passion for lucre', as he campaigned against Sunday working during the 1840s.[62] Unfortunately the evidence available is insufficiently detailed to allow a rigorous proof that this was the predominant kind of relationship between church and business. One must therefore be content with a more impressionistic approach: on this basis, Poulat appears broadly correct as far as the industrial and commercial bourgeoisie is concerned. Clerics and businessmen tended to live in separate, if not hostile worlds.

A preliminary indicator that this was the case has been provided by the Abbé Fernand Charpin. His analysis of the delay in baptizing infants shows industrialists and merchants to be one of the 'undisciplined' occupational groups in nineteenth-century Marseilles. In 1821, 66.7 per cent of them registered baptisms within the required three days: some way behind 'faithful' groups such as sailors, with 81.6 per cent, or farmers, with 74.0 per cent, but ahead of the extremely lax doctors and lawyers with their 58.6 per cent. However, Charpin also notes that during the 1850s and 1860s, businessmen were slower than most in the general slide towards 'indiscipline'. In 1871 approximately one-third of their baptisms were

---

[61] E. Poulat, *Eglise contre bourgeoisie* (Paris, 1977), p. 9.

[62] Y.-M. Hilaire, *Une chrétienté au XIXe siècle? La vie religieuse des populations d'Arras, 1840–1914* (2 vols., Lille, 1977), vol. 1, p. 116: Droulers, *Action pastorale*, p. 212.

registered on time at this period, compared to only one-sixth among the liberal professions. [63] Of course what Charpin is measuring here is an action that may be influenced by political events as much as by religious beliefs. [64] Yet it remains an important piece of evidence for our purposes, since we are interested in the relationship between businessmen and the Catholic church as a social institution. There are also various local studies which tend to confirm the general drift of the argument from literary sources. Adeline Daumard asserts that in Paris religion played a limited role in the life of the bourgeoisie during the first half of the century. In Rouen, at the same period, Jean-Pierre Chaline confirms the general indifference of the bourgeoisie to religion. In the Tarn, Jean Faury finds that although the handful of *grands bourgeois* in the department was firmly in the 'clerical' camp, the small and medium bourgeoisie were often won over to anticlerical ideas under the Third Republic. Even in the Nord, Bonnie Smith is eager to stress that beside the kernel of fervent Catholics, there was a silent majority of employers with little interest in religious matters. [65]

The overall pattern that emerges is of an industrial and commercial bourgeoisie that generally distanced itself from the activities of the Catholic church, rarely attending mass or confession. Like most of the population the business community maintained a 'seasonal conformism' throughout the century: it almost invariably turned to the church for the four major rites of baptism, first communion, marriage and burial. There was some ebb and flow in the relationship, as the bourgeoisie tended to remain aloof from the clergy during periods of social peace, but closed ranks with them during a crisis. Thus the 'Voltairian' Restoration gave way to the *rapprochement* in the wake of 1848; the disillusionments of the 1860s were followed by the return to Catholicism among many members of the *bonne bourgeoisie* after 1870. In the west André Siegfried detected a more linear shift among the bourgeoisie from scepticism in religious matters to clericalism. Here the agnostic generation of the 1830s and 1840s was succeeded by one that was personally indifferent to Catholicism, but which was prepared to

[63] F. Charpin, *Pratique religieuse et formation d'une grande ville: le geste du baptême et sa signification en sociologie religieuse (Marseille, 1806–1958)* (Paris, 1964), ch. 5.

[64] T. Zeldin, *France, 1848–1945*, vol. 2, *Intellect, Taste and Anxiety* (Oxford, 1977), pp. 988–92.

[65] A. Daumard, *La bourgeoisie parisienne de 1815 à 1848* (Paris, 1963), pp. 347–51; Chaline, *Bourgeois de Rouen*, pp. 260–71; Faury, *Cléricalisme*, p. 393; Smith, *Ladies*, p. 27.

support the political activities of the church, leading finally to a Catholic and clerical generation under the Third Republic.[66] At this later period there are grounds for talking of two bourgeoisies in France: the one rich and close to the Catholic church, the other solidly middle class and anticlerical.[67] These nuances do not however alter the conclusion that a *nouvel esprit* that was at once materialist and indifferent to religion appeared with the factory system and industrial labour. Whereas in some areas, like the Ruhr or the southern Netherlands, industrialization did not cause 'mass apostasy', in France this tended to be the case.[68]

Theodore Zeldin has usefully suggested that, beyond the clericalism and anticlericalism that polarized the French population, there lay a division that was more fundamentally religious:

> The division between those who were preoccupied by the problems of death, guilt, conscience, the distinction of the valuable from the trivial and the place of the individual in the universe, and those who were not.[69]

Entrepreneurs 'living and breathing business' could hardly avoid falling into the latter category.[70] They saw themselves as hard-headed, practical men: tough competitors on the market who 'had to meet a payroll'. While they were not necessarily unsympathetic to the teachings of the church, there was a propensity among committed Catholic businessmen to concentrate on the social dimension: the 'good works' traditionally associated with Christian charity (and even these were often left to wives and daughters). More typical was the 'respectful indifference' towards Catholicism of Casimir Périer and other male members of his family.[71] Otherwise

---

[66] A. Siegfried, *Tableau politique de la France de l'ouest sous la troisième république* (Paris, 1964 [1913]), pp. 471–72.

[67] Y.-M. Hilaire, 'La pratique religieuse en France de 1815 à 1878', *L'information historique* (1963), 57–69 (pp. 67–8); Braudel and Labrousse, *Histoire économique*, vol. 4, part 1, p. 444; G. Cholvy and Y.-M. Hilaire, *Histoire religieuse de la France contemporaine*, vol. 1, *1800–1880*, pp. 202–3 and vol. 2, *1880–1930* (Toulouse, 1985–86), p. 175; Gibson, *French Catholicism*, pp. 195–212.

[68] F. Boulard, *Premiers itinéraires en sociologie religieuse* (Paris, 1954), p. 31; R. Rémond, 'The Problem of Dechristianization: The Present Position and some Recent French Studies', *Concilium*, vii (1965), pp. 77–80 (p. 79).

[69] Zeldin, *France*, vol. 2, p. 994.

[70] R.R. Locke, *Les fonderies et forges d'Alais à l'époque des premiers chemins de fer, 1829–74* (Paris, 1978), p. 37.

[71] P. Barral, *Les Périer dans l'Isère au XIXe siècle* (Paris, 1964), p. 50.

their *credo* was firmly rooted in the modern world. They believed in the virtues of liberalism, in the possibilities of unlimited progress, in the benefits of science and technology.[72] Even Augustin Cochin was impressed by *les créations merveilleuses de l'industrie*. At Saint-Gobain he grappled enthusiastically with the latest technology and strove to promote efficient management.[73]

The Catholic clergy, by contrast, was naturally more concerned with the spiritual than the material world, with saving souls rather than accumulating wealth. This type of preoccupation had never prevented the church from taking its social responsibilities seriously: it had a long tradition of involvement in such fields as poor relief, education and caring for the infirm. Yet this experience did not prepare it sufficiently to cope with industrial civilization. All too often the clergy failed to hide its yearnings for the power and wealth enjoyed by the church in medieval times. They were painfully slow to distinguish the new working class from the age-old poor – though ironically when they did confront the 'social question' they risked opposition from employers, who were fiercely conservative in this sphere. As already noted, leading Catholics frequently anathemized contemporary notions of progress, liberalism and even science. In short, the Catholic church appeared to 'refuse the nineteenth century'.[74]

To explain this divergence one can point to a number of underlying influences. In the first place priests and nuns were rarely recruited from the bourgeoisie. This form of distancing between the lay urban elites and the clergy can be traced back to the eighteenth century. By the time of the Third Republic nine out of ten parish priests came from modest social backgrounds, being the sons of peasants and artisans.[75] Bishops tended to be drawn from a more select social background: during the 1840s nearly half still came from noble families. Yet even at this level of the ecclesiastical hierarchy a marked 'proletarianization' occurred from 1830 onwards. During the period 1870 to 1883 over half of the episcopacy were

---

[72] See, for example, Dansette, *Histoire religieuse*, pp. 202, 325–30, 403–4; Braudel and Labrousse, *Histoire économique*, vol. 3, part 1, pp. 137–59.

[73] Daviet, *Saint-Gobain*, pp. 72–73.

[74] Rémond, *Right Wing*, pp. 56–57; Crubellier, *Histoire culturelle*, pp. 376–77; Cholvy and Hilaire, *Histoire religieuse*, vol. 1, *passim*.

[75] T. Tackett, *Religion, Revolution and Regional Culture in Eighteenth-Century France* (Princeton, 1986), pp. 256–57; F. Lebrun (ed.), *Histoire des catholiques en France du XVe siècle à nos jours* (Toulouse, 1980), pp. 305–10; Latreille and Rémond, *Histoire du catholicisme*, p. 427.

enfants du peuple leaving only one-third whose fathers were bourgeois or big rural landowners, and one-eighth from the nobility.[76] In the second place, the training of priests and businessmen was destined to produce two very different mentalities. Merchants and industrialists might have attended one of the *grandes écoles* or a university. More typically their formative years were spent learning *sur le tas* (on the job). A more-or-less extended secondary schooling would be followed by long spells working abroad, or gaining experience in the various departments of a large firm. It was an eminently practical training, a matter of 'learning by doing' in the real world.[77] Meanwhile the aspiring priest was being cloistered in a seminary and taught to hold himself aloof from this same secular world. His training was still rooted in the seventeenth-century world of the Counter-Reformation. The priest was to be 'a man of prayer, sacrifice and contemplation', which made him ill-fitted to provide leadership in an increasingly secularized society.[78] Finally the two sides were held apart by conflicting interpretations of the Revolution. The church was implacably hostile, after the traumas of persecution and the loss of most of its material stake in society. Businessmen in their turn trembled at the memory of the Terror. But some at least had profited from the sale of *biens nationaux*, and the majority, whether Orleanist, Bonapartist or Republican, saw themselves in various ways as the heirs of 1789.

Two worlds, then, sheltering behind the inscrutable facades of the seminary and the factory.[79] These institutions had several features in common. Both attempted to cloister themselves from the rest of the community; both had a detailed work routine; and both enforced strict discipline on their inmates. They were led by men who preached the values of hard work, obedience and education (though both were considered as hotbeds of debauchery by hostile observers). Priests and businessmen could therefore cooperate in some circumstances. More often than not, the two worlds went their separate ways, the one dedicated to God, the other to Mammon.

Conclusion

If we return to M. Colrat, and his notion that the French middle classes

---

[76] Tudesq, *Grands notables*, vol. 1, pp. 436–37; Gadille, *La pensée*, vol. 1, pp. 26–27; Gibson, *French Catholicism*, pp. 61–63.

[77] Bergeron, *Les capitalistes*, pp. 56–79.

[78] D. Julia and W. Frijhoff, 'The French Priest in Modern Times', *Concilium*, vii (1969), 66–71 (p. 67); Zeldin, *France*, vol. 2, pp. 986–98; Gough, *Paris and Rome*, ch. 1.

[79] Heywood, 'Catholic Church', 517–18; Gibson, *French Catholicism*, pp. 87–91.

were at once faithful Catholics and passionate anticlericals, we find this
to have been largely fanciful. Although an excellent device for puffing up
bourgeois pride, it also served to conceal a more humdrum reality. Certainly
there were always fervent Catholics among the business community, but
they usually enjoyed cordial relations with the local clergy. There were also
many virulent anticlericals among the bourgeoisie, but increasingly their
residual Catholic spiritualism was replaced by some form of 'scientism'.
In between was the great mass of businessmen whose links with the
church were purely formal: the key words here would have to be
'scepticism' and 'indifference'. The Catholic church for its part was
equivocal in its relations with modern capitalism. Most of the clergy
was more at home with the landed aristocracy than with the new
bourgeoisie. Hostile to the values of the urban and industrial society
emerging around them, these men did their best to ignore it, finding
daily consolation in the pages of *L'Univers*. Yet there were priests in urban
areas who could earn the respect of the working class; and a majority of
Catholics sought compromise in various ways with the nineteenth-century
world of liberalism, industrialism, revolution and eventually democracy.

This multiplicity of stances in both camps led to an uneasy relationship
over the course of the nineteenth century. Although church and business
could be mutually supportive, the cultural setting proved unfavourable for
an extensive programme of cooperation. Businessmen might find their
Catholic faith a source of strength in their careers; but they were more likely
to perceive the attitudes and values of religious leaders as an obstacle to
enterprise. They might be tempted to use the church as an ideological prop
for the existing order; but the risk was that both they and their employees
would prove too lukewarm in their Catholicism for the strategy to work. On
the other side of the coin, businessmen could be a useful source of funds
and leadership for the church; yet they might equally promote a materialist
view of the world that was alien to Christian doctrine. The fundamental
problem was that businessmen were generally in the vanguard of social
change during the nineteenth century, while the Catholic church was still
cast in the seventeenth-century mould of the Counter-Reformation. A few
businessmen attempted to marry the old and the new: the guild system
appearing as a 'mixed union' in a factory, traditional charitable works
anticipating modern welfare schemes in the 'Christian factory' and so on.
The majority evidently found the church out of step with the world they
knew. Not for the first (or the last) time, Christianity proved difficult to
reconcile with capitalism.

5

The Emergence of Catholic Politics in the Midi, 1830–70

Brian Fitzpatrick

Some words of explanation about the title of this essay might be helpful. Those familiar with the history of the Midi know that religion was central to the region's political debate from the Reformation to recent times. Faced with the sudden emergence of considerable concentrations of Calvinists, who set out to give their religious beliefs political expression by seeking to establish Protestant rule in many towns and districts, the Catholic population aligned itself with the French monarchy in its endeavours to curb the growth of Calvinist influence.[1] From the earliest days Catholic-Protestant relations were marked by violent conflict as the communities struggled to gain power or to retain it. The Protestant-inspired *Michelade* of 1567 was matched by the south's emulation of the *Saint-Barthélémie* in 1572. After the revocation of the Edict of Nantes in 1685, the southern Catholic community could call upon the legal and military might of the monarchic state to maintain its supremacy in public affairs.

The conflict between Catholics and Protestants was essentially about the monopoly of power and public office, and it remained largely so for most of the nineteenth century. Doctrinal questions underpinned political assumptions certainly, as they did in all early-modern European states, but they had faded into the background by the eighteenth century, and

---

[1] See P. Wolff, (ed.) *Histoire des protestants en France* (Toulouse, 1977) and E. Leroy Ladurie, *Les paysans du Languedoc* (Paris, 1966) particularly part 2.

were only resurrected as a result of the French Revolution, which was 'Protestant' in its rejection of the notion of a divinely ordained social and political order. Much of nineteenth-century royalist thought focused on the need to restore theocracy as the basis of government; it might be argued that the reign of Charles X was a crude attempt to do this.[2]

In practical terms, the Revolution liberated the south's Protestants and deepened confessional antagonisms in the Midi. Throughout the nineteenth century, Protestants welcomed, identified with and benefited from regimes which acknowledged the principles of 1789, while Catholics, in the main, backed factions which wanted to reassert the primacy of Catholics in local life. Every change of national regime tended to involve changes in the religious composition of public office holders. In broad terms, the First and Second Bourbon Restorations were 'Catholic', while the First Empire, the Hundred Days and the July Monarchy attracted Protestant support. The Second Republic and Second Empire cannot be so easily simplified. The introduction of adult male suffrage and the emergence of class-based 'red' Republicanism led to some relegation of confessional discord among socially conservative groups during the Second Republic, while Louis-Napoleon's conscious wooing of the Catholic interest rallied many Catholics, at least initially, to the Second Empire.

Sectarian hostilities were never completely transcended, however, and in this respect it is possible to speak of 'Catholic' politics in the Midi as the persistence of the traditional political anti-Protestantism which had existed since the Reformation, exacerbated by the events and consequences of the French Revolution. For much of the nineteenth century the chief outlet for this traditional stance was the profession of Ultraroyalist and Legitimist views and tactics, although these proved unable to restore the hegemony many Catholics sought. There were two key elements in the failure of southern Royalism to achieve its counter-revolutionary goal. The first was the Bourbons' pragmatic acceptance of much of the Revolution's ideological and institutional creation; the second, largely a consequence of the first, was the failure of southern Royalists to secure complete control of the southern departments in the summer of 1815, during the so-called White Terror.[3]

---

[2] See B. Reardon, *Liberalism and Tradition. Aspects of Catholic Thought in Nineteenth Century France* (Cambridge, 1975) and S. Rials, *Révolution et contre-révolution au XIXe siècle* (Paris, 1987).

[3] B. Fitzpatrick, 'Réflexions sur le "Royaume du Midi en 1815"', *Mémoire*, 5 (1986), pp. 71–90.

This essay is not concerned with the persistence of a primarily traditional, political anti-Protestantism in which Catholicism and Royalism were assumed to be natural bedfellows. Rather it explores the emergence of a trend which set Catholic doctrinal and ecclesiastical concerns above secular, dynastic and party issues. The 'new' Catholic politics in the Midi was part of a larger movement which affected France and other parts of Europe, and which became known very quickly as Ultramontanism. While it displayed tendencies and characteristics common to Ultramontanism in general, the southern Catholic movement built on existing practices and prejudices. It necessarily reflected such meridional preoccupations as a deep-seated suspicion of the central state and a widespread rejection of the Revolutionary settlement, or imposition, as many Catholics saw it. Key elements in the success of Ultramontanism in the south were the legacy of popular, mass Royalism; the persistence of the 'Protestant question'; and the forceful personality of churchmen like Mgr. de Clermont-Tonnerre, archbishop of Toulouse from 1820 to 1830; his successor, d'Astros (1830–51); Plantier, bishop of Nîmes from 1855 to 1875; and his remarkable aides, the Abbés d'Alzon and Cabrières, the latter of whom became bishop of Montpellier in 1874.

The wider context requires a brief comment. In France, as in other European states, religion had been restored to official status in the 1814 to 1815 period as a prop for the principle of dynastic legitimacy and the practice of social conservatism.[4] In the main this nakedly political use of religion proved to be a failure in the long run. While the excessively clerical character of regimes like that of Charles X of France, from 1824 to 1830, contributed to their downfall, their resort to religion and to clerical control discredited the church while utterly failing to counter the 'Revolutionary mentality'. To young members of the French Catholic intelligentsia like Lamennais Catholicism, by its association with the state, was the hostage of an ineffective, decrepit monarchy. At the same time the implementation of the 1801 Concordat had involved the papacy in French ecclesiastical affairs more deeply than a number of French churchmen of the old school wished. The concordatory hierarchy had been created as a result of negotiations between Rome and Paris which took no account of the views of the constitutional bishops in post. These were invited to resign or be sacked by Pius VII if they were deemed to be unsuitable

---

[4] For church-state relations in the period 1814 to 1848, see J. Leflon, *Histoire de l'église*, 20, *La crise révolutionnaire, 1789–1846* (Paris, 1951).

for episcopal office under the Concordat. This *de facto* extension of papal power was not confined to France. In 1821 Rome overturned Maximilien-Joseph's attempt to subordinate Catholic interests to those of the state in the Bavarian constitution of 1818. Frederick William III of Prussia failed to impose his will on Rome in the 1830s in the matter of Catholic requirements in marriages between Protestants and Catholics, despite imprisoning two elderly bishops.

In France itself the 1830 Revolution and the establishment of the July Monarchy increased the scope of papal influence. When leading French churchmen like Cardinal Latil, Cardinal de Rohan and Mgr. de Forbin-Janson, all outspoken Royalists, fled the country fearing the worst from a revolution directed against the Bourbons and the Catholic church, Pius VIII condemned their dereliction of their pastoral duties. He later directed the French hierarchy to give its full recognition to the new regime and to swear allegiance to Louis-Philippe as and when required to do so in their positions in public life. To set the tone of relations between Orleanist Paris and Rome the Pope conferred on Louis-Philippe the title of *Roi très chrétien*, demonstrating plainly that Rome viewed the citizen-king as the legitimate successor to Charles X and that it was unwilling to bend to the sensibilities of 'political' churchmen.[5] This resolute pursuit of Catholic interests as defined by Rome was repeated in 1834 when Pius VIII's successor, Gregory XVI, rejected Lamennais' appeal for support for his modernizing ideals expressed in the newspaper *L'Avenir*. Taken together, the recognition of the July Monarchy and the condemnation of Lamennais represented Rome's policy of standing above national, domestic and dynastic issues in order to achieve purely 'Catholic' objectives.

Rapid recognition of the regime by the Pope did little to diminish the anti-clerical character of the July Monarchy in its early days. In efforts to distance itself from the Catholic church, army chaplains were withdrawn, scholarships to Catholic colleges abolished, certain educational establishments run by religious closed, and religious symbols removed from public buildings, while Roman Catholicism was demoted from its position as official religion of the state. The removal of the mission crosses erected during the Restoration to mark the passage of Père Rauzan's ostentatiously pro-Bourbon *Mission de France* probably provoked

---

[5] Leflon, *Histoire de l'église*, pp. 419–21.

the greatest unrest. The process was drawn out and provided opponents of the new regime with ample time to mobilize resistance.[6] In Nîmes, for example, the prefect's inability to persuade the parishes to place the crosses inside their churches as the law required led to a carefully prepared weekend of rioting.[7] Such incidents, along with the random attacks on church property which began in places during the weeks following the July Revolution, brought religious issues to the forefront of politics and provided conservative opponents of the regime with a much more considerable weapon than the jaded Bourbon cause could. While Legitimists rushed to the assistance of the church, the latter, with few exceptions, devoted itself to adapting to changed circumstances. The requiem mass said by the curé of Saint-Germain l'Auxerrois for the duc de Berry in February 1831 illustrates this point clearly. The archbishop of Paris, Mgr. Quélen, had forbidden the use of political symbols at the anniversary service and the curé involved had tried to prevent the Legitimists from displaying emblems they had brought surreptitiously into the church. The violence which ensued was entirely the fault of the Legitimists who wanted to make the service into a political protest.[8] In practice purely political action by the Legitimists failed to achieve very much. Plans to overthrow the July Monarchy culminated in the failure of the duchesse de Berry's expedition across the Midi in 1832. The expedition, which involved most of the southern towns, was an embarrassing fiasco. The authorities were aware of the planned landing near Marseille and the ringleaders of the plot were arrested without difficulty.[9] The failure of the insurrection left the Legitimists bereft of convincing policies, precisely at a time when religious questions came to the fore again, this time in the shape of Guizot's law on primary education. The law established a primary school in every *commune* and made the local authorities responsible for its provision. The religious complexion of the school was also left up to the local community. Clergy and Legitimists found a common cause in their insistence on Catholic education for the sons of the lower classes.

[6] J.M. Phayer, 'Politics and Popular Religion: The Cult of the Cross in France, 1815–1848', *Journal of Social History*, 11 (1978), 346–65.

[7] B. Fitzpatrick, *Catholic Royalism in the Department of the Gard, 1814–1852* (Cambridge, 1983), pp. 107–8.

[8] Leflon, *Histoire de l'église*, pp. 440–41.

[9] G. Bertier de Sauvigny, 'La conspiration des légitimistes et de la duchesse de Berry contre Louis-Philippe', *'Etudes d'histoire moderne et contemporaine*, 3 (1950), xvii–125; Fitzpatrick, *Catholic Royalism*, pp. 110–21.

Fear that control of the schools would fall into the hands of Protestants led to a campaign across the Midi. Its aim was to persuade Legitimists to overcome what scruples they felt concerning the oath of allegiance so that Catholics would be represented on the local councils and would be able to influence the choice of schoolteachers and the moral tone of the schools. Specific reference was made to the hierarchy's acceptance of the oath, and the principal Legitimist newspaper, the *Gazette du Languedoc*, breathed a sigh of relief when sufficient Legitimist candidates were returned in the local elections of 1833 to ensure Catholic control of most primary schools.[10]

The primary schools issue was responsible for considerably reducing the abstentionist stance of southern Legitimists. By the end of the 1830s there were Legitimist representatives on one or more of the elected councils in almost all of the southern départments; Toulouse had nine Legitimist councillors, Nîmes fifteen.[11] At the same time the Guizot education law, by establishing the right of groups and individuals to open their own schools as long as qualified teachers were employed, had whetted the church's appetite. Very quickly, in the 1840s, Catholics began to petition and mobilize for the right to establish Catholic colleges with the same rights as the Catholic primary schools. As the only other live political issue which exercized the Legitimists was electoral reform, the clergy could once again, but with increased confidence, enrol the Legitimists behind their specifically religious demands. It is clear that, by the 1840s, southern Legitimism was becoming little more than the lay political arm of the Catholic church. Digests prepared for the Minister of Police in 1844 are revealing:

Il s'est formé à Toulouse, dit-on, un comité catholique fonctionnant à part du comité carliste. Les hommes qui le composent sont ecclésiastiques pour la plupart et correspondent avec des comités de Nîmes et d'Avignon pour tout ce qui concerne les questions religieuses du jour. C'est en effet de Toulouse et de Lyon qu'arrivent toutes les publications catholiques de Paris sur les lois en discussion.[12]

[10] *Gazette du Bas Languedoc*, 27 October, 21, 22, 23 November 1833.

[11] A.J. Tudesq, 'L'opposition légitimiste en Languedoc en 1840', *Annales du Midi* (1956), 391–407.

[12] A.N. F19 5061, report dated 24 May 1844.

Some days later the writer observed that:

> Tout ce mouvement plaît beaucoup aux légitimistes de ce pays, et nous les voyons toujours mettre leur bourse à la disposition du clergé. Les brochures publiées à Nîmes, à Avignon sur la liberté de l'enseignement ont toutes été imprimées avec l'argent des légitimistes.[13]

At roughly the same time a depressed *procureur-général* at Avignon reported his failure to secure the conviction of a priest who had illegally published a pamphlet entitled *De l'abolition du monopole universitaire* because 'le personnel du jury, presque entièrement composé de légitimistes, ne permettait pas d'espérer un résultat plus heureux'.[14] Moreover, it was noted that 'les publications ayant un vernis légitimiste augmentent en proportion des efforts cléricaux', and that, 'Les discours de M de Montalembert ont été répandus dans nos campagnes avec une profusion incroyable', while 'Nous avons vu le discours réhabilitant les Jésuites traîné jusque dans les petits cabarets où les paysans en commentaient quelques passages en patois languedocien'.[15]

In social matters also the paucity of genuinely 'Legitimist' policies left the initiative to the church; once again, Legitimists became followers rather than leaders. The tone was set by churchmen like Mgr. d'Astros in Toulouse, who built on existing confraternities and encouraged the new associations of the 1830s and 1840s such as the Societies of Saint-Vincent de Paul and Saint François-Xavier, for example, while Legitimists rarely went beyond making statements on the need to 'moralize' the working class to prevent it falling into the clutches of the 'reds'.[16]

In certain cases Legitimists undoubtedly saw the rise of Catholic social organizations as an opportunity to extend or consolidate their influence on the working classes. Austin Gough has demonstrated this in his colourful essay on Bishop Pie of Poitiers and there is evidence that, for a while, Toulouse Legitimists sought to achieve the same end. In practice Legitimists were serving the church, like it or not. In the main,

---

[13] *Ibid.*, 30 May 1844.

[14] A.N. BB18 1421, *Procureur-général de la cour royale de Nîmes*, 2 May 1844.

[15] A.N. F19 5061, report of 24 May 1844.

[16] See J.-B. Duroselle, *Les débuts du catholicisme social en France, 1822–1870* (Paris 1951), pp. 198–209; P. Pierrard, *L'église et les ouvriers en France, 1840–1940* (Paris, 1984), *passim*.

the authorities were content to do nothing more than keep a close watch on the Catholic *oeuvres*.[17]

In most southern *départements* the charitable organisations were founded in the late 1830s or in the 1840s by individuals who were devout Catholics first and foremost.[18] By the time the political potential of organizations like the Societies of Saint-Vincent de paul and Saint-François-Xavier became apparent in cities like Toulouse, Montpellier, Nîmes and Avignon, that is to say in the 1850s, the clerical interest was already far more powerful than the Legitimist interest. It had a wider appeal than Legitimist politics *tout court* in view of the threat of class conflict which the period of the Second Republic had revealed so starkly. Consider this assessment, made in 1855, of the strength of Legitimism in Toulouse, long deemed the capital of southern extreme Royalism:

> Son état major est assez nombreux . . . mais en réalité ce parti ne possède guère de puissance, son armée est bien peu sûre. Pour avoir l'apparence d'une popularité, les meneurs se sont emparés de la direction d'une société de secours mutuel, dit de Saint François-Xavier, qui compte environ deux mille sociétaires. Ils agitent beaucoup en sa faveur, mais ils en sont si peu sûrs qu'ils dissimulent avec grand soin le but politique de toute cette activité et ne cessent de donner à la police l'assurance que la société ne sort pas du cercle de son action statuaire. Ils savent, en effet, qu'au moment donné, une grande partie des sociétaires ne les suivraient pas sur le terrain politique, ou se tourneraient contre eux.[19]

Reports on the clergy of Toulouse, written at the same time, indicate an air of satisfaction and docility: 'En général le clergé se renferme dans le cercle de ses attributions religieuses et ne vise pas, du moins pour le

---

[17] A. Gough, 'The Conflict in Politics: Bishop Pie's Campaign against the Nineteenth Century', in T. Zeldin, ed. *Conflicts in French Society* (London, 1970), pp. 94–168; on official attitudes to Catholic organizations with a known or suspected Legitimist connection, see A.D. Haute Garonne X CP 84, Bienfaisance (Cotes provisoires).

[18] The first conference of the Society of Saint-Vincent de Paul was founded in Toulouse in 1837 by a young lawyer, Firmin Boutan, who remained president of the conference until 1888. Politically he was a moderate Legitimist. The first conference in Nîmes was founded in 1837 by the son of a business family, Léonce Curnier. In 1852 Curnier stood as a *légitimiste rallié* in Nîmes with the approval of the local bishop, Cart, and that of his uncle, Mgr. Sibour, archbishop of Paris. A.N. F1cIII Gard 5. Sibour to the Minister of the Interior, 5 February 1852.

[19] A.N. F1cIII Haute Garonne 9, Prefect to Minister of the Interior, 1 February 1855.

moment, à l'influence politique'.[20] 'On remarque que le clergé, qui semble dans ce pays plus identifié avec la cause légitimiste qu'ailleurs, a cédé, et cède tous les jours d'avantage à l'affection que lui commandent les bienfaits éclairés de l'Empereur pour la religion'.[21] The Catholic working classes of the city were described as obedient to the leadership of their clergy.[22] It was not until the Italian question arose in 1859 that French Legitimism recovered a militant posture. Then, too, the issue was essentially Catholic, with Chambord, who had already espoused Ultramontanism by the late 1830s, himself giving full support to a new alliance between throne and altar, one in which the altar was in fact the dominant partner. Persigny's action in 1861 to weaken the role of the central provincial councils in the organization of the Society of Saint-Vincent de Paul had little to do with his fears of Legitimism per se but reflected fear that the clergy, enraged by the regime's anti-papal policy in Italy, might use its abundantly obvious influence over Legitimists in the society to persuade these to take action of one kind or another against the state.

This account of the development of clerical supremacy over dynastic imperatives from the early 1830s contrasts with Michel Denis' description of the emergence of 'Catholic' politics in the Mayenne, when he writes:

C'est à l'approche des élections d'avril 1848 que les légitimistes mayennais découvrent un début d'autonomie d'action chez les catholiques sur lesquels ils croyaient pouvoir compter.[23]

Much of the difference undoubtedly stems from the character of southern Royalism which was militant, a 'mass' movement with widespread support in the towns, and a vehicle for articulating essentially local grievances and aims rather than expressing dynastic loyalty as the more 'château-orientated' variety did.

Outstanding among the local grievances Royalism articulated was the 'Protestant problem' which retained its urgency in Lower or eastern

---

[20] *Ibid.*, Prefect to Minister of the Interior, 27 January 1855.

[21] *Ibid.*, Prefect to Minister of the Interior, 12 July 1854. A report from the *procureur-général* of Toulouse in 1858 observed that the town's Legitimists were wooing the clergy from a position of marked deference: A.N. BB30 388, 12 July 1858.

[22] A.N. F1cIII Haute Garonne 9, Prefect to Minister of the Interior, 8 July 1858.

[23] M. Denis, *Les royalistes de la Mayenne et le monde moderne (XIXe et XXe siècles)* (Paris, 1977), p. 379.

Languedoc notably.[24] Emancipated by the Revolution, the Protestants continued to provide the cement for an otherwise unlikely cross-class alliance of Catholic interests which refused to accept the outcome of the French Revolution, largely because it had stripped the Catholic community of power. The Protestant presence in Lower Languedoc undoubtedly explains the ability of Royalism to flourish for longer and in a more militant form in the eastern end of the province than in the *toulousain* for example. Events like the July Revolution, with its heavily anti-Catholic flavour, reinforced the prejudices of Catholics, just as the White Terror of 1815 and Catholic demands during the Bourbon Restoration had done nothing to reassure Protestants that their position in the post-Revolution world was secure. The result was an inter-community rivalry which assumed that one community's gains were achieved at the expense of the other, and the description of political regimes as either 'Protestant' or 'Catholic' according to the opportunities they offered one or other of the communities.

Beyond the struggle for political hegemony, Catholics and Legitimists were intellectually hostile to Protestantism. One of the leaders of the Royalist campaign to take full political control of the Midi in 1815, the marquis de Villeneuve, indicated in notes made during the Hundred Days that French Protestantism had been considered to be fundamentally hostile to the monarchic principle from the earliest days, and that it should continue to be so regarded.[25] Villeneuve was not alone in his profound suspicion of the Protestant mentality. In 1837 the Legitimist *Gazette du Bas Languedoc* carried an article on pauperism in which the writer concluded:

Si donc aujourd'hui le paupérisme nous menace de catastrophes imminentes, c'est au catholicisme qu'il faut demander le moyen de les prévenir. On peut aller plus loin et affirmer que tous les systèmes désastreux dont nous recueillons les fruits ont eu pour germe la pensée protestante. L'effet elle-même de la Réforme est d'isoler et de désunir. Elle n'a d'autre principe d'unité que la haine contre ses adversaires.[26]

[24] For an overview of the role of religion in the period with which this essay is concerned, see G. Cholvy, 'Religion et politique en Languedoc méditerranéen et Roussillon à l'époque contemporaine', A. Encrevé, 'Protestantisme et politique: les protestants du midi en décembre 1851', and J.D. Roque, 'Positions et tendances des protestants nîmois au XIXe siècle', in Université Paul Valéry, *Droite et gauche de 1789 à nos jours* (Montpellier, 1975).

[25] A.D. Gard, Archives de La Tour -Saint Chaptes, papers of Louis Pons de Villeneuve. M.S. notes, 1815–18.

[26] *Gazette du Bas Languedoc*, 21 June 1837.

The spread of materialism and secularism in the course of the nineteenth century reinforced Catholic prejudices as did the tendency of a significant proportion of the Protestant population of Lower Languedoc to embrace 'red' Republican doctrines. In 1850 the Protestant stronghold of Saint-Jean-du-Gard was described as 'une république qui se gouverne à part; le socialisme est l'opinion générale', while at equally Protestant Vézénobres, 'les pasteurs, les instituteurs ont fait des localités des foyers du socialisme'; and 'Dans cette partie de l'arrondissement de Nîmes qu'on appelle la Vaunage, partie presqu'exclusivement protestante, un grand nombre de maires sont du parti rouge, plusieurs font partie des sociétés démagogiques qui infestent le pays, quelques uns sont à la tête des agitateurs'.[27] It was the Protestants who provided the nucleus of the insurrection against Louis-Napoleon's coup in December 1851, and Raymond Huard has noted that Protestant pastors could no longer automatically be relied upon as defenders of order in the second half of the century.[28]

The Italian question and the liberalization of the Second Empire's politics gave liberal and radical southern Protestants an unexpected outlet, and further convinced the Catholics that Protestantism sided naturally with the anti-Catholic forces of the nineteenth century.[29] Moreover, the Italian question coincided with the tercentenary of the Reformation, the celebration of which infuriated an already volatile Catholic opinion and provoked an intemperate attack from the bishop of Nîmes, Mgr. Plantier, who could not admit the right to celebrate error.[30]

Yet, in spite of the tide of secularism and modernism which churchmen believed was gathering to batter the Catholic world, some of them thought they could detect a glimpse of victory. Even while they celebrated three centuries of reformed Christianity, the Protestants of the south of France appeared to be going into decline, numerically and morally. Having accounted for 30 per cent of the Gard's population in 1846,

[27] Fitzpatrick, *Catholic Royalism*, p. 176.

[28] R. Huard, *Le mouvement républicain en bas Languedoc, 1848–1881* (Paris, 1982), p. 172.

[29] Republicanism won the largest share of the Protestant vote in the Nîmes municipal elections of 1865; the Republican candidates were all Protestant: Roque in *Droite et gauche*, p. 214.

[30] Mgr. Plantier, *Lettre aux protestants du Gard à l'occasion de leur jubilé séculaire* (Nîmes, 1859) and *Nouvelle lettre aux protestants du Gard* (Nîmes, 1859).

their size had fallen to just less than 29 per cent by 1866.[31] The decline was keenly noted by zealous Catholics like Emmanuel d'Alzon, whose obsession with the Protestants was such that he kept statistics of births in the two communities.[32] At the same time Protestantism was losing members to secular political ideologies, notably to Republicanism, while splits and schisms appeared to occur constantly within the body of believers. It was, said d'Alzon and others, the result of leaving the individual free to make what he could of the Bible and the world, the consequence of not having a central teaching authority and a unified body of doctrine. Encouraged by the English Oxford Movement, and by the restoration of Catholic hierarchies to Britain and Ireland, d'Alzon was the standard-bearer of Catholic politics in Lower Languedoc for most of the second half of the nineteenth century.

Emmanuel d'Alzon represented the most extreme case of the triumph of Catholic issues over Legitimism in the Midi. The son of a Legitimist family, he was profoundly influenced by Lamennais. But like other future Ultramontanes, he did not follow the master into schism with Rome. Rather d'Alzon aligned himself with Rome from the early 1830s, when he was ordained. He commented in 1834: 'Il faut toujours travailler pour Rome, quelquefois sans Rome, jamais contre Rome'.[33] From his appointment as honorary vicar-general of the diocese of Nîmes in 1835 until his death in 1880, d'Alzon laboured uncompromisingly for what he saw as the interests of the Catholic church in Lower Languedoc, founding an important college, a religious congregation, the Assumptionists – which later achieved notoriety in the Dreyfus affair – and devotional and charitable organizations for the young and the working classes. He did not shy from entering into fierce controversies with the Second Empire, over the Italian question, the restrictions on the Society of Saint Vincent de Paul, and on the performance at Nîmes in 1861 of a play by Emile Augier, *Le fils de Giboyer*, in which church and the Legitimist party were ridiculed.

The extent of d'Alzon's Ultramontanism may be seen in his readiness to interfere in the affairs of other churchmen whom he felt were not zealous enough, as he did in 1861 in the neighbouring diocese

[31] Huard, *Le mouvement républicain*, pp. 170, 490.

[32] R. Rémond, E. Poulat (eds.), *Emmanuel d'Alzon dans la société et l'église du XIXe siècle* (Paris, 1982), pp. 29–30.

[33] *Ibid.*, p. 31.

of Montpellier with his own equally Ultramontane bishop, Plantier.[34] Given the concerns of this essay, d'Alzon's political evolution is worth noting. In 1861 he still looked to the Legitimists to articulate clerical interests in the political domain.[35] By 1868, disillusioned with the Empire's liberalism, yet encouraged by the progress made by the Catholic church in Britain and the United States, he preached a sermon in the church of Saint-Charles at Nîmes in which he was reported to have said: 'La démocratie peut et doit être acceptée par les catholiques' and referred to the United States, a secular society in which Catholicism flourished. He further said that 'la démocratie est fatalement liée avec le catholicisme', citing a number of popes whose origins were plebeian. The sermon proposed ending the concordatory regime in France in order to give the church greater freedom and to enable the Pope alone to appoint the bishops.[36]

Emmanuel d'Alzon's own Ultramontanism was matched by the enthusiasm of one of his pupils at the Assumptionist College in Nîmes, the Abbé de Cabrières, who became Bishop Plantier's secretary and then, in 1874, bishop of Montpellier. The three men were, however, the only significant exponents of full-blooded Ultramontanism to shape the Catholic politics of the Midi, and their influence as 'Romanizers' was felt primarily in the 1860s, when church-state relations had deteriorated. Long before, the Catholic interest had been promoted by churchmen who had little inclination to promote the centralism and uniformity which Ultramontanism ultimately achieved, but who sought rather to secure for the church a freedom from 'party' politics so that it might fulfil its pastoral role in the post-Revolution world.[37]

---

[34] A.N. FicIII Hérault 15, Prefect to Minister of the Interior, 3 May 1861; A.N. F19 5835, Prefect of the Hérault to the Minister of Education and Religious Affairs, 9 June 1861. Plantier (1855 to 1875 in Nîmes) was known to support d'Alzon's zeal. Apprised of the manufactured outcry over the play *Le fils de Giboyer*, the Minister of Education and Religious Affairs wrote to Persigny: 'Dans l'état des choses à Nîmes, état bien connu de vous, il est trop manifeste que nous n'avons rien à espérer de la discipline ecclésiastique ni de l'intervention de l'évêque réprimant son vicaire-général': A.N. F19 5835, letter of 30 January 1863.

[35] A.N. F19 5835, Prefect of the Hérault to Minister of Education and Religious Affairs, 9 June 1861.

[36] A.N. F19 5835, Police report to Minister of Education and Religious Affairs, 16 December 1868.

[37] Austin Gough has published an excellent study of the rise of Ultramontane Catholicism in: *Paris and Rome: The Gallican Church and the Ultramontane Campaign, 1848–1853* (Oxford, 1986).

In the archdiocese of Toulouse the movement began as early as the 1820s. Toulouse itself was synonymous with Catholic Royalism. From the days of the French Revolution, Catholic opinion had been shaped by shadowy organizations like the *Associatio amicorum* and the *Congrégation*, which retained their influence on some clergy and laymen well into the nineteenth century, complementing the more ostentatious vehicles of southern religious fervour, the confraternities of *pénitents*.[38] The events of 1815 revealed the extravagant and violent brand of Royalism which went hand in hand with this fervour. In 1820 the septuagenarian aristocrat, Mgr. de Clermont-Tonnerre, was appointed to the see. His Legitimism notwithstanding, the new prelate put loyalty to the church first and openly criticized the Martignac government in 1828 for its ban on the Jesuits and for seeking to restrict enrolment in the *petits séminaires* to clerical aspirants. In the words of Mgr. Chansou:

> Le cardinal de Clermont se présente donc comme le porte-parole d'une Eglise de France qui, tout en collaborant étroitement avec la monarchie, est soucieuse de sauvegarder, de développer son autonomie.[39]

Clermont-Tonnerre's successor continued this policy. Mgr. d'Astros arrived in Toulouse in the wake of the 1830 Revolution, determined to obey and to enforce Pius VIII's instruction to the French church to give its allegiance to the July Monarchy. His own attitudes became clear very quickly. In 1832 he forbade any commemorative requiem masses for Louis XVI, but deplored the prefect's decision to prohibit the annual Corpus Christi procession that year because of Legitimist unrest in the Midi.[40] At the same time he was resolutely opposed to the Ultramontanism of Lamennais, and took the lead in enumerating the errors of the *Avenir* movement, contributing significantly to their condemnation by the Pope. In practical terms d'Astros' achievement was in exercising a strict discipline over the diocesan clergy, many of whom were temperamentally disposed to Legitimist ideals; and extending

[38] J. Godechot, 'Quel a été le rôle des Aa pendant l'époque révolutionnaire?' in J. Godechot, *Regards sur l'époque révolutionnaire* (Toulouse, 1980), pp. 85–94; J. Godechot, *La révolution française dans le midi toulousain* (Toulouse, 1986); G. Bertier de Sauvigny, *Le Comte Ferdinand de Bertier et l'énigme de la congrégation* (Paris, 1948).

[39] In Ph. Wolff (ed.), *Le diocèse de Toulouse* (Paris, 1983), p. 196.

[40] P. Droulers, *Action pastorale et problèmes sociaux sous la monarchie de juillet chez Mgr. d'Astros, archévêque de Toulouse* (Paris, 1954), pp. 49–54.

the influence of the church in some working class milieux through the charitable and mutual aid organizations he promoted. Growing sections of the working class certainly escaped or turned away from this paternalism, but in the long run clerical influences proved stronger than Legitimist influences among those social groups who remained susceptible to paternalism.[41]

In 1849 Mgr. Mioland, d'Astros' coadjutor, succeeded to the archiepiscopal chair. While he personally professed the same independence as d'Astros, the appeal of Ultramontanism had taken root among the diocesan clergy, not least because of their success in mobilizing lay support in the 1840s over the Catholic education issue. On Mioland's death in 1861 the new archbishop, Desprez, introduced the Roman liturgy and Ultramontane theology immediately, to the satisfaction of the majority of his clergy. The period of his episcopacy saw a concerted effort to build up a strictly Catholic, pro-papal party in the *toulousain*, a task to which the region's Legitimists contributed in no small measure.[42]

In the diocese of Montpellier the conflict between 'Gallican' and 'Ultramontane' tendencies became a public affair, with most of the clergy openly opposing the benign attitudes of bishops Thibault (1835–61) and Le Courtier (1861–73) to the government provided it respected the primacy of the church in spiritual matters. Thibault displayed warmth and respect in his attitude to the Protestants in the diocese, while Le Courtier was one of the minority of bishops who voted against the doctrine of infallibility at the First Vatican Council. These were dangerous attitudes in the diocese adjacent to d'Alzon's and Plantier's Nîmes and occasioned unconstitutional 'raids' by the Nîmes clergy anxious to encourage the Ultramontanes. Thibault's funeral was boycotted by his clergy; Le Courtier was forced out and replaced by the uncompromising Ultramontane from the diocese of Nîmes, the Abbé de Cabrières.[43] Throughout the struggle in the diocese the Ultramontane faction enjoyed the support of the Legitimists. These were skillfully manipulated by d'Alzon who at that time still believed

---

[41] See R. Aminzade, *Class, Politics and Early Industrial Capitalism: A Study of Mid-Nineteenth Century Toulouse* (Albany, 1981).

[42] See Chansou and Sempéré in Wolff, *Le diocèse de Toulouse*, pp. 215–18.

[43] See G. Cholvy, *Le diocèse de Montpellier* (Paris, 1976), pp. 198–227; A.N. F1cIII Hérault 15, Prefect to the Minister of the Interior 5, 11 May 1861, *Rapport périodique*, 1–15 January 1863.

that Legitimism was the most suitable vehicle for advancing the clerical cause.[44]

There were other factors which help to account for the emergence of Catholic or strictly religious politics in the period, but these were common to other parts of France, and indeed Europe, as well. Obviously, in the 1860s, the plight of Pius IX attracted the attention and support of Catholics world wide; such instruments as Peter's Pence [*le denier de Saint-Pierre*] promoted and expressed that concern, as did the growing work of the Lyon-founded Society for the Propagation of the Faith. At the same time the spate of apparitions and the triumphalist proclamation of doctrine publicized Catholicism and enhanced its image in the eyes of many people.

Important, too, was the new generation of priests. Their experience was entirely located in the often unsatisfactory workings of the Concordat, which many viewed as a straitjacket with few benefits in the unstable political climate of nineteenth-century France beyond the obvious material ones. In the archdiocese of Toulouse an average of twenty-two priests were ordained each year between 1830 and 1880 against seventeen deaths per annum; while two-thirds of the clergy were over sixty years old in 1816, only half were in 1830.[45] In the diocese of Montpellier, an average of twenty-five priests were ordained each year in the period from 1825 to 1834; by 1848, only 6 per cent of the clergy were sixty years old or more.[46]

Catholic politics in the Midi reflected essentially local traits which this essay has tried to draw out. The tradition of mass royalist political involvement and the existence of royalist organizations gave the clergy access to a mass audience and a useful vehicle for their demands. The Protestant presence, strong in the east, weaker in the west, but still part of the Catholic collective memory, provided the cement and made easy a

[44] See, for example, A.N. F19 5835, Prefect of the Hérault to the Minister of Education and Religious Affairs, 9 June 1861: 'Monsieur d'Alzon, vicaire-général de Nîmes, m'a écrit hier pour m'annoncer sa résolution de se porter candidat aux élections pour le conseil général dans le deuxième canton de Montpellier . . . Bien que connu dans tout le Midi par l'exaltation de ses principes politiques et par l'ardeur de son prosélytisme ultramontain, cet ecclésiastique a voulu accentuer plus fortement encore sa démarche et lui donner une signification non équivoque d'hostilité en chargeant un des principaux chefs du parti légitimiste de cette ville, Monsieur le vicomte de Ginestous, de me remettre en personne la lettre par laquelle il pose sa candidature'.

[45] Wolff, *Le diocèse de Toulouse*, pp. 198, 209.

[46] Cholvy, *Diocèse de Montpellier*, p. 203.

shift of focus, away from the primacy of secular political objectives to the primacy of Catholic religious goals. One point in particular seems significant. Strictly Catholic politics emerged relatively early in the century in the Midi and, for a number of its exponents, had little to do with Roman affairs. It would be misguided to suggest that there was an inevitability in the triumph of Ultramontanism. As Austin Gough has demonstrated, the Ultramontane assault on the French church was sudden and swift.[47] Certainly the ground had been prepared unwittingly by those who had fought to distance the church from particular political regimes, but the bitterness of the conflict in the diocese of Montpellier during the 1850s and 1860s reveals that many influential clerics believed firmly that Catholic politics was about Catholicism in France, and nothing more. They were as surprised as anybody at the way things turned out.

---

[47] Gough, *Paris and Rome.*

6

Why Republicans and Catholics Couldn't Stand Each Other in the Nineteenth Century

Ralph Gibson

The first thing to do, before enquiring why Republicans and Catholics couldn't stand each other, is to establish that it was in fact the case that they couldn't. Theodore Zeldin, and some others, have doubted it. They argue that behind a façade of bitter polemic, and even of concrete mutual persecution, both sides were in agreement about a lot of fundamental issues. This was (it is alleged) particularly true where common-or-garden moral issues were concerned. They agreed about most aspects of family morality, paternal authority, the infantilization of women, dutifulness in children and the undesirability of extra-marital sex. They agreed about the evils of alcoholism, the awfulness of sexual crimes, the sanctity of property. They were both, as Zeldin remarks, 'occupied by the problems of death, guilt, conscience, the distinction of the valuable from the trivial and the place of the individual in the universe';[1] as such they were united against those who were not. There is thus a persuasive revisionism which argues that the apparently bitter conflicts about which so much history has been written were really only froth and bubble and that, at a fundamental level, Republicans

---

[1] T. Zeldin, *France, 1848–1945* (2 vols, Oxford, 1973–77), vol. 2, p. 994. See also J. Faury, *Cléricalisme et anticléricalisme dans le Tarn (1848–1900)* (Toulouse, 1980), p. 493.

and Catholics were united by more issues than those which divided them.[2]

This revisionism is healthy, but it must not go too far. Zeldin himself points out that disagreements about issues which may have been objectively relatively minor nevertheless led to those concerned becoming 'enemies so violent that they became quite incapable of understanding or sympathizing with each other'.[3] Jean Faury observes that even though Republicans and Catholics might agree on a fair amount of sexual repression, the former did not share the visceral hostility to the human body that so marked the traditions of the Catholic Reformation.[4] More fundamentally, although they may have shared many moral positions, it did matter that the theoretical underpinnings of their moral systems were utterly incompatible.

Most crucially of all, Republicans and Catholicism were both, in their different ways, religious phenomena and the conflict between them could easily take on the levels of bitterness of a religious war. René Rémond has argued persuasively that the anticlericalism of Republicans was not merely a rejection of 'clericalism', but constituted 'une idéologie politique positive' in its own right.[5] I would go further, and argue that Republicans, at least of the educated and articulate kind, often had a coherent belief system which effectively amounted to a religion. Consider the credo of Zola's Dr. Pascal:

> Je crois que l'avenir de l'humanité est dans le progrès de la raison par la science. Je crois que la poursuite de la vérité par la science est l'idéal divin que l'homme doit se proposer . . . Je crois que la somme de ces vérités, augmentées toujours, finira par donner à l'homme un pouvoir incalculable, sinon le bonheur.[6]

[2] See T. Zeldin (ed.), *Conflicts in French Society: Anticlericalism, Education and Morals in the Nineteenth Century* (London, 1970), pp. 9–10, 36, 88, 93, 228–29; Zeldin, *France, 1848–1945*, vol. 2, pp. 983, 1031; F. Lebrun (dir.), *Histoire des catholiques en France du XVe siècle à nos jours* (Toulouse, 1980), pp. 372–73; Faury, *Cléricalisme et anticléricalisme*, pp. 267–68, 493.

[3] Zeldin, *France 1848–1945*, vol. 2, p. 1039.

[4] Faury, *Cléricalisme et anticléricalisme*, pp. 276–78. See also R. Gibson, *A Social History of French Catholicism, 1789–1914* (London, 1989), pp. 92–94. For the following point, see P. Bountry, *Prêtres et paroisses au pays du curé d'Ars* (Paris, 1986), p. 446.

[5] R. Rémond, *L'anticléricalisme en France de 1815 à nos jours* (Paris, 1976), pp. 4, 7, 17, 32, *passim*.

[6] E. Zola, *Les Rougon-Macquart* (5 vols., Paris, 1960–67), Bibliothèque de la Pléiade, vol. 5, p. 953.

To my mind, the litmus test of a religion is whether it can carry a believer over the last great hurdle. It is thus instructive to look at the rhetoric surrounding the *enterrements civils* under the Third Republic. Here is the old philosopher Quinet, in 1875, after the Prefect of the Moral Order had attempted to prevent a civil burial ceremony at Lyon:

> Barbarie vaine! Il dépend de tout homme de se préparer, pour l'heure suprême, un magnifique cortège qu'aucune puissance humaine n'empêchera de passer et de resplendir dans la nuit. Travaillons à nous faire cortège à nous-même. Je convie autour de moi, quand viendra le moment, les pensées les plus hautes et les meilleures où j'ai pu m'élever, les vérités que j'ai rencontrées et servies, les idées immortelles qui m'ont apparu depuis ma jeunesse jusqu'à mon dernier jour. Qu'elles viennent et me protègent contre l'outrage au-delà de la mort. [7]

This is the kind of discourse that one may reasonably call religious; it is not dissimilar from Catholic discourse about the good death. It suggests that Catholics and Republicans were divided by competing religious beliefs. It is thus not surprising to find them capable of similar levels of intolerance. The textbooks contain enough examples of Catholic intolerance; let me quote one striking example from the Republican side. The 1892 congress of *Libre-Pensée* groups of the south-east called not only for the separation of church and state, but also for the *suppression* of churches in the state, on the grounds that 'c'est respecter la liberté de conscience que d'empêcher d'induire en erreur les consciences'. [8] There is surely not much difference between that and Pius IX's Syllabus of Errors.

There were thus many ways in which Republicanism was a religion in the same sense that Catholicism was, and this may account for some of the bitterness between adherents of the two faiths. This is however only a very partial explanation of why they couldn't stand each other; in particular, it is probably only true of an intellectual élite. There were

---

[7] Quoted by J. Lalouette, 'Les enterrements civils dans les premières décennies de la troisième république', *Ethnologie française*, xiii, no. 2 (1982/3), p. 120. See also G. Cholvy et Y.-M. Hilaire, *Histoire religieuse de la France contemporaine*, (3 vols., Toulouse, 1985–88), vol. 2, p. 28, and the death of Luce in Roger Martin du Gard, *Jean Barois* (Paris, 1969, Livre de Poche), pp. 496–99.

[8] P. Lévêque, 'Libre-pensée et socialisme (1889–1939), quelques points de repère', in *Christianisme et monde ouvrier* (Paris, 1975), pp. 117–55 (p. 126).

many other factors at work, some of them very old and very deeply entrenched.

René Rémond remarks that any clergy which sets itself up as a body apart is likely to provoke resentment.[9] The Catholic clergy created by the canons of the Council of Trent certainly did that: the clergy was marked off, in a way it had not been before, by specialized education, dress, effective celibacy and by a systematic rejection of the world. Under the *ancien régime*, it had already provoked a widespread anticlericalism, which developed many of the general criticisms of the clergy which would still be popular in the nineteenth century. Such criticisms focused on the avarice of priests, on their hypocricy (a criticism taken up with immense success by Molière in *Tartuffe* and later by Stendhal in *Le Rouge et le Noir*), and on what the French delightfully refer to as *concupiscence*. This was what Jean Faury has called 'un fonds ancien instinctif, viscéral, qui est tout le contraire d'un movement rationnel de l'esprit: le besoin de défier et de transgresser le sacré, qui se cristallise dans la haine du prêtre'.[10] It would continue to be very popular in the nineteenth century, as the success of the re-edition of the *Bon sens du curé Meslier* in the 1830s would testify.[11] Such traditional anticlericalism continued into and right through the nineteenth century (and indeed today): it is powerfully expressed in the verse of a popular song which the anarchist Ravachol sang at the foot of the guillotine in 1892:

> Si tu veux heureux,
>   Nom de Dieu!
> Prends ton propriétaire,
>   Nom de Dieu!
> Fous les églises par terre,
>   Sang Dieu!
> Et l'bon Dieu dans la merde,
>   Nom de Dieu!
> Et l'bon Dieu dans la merde![12]

[9] Rémond, *L'anticléricalisme*, pp. 20–21.

[10] Faury, *Cléricalisme et anticléricalisme*, p. 437.

[11] See C. Marcilhacy, *Le diocèse d'Orléans au milieu du XIXe siècle: les hommes et leur mentalités* (Paris, 1964), pp. 455–60.

[12] P. Pierrard, *L'eglise et les ouvriers en France (1840–1940)* (Paris, 1984), p. 423 (and pp. 414–24), or Rémond, *L'anticléricalisme*, pp. 216–17.

Not a word about capitalists; popular hatred in Paris under the Third Republic was centred on the landlord and on the Catholic clergy.

The anticlericalism of such a popular song was the continuation of a very old tradition of popular anticlericalism which may be seen, at least in part, as a reaction against a clergy which set itself apart and held itself aloof. It was, furthermore, a clergy which had a very high opinion of itself: seminary training had imbued it with a sense of the 'eminent dignity of the priest', such that even the curé d'Ars, himself a model of humility, used to say that if he met a priest and an angel he would greet the priest before the angel.[13] The Tridentine church was a very hierarchical organization, particularly where relations between clergy and laity were concerned; the role of the latter was simply to watch and pray. As Pius X reminded French Catholics in 1906, the church was:

> an essentially unequal society, that is to say, a society composed of two categories of people: the pastors and the flock . . . the mass has no other duty than to let itself be led and, like a docile flock, to follow its pastors.[14]

The intensely hierarchical ideology and structure of the Tridentine church had no doubt always alienated men (women a lot less). In the nineteenth century it would particularly alienate Republicans. Republicans may on occasion have been pretty hierarchical themselves, but they were at least in principle committed to an ideology of popular sovereignty, where power flowed from the bottom up and not from the top down. There was thus a clear intrinsic clash between their ideology and that of the Catholic church (at least in its Tridentine form).[15] Perhaps more importantly, Republicans were mostly men, and they were part of a male culture which prescribed a certain independence of spirit, a refusal to submit oneself to the authority of another man (whereas women were systematically trained to do just that). They thus found it very difficult to accept a clergy imbued with a sense of its own 'eminent dignity'. This was particularly true where confession was concerned: it involved the abandonment of one's will and judgement to another man.

[13] A. Monnin, *Esprit du curé d'Ars* (Paris, 1864), ch. 9.
[14] Lebrun, *Histoire des catholiques*, pp. 86–87 (quotation by R. Sauzet from *Vehementer nos*, 11 February 1906).
[15] R. Aubert, *Le pontificat de Pie IX (1846–1878)* (Paris, 1952), p. 129.

That is partly why confession was such a regular object of anticlerical abuse.[16]

Hostility to clerical authority was all the stronger in the nineteenth century in that the clergy itself was socially very different from its *ancien régime* predecessor. Eighteenth-century curés had been on the whole of bourgeois origin: authority over the mass of the people came naturally to them and the faithful tended to respect the priest and to accept his authority for social as well as theological reasons. Nineteenth-century curés came, increasingly, from the better-off peasantry and elements of the rural artisanate.[17] Men of the village who had known them as lads (probably rather stand-offish ones) found their newly-acquired status and authority rather hard to take. As Mgr. Calvet wrote of the clergy of the diocese of Cahors in 1905.

> Comme il est sorti des rangs du peuple et qu'il s'est élevé au-dessus du peuple, la jalousie le poursuit, implacable.[18]

Furthermore, priests who had been socially mobile might indeed become arrogant. The point was made, with some if not total justification, by an anticlerical polemicist in 1847:

> Le prêtre catholique, sorti de parents humbles, se trouve à une si prodigieuse distance de son point de départ qu'il peut à peine l'apercevoir derrière soi.[19]

This is probably why so many anticlerical outbursts in nineteenth-century France (particularly in the countryside) centred on the clergy's *esprit de domination*. Thus in March 1848 the inhabitants of a village in the diocese of Belley petitioned against their curé:

> M. Tournier se réservant sans doute à lui tout seul d'être l'unique dans la commune à tout gouverner . . . les maisons dont les pères de famille n'avaient

[16] Of course it always had been: see J. Delumeau, *L'aveu et le pardon: les difficultés de la confession, XIIIe–XVIIIe siècle* (Paris, 1990). For the nineteenth century, two of the most interesting treatments are T. Zeldin, 'The Conflict of Moralities: Confession, Sin and Pleasure in the Nineteenth Century', in Zeldin (ed.), *Conflicts in French Society*, pp. 13–50 and P. Boutry, *Prêtres et paroisses*, part 3, ch. 1.

[17] See Gibson, *French Catholicism*, pp. 68–76.

[18] Mgr. J. Calvet, 'Monographie religieuse d'un diocèse français: le diocèse de Cahors', *Revue catholique des églises*, 2e année, no. 12, février 1905, pp. 65–87 (p. 85).

[19] Rémond, *L'anticléricalisme*, p. 67.

pas voulu courber la tête sous sa tyrannie et être gouvernés par lui . . . ont dû subir ses sentiments haineux et vindicatifs . . . Les habitants lui ayant reconnu un caractère hautain, fier, haineux et vindicatif se sont lassés de sa tyrannie.[20]

This petition was composed during a crucial period in national politics, but there is no sign that it was the curé's reaction to the events of February that concerned his parishioners; they were simply expressing accumulated resentment of his *esprit de domination*. The clergy themselves were often aware of the problem: a curé of the diocese of Orleans reported in 1850 that his flock refused religious instruction, 'parce que le curé les dominerait et ils ne veulent pas être dominés en quoi que ce soit'.[21] This refusal by men to accept clerical domination may have been at the heart of a whole series of local squabbles, as curés tried to assert their authority and as parishioners, often led by their mayors, stoutly resisted it.[22]

The social origin of the clergy, and perhaps the growth of an aggressive individualism among a peasantry which increasingly owned land and the *nouvelles couches sociales* who proliferated in an increasingly market economy, made this a particularly acute problem in the nineteenth century. It had a lot to do with hostility between Catholics and Republicans. Yet this was in essence an old problem, dating back to the creation of a new kind of clergy in the Catholic Reformation. Their inability to stand each other was clearly also attributable to a much more recent past: the Enlightenment and the French Revolution. There is little need to say very much about these factors at this juncture, since they are well known, but it is important to emphasize the degree to which the traditions of such past generations weighed like a nightmare on the brain of the living. The anticlericalism of Voltaire was massively influential in the century after his death: it was calculated, for example, that over one and a half million copies of his works sold in the decade

---

[20] Boutry, *Prêtres et paroisses*, p. 367.

[21] C. Marcilhacy, 'L'anticléricalisme dans l'Orléanais pendant la première moitié du XIXe siècle', *Archives de sociologie des religions*, 6 (1958), 91–103 (p. 99). See also Marcilhacy, *Orleans*, pp. 256–62, and A. Corbin, *Archaïsme et modernité en Limousin au XIXe siècle, 1845–1880* (Paris, 1975), vol. 1, pp. 646–47, 650.

[22] See R. Magraw, 'The Conflict in the Villages: Popular Anticlericalism in the Isère (1852–70)', in Zeldin (ed.), *Conflicts in French Society*, pp. 169–227, and B. Singer, *Village Notables in Nineteenth-Century France: Priests, Mayors and Schoolmasters* (Albany, 1983), chs. 4, 5.

1814–25,[23] and his popularity was to remain undimmed for the rest of the century. Even more crucially, the ideological and physical violence of the Revolution created insuperable barriers between Republicans and Catholics for the next hundred and fifty years. It has to be remembered that between two and three thousand members of the clergy had been murdered in various ways in the 1790s,[24] to say nothing of the other anticlerical violence of the age. The Republicans on their side could not claim quite so many martyrs, but they were permanently distressed by the failure of their Promethean dream in the 1790s; the temptation to thrust the responsibility for that failure onto the Catholic church was immense. Catholics thus saw Republicans as the murderers of priests, and Republicans saw Catholics as the murderers of an ideological dream. That Revolutionary legacy would dominate the nineteenth century.

It is true that by the time of the Third Republic memories of the Revolution were almost entirely dependent on the written word. Republican resentment against Catholics had however been refuelled by more recent events: the crude alliance in the 1850s between the church and the Second Empire. Most Republican leaders and ideologues had had personal experience of persecution under Napoleon III and their hatred of Bonapartism was profound. Despite the partial rupture between church and régime in 1859, it was the alliance of eagle and altar in the 1850s that stuck in most Republicans' minds and in their craw. Zola is perhaps the most prominent example.[25]

It was not just the clergy's politics under the Second Empire that refuelled Republican resentment. The mid century had seen the triumph in France of a new style of Catholicism, usually referred to as Ultramontane. Ultramontane Catholicism was not only politically reactionary; it was many other things as well which Republicans found repellent. It was internationalist and loyal to Rome rather than to France. It was, in the eyes of bourgeois Republicans with a good education, intellectually

[23] J. Bruhat, 'Anticléricalisme et mouvement ouvrier en France avant 1914: esquisse d'un problématique', in *Christianisme et monde ouvrier* (Paris, 1975), pp. 79–115 (p. 93). See also P. Guiral, 'Quelques notes sur le retour en faveur de Voltaire sous le second empire', in *Hommage au doyen Etienne Gros* (Aix-en-Provence, 1959), pp. 193–204.

[24] B. Cousin et al., *La pique et la croix: histoire religieuse de la révolution française* (Paris, 1989), p. 168.

[25] See G. Cholvy, *Religion et société au XIXe siècle: le diocèse de Montpellier* (Service de reproduction des thèses, Université de Lille III, 1973), pp. 731–32, 1249–50.

disreputable: in particular, Ultramontane spokesmen like Louis Veuillot and his followers uncritically accepted the miraculous. The miracles of La Salette (1846) and Lourdes (1858), much trumpeted by Ultramontanes, were greeted by Republicans with hoots of derision; La Salette was, in the words of the *Journal de Rouen* in 1862, 'un insulte aux progrès de la science et un outrage à la raison humaine'.[26] All the evils of Ultramontanism appeared to Republicans to be summed up in the Syllabus of Errors of 1864; for Larousse's *Grand dictionnaire universel du XIXe siècle*, the Syllabus was 'révoltant pour la conscience et la raison humaine . . . un abîme infranchissable est désormais creusé entre la papauté et le monde moderne'.[27]

Perhaps the fundamental objection to Ultramontanism was its central doctrine that 'Christ must also reign upon earth'. It was essentially theocratic: France must found her public polity on the kingship of Christ, with all its political consequences.[28] This was not necessarily a dominant doctrine in the French church in the second half of the nineteenth century, but it was noisily voiced, and many clerics who did not entirely subscribe to it nevertheless lined up with the Ultramontanes in solidarity against the Republican and anticlerical enemy.[29] This was happening at the same time as Republican doctrines about 'religion, affaire privée' were becoming ever clearer and stronger. Such had not been the ideology of the Revolutionaries of 1789: they had firmly believed that religion was and should be a matter of public policy.[30] But the liberal individualism to which Republicans increasingly subscribed found any kind of theocratic doctrine fundamentally unacceptable – just at the moment when such doctrines were being noisily voiced by Ultramontane Catholics, in a way that was entirely new in French Catholicism (their Gallican predecessors would have found it nearly as objectionable as did the Republicans).

[26] Cited in J.-P. Chaline, *Les bourgeois de Rouen: une élite urbaine au XIXe siècle* (Paris, 1982), p. 276.

[27] Cited in E. Poulat, *Eglise contre bourgeoisie: introduction au devenir du catholicisme actuel* (Paris, 1977), p. 173.

[28] A. Gough, 'The Conflict in Politics: Bishop Pie's Campaign against the Nineteenth Century', in Zeldin (ed.), *Conflicts in French Society*, pp. 94–168 (p. 96).

[29] J. Gadille, *La pensée et l'action politique des évêques français au début de la IIIe République, 1870–1883* (2 vols., Paris, 1966), vol. 2, pp. 260, 263 and vol. 1, book one, ch. 3.

[30] A theme extensively developed in Cousin et al., *La pique et la croix*.

I have suggested that the ideology of Republicanism was liberal individualism. This is not entirely true, inasmuch as most Republicans under the Third Republic were increasingly committed to the idea of the nation. They were particularly concerned with the moral unity of the nation. That was what made education such a crucial issue: Catholics must not be allowed to create *deux jeunesses*.[31] Such a division in the moral unity of the nation would be all the more serious, in Republican eyes, because the church was an international institution whose primary loyalties were not to France. This accusation was at any rate tirelessly repeated (at least until the Dreyfus Affair lined up the clergy on the side of the army), and one must suppose that Republicans meant what they said when they accused Catholics of being disloyal to the nation. There was of course no basis for it in fact: Catholics had indeed been *anti-patriote* in the 1790s, but by the time of the Third Republic they had proved their patriotism in the Franco-Prussian war, and would do so again in 1914.[32] But Ultramontane devotion to the cause of the temporal power of the Pope rendered them vulnerable to accusations that they put French interests second.[33] It was an accusation that was particularly telling against the religious orders, especially those with international ramifications, who, as Lockroy said in the Chamber of Deputies in 1880, 'ont une patrie céleste qu'ils préfèrent à la patrie terrestre, et qui . . . obéissent à un chef étranger'.[34] In a Republic that was busily engaged in turning the particularist loyalties of the peasants toward the nation-state, and which was increasingly worried about the industrial and demographic giant across the Rhine, the accusation was a deadly serious one. It was, furthermore, an accusation that rang bells in the consciousness of at least some ordinary Frenchmen. Folk-memories of Catholic hostility to the *patriotes* of the Revolution was a long time a-dying. Curés in the early 1870s frequently reported that they were accused of

[31] R. Anderson, 'The Conflict in Education. Catholic Secondary Schools (1850–70): A Reappraisal', in Zeldin (ed.), *Conflicts in French Society*, pp. 51–93 (p. 54), and Rémond, *L'anticléricalisme*, pp. 113–14.

[32] See M.-C. Pierre, 'Les idées politiques de Mgr. Turinaz (évêque de Tarentaise, 1873–1882, évêque de Nancy, 1882–1918)', doctorat de IIIe cycle, Université de Nancy II, 1982, pp. 50–54, and 4e partie, ch. 3; also M. Despland, 'A Case of Christians Shifting their Moral Allegiance: France, 1790–1914', *Journal of the American Academy of Religion*, lii. no. 4, 671–90.

[33] Y.-M. Hilaire, *Une chrétienté au XIXe siècle? La vie religieuse des populations du diocèse d'Arras (1840–1914)* (Lyon, 1977), vol. 1, p. 342.

[34] A. Prost, *L'enseignement en France, 1800–1967* (Paris, 1968), p. 212.

collaborating with the Prussians and that the accusation had resulted in a sharp fall in religious practice.[35] Yet more surprisingly, the accusation seems to have stuck in 1914, at least in isolated parts of the Limousin, where it was reported that curés were believed to be sabotaging railway lines and sending money to the Germans.[36]

There were many other sources of conflict between Catholics and Republicans which could be examined, particularly the tie-up between elements of the Catholic church and elements of the industrial bourgeoisie,[37] or the way in which Republicans with a very strong belief in *l'état* came to resent the way in which the church, under the Third Republic, increasingly took on the nature of a state within a state. In these respects, however, as in those which I have examined in more detail, the conflict was essentially over the public role of the church. We have recently grown used to the idea that the private role of the church may have been even more crucial in alienating Republicans, at least where men were concerned. In particular, the struggle between the two was to a very considerable degree a struggle between two groups of men for the control of French women. Women often found in the church a refuge from a male-dominated world. Theodore Zeldin pointed this out very clearly:

> In a world where the male reigned supreme, the church in fact presented a haven where women were treated as equals, and given opportunities to lead lives independent of their menfolk, organizing and participating in exclusively feminine charities and societies.[38]

I would add that the female religious orders, which in the nineteenth century flourished like the green bay tree, provided a marvellous opportunity for women to lead independent lives (which is probably why they were so

---

[35] F. Boulard et al., *Matériaux pour l'histoire religieuse du peuple français, XIXe-XXe siècles* (2 vols., Paris, 1982–87), vol. 1, pp. 76, 147, 319–20, 342, 344, 369; see also Faury, *Cléricalisme et anticléricalisme*, p. 88, and A. Corbin, *Le village des cannibales* (Paris, 1990), pp. 61–64.

[36] L. Pérouas, *Refus d'une religion, religion d'un refus: en Limousin rural, 1880–1940* (Paris, 1985), pp. 192–93.

[37] See Colin Heywood's essay above, pp. 67–88, and his 'The Catholic Church and the Formation of the Industrial Labour Force in Nineteenth-Century France: An Interpretative Essay', *European History Quarterly*, 19 (1989), 509–33; for a slightly different view, see Gibson, *French Catholicism*, ch. 7.

[38] Zeldin, *France, 1848–1945*, vol. 2, p. 992.

successful).[39] Republican men, who preferred their womenfolk to be under their own exclusive control, could get very resentful. They particularly resented the power which they thought the confessional gave priests over women. Michelet is the most notorious example and his much-cited testimony is worth quoting again:

> Le confesseur d'une jeune femme peut se définir hardiment, l'envieux du mari, et son ennemi secret . . . Cet homme sait maintenant sur cette femme ce que le mari n'a pas su, dans les longs épanchements des nuits et des jours . . . Elle aussi, elle sait bien qu'il y a un maître de sa pensée intime. Jamais elle ne passera devant cet homme sans baisser les yeux . . . Chose humiliante, de n'obtenir rien de ce qui fut à vous que sur autorisation et par indulgence, d'être vu, suivi dans l'intimité la plus intime par un témoin invisible qui vous règle et vous fait votre part, de rencontrer dans la rue un homme qui connaît mieux que vous vos plus secrètes faiblesses, qui salue humblement, se détourne et rit.[40]

Michelet's fantasies were perhaps unusually precise, but the resentment of a clerical rivalry exercising power over women who were regarded as exclusive possessions was very widespread. In 1899 a Socialist militant gave vituperative expression to the same hostility:

> Tandis que, tranquilles et contents, nous vaquons à nos affaires, nos femmes, fascinées par ces hommes de mensonge, vont s'abattre dans les confessionaux, et, à notre insu, trahissent tous les secrets de notre vie, qui leur sont, hélas, trop facilement extorqués. Alors que nous croyons avoir mis les nôtres dans la voie de la vérité, nous sommes indignement trompés, car notre oeuvre est détruite en quelques minutes par les fables de ces hommes sinistres: ils volent la conscience de nos femmes.[41]

'They steal away the conscience of our women.' No testimony could be more direct as to the way in which anticlerical men perceived the male clergy as rivals for control of their womenfolk. Therein lay, without doubt, one of the deepest roots of hostility between them.

---

[39] See C. Langlois, *Le catholicisme au féminin: les congrégations françaises à supérieure générale au XIXe siècle* (Paris, 1984); O. Arnold, *Le corps et l'âme: la vie des religieuses au XIXe siècle* (Paris, 1984); Y. Turin, *Femmes et religieuses au XIXe siècle: le féminisme 'en religion'* (Paris, 1989).

[40] J. Michelet, *Le prêtre, la femme et la famille* (Paris, 1862, 8th edn.), pp. 211–15.

[41] Faury, *Cléricalisme et anticléricalisme*, p. 271; see also Pérouas, *Refus d'une religion*, p. 189.

Clerical control of women through the institution of confession was of course supremely resented when it came to sexual matters. This was above all true of the issue of contraception, almost universally practised in rural France. Clerical attitudes to the issue did in fact soften in the course of the century, as pressure on the clergy built up and as Liguorist moral theology gave them a way out; by the end of the century, many priests had even given up tackling men in confession with respect to the sin of Onan.[42] But men continued profoundly to resent what they saw as interference in a wholly intimate and personal matter. The clergy was well enough aware of this. Bishop Bouvier of Le Mans, the acknowledged specialist in the matter, sought guidance from Rome in 1842, pointing out that young people:

> normally feel very offended when their confessors interrogate them on the manner in which they use their matrimonial rights; they cannot be got by warnings to moderate their exercise of the conjugal act, and they cannot decide to increase the number of their children too much. To the murmurs of their confessors they reply by abandoning the sacraments of penitence and Eucharist . . . religion suffers considerable prejudice from this.[43]

Rome replied advising confessors to be extremely circumspect in such matters, and on the whole they probably were. Yet sex in general, and contraception in particular, remained a sticking point. At Bonnot in the Limousin, during the mission of 1898, the Fathers spoke much, both in public and in private, about the sins of the flesh; there were very few communions by men. When a new priest arrived in the parish in 1904 men came to him promising to leave him in peace if he did not talk of 'ces choses'.[44]

It was in such intimate matters that many of the deepest roots of the hostility felt by Republican men towards the Catholic clergy were to be found. The sense that priests controlled their wives and daughters, and the fear that priests would interfere in a part of their lives which men of the time regarded as absolutely personal and private, could culminate in

---

[42] J. Stengers, 'Les pratiques anticonceptionnelles dans le mariage au XIXe et au XXe siècle: problèmes humains et attitudes religieuses', *Revue belge de philologie et d'histoire*, xlix, pt. 2 (1971/2), 403–81.

[43] Quoted by Zeldin, in *Conflicts in French Society*, p. 33. See also Hilaire, *Une chrétienté*, p. 460, and P. Lévêque, *Une société en crise: la Bourgogne au milieu du XIXe siècle (1846–1852)* (Paris, 1983), vol. 2, p. 458.

[44] Pérouas, *Refus d'une religion*, p. 191.

a fierce anticlerical hatred. It was not the only reason why Republicans and Catholics couldn't stand each other: they were divided by competing religious faiths; by the natural resentment of a clergy with pretentions to separateness; by legacies of the Enlightenment and Revolution and by the more recent legacy of the Second Empire; by Ultramontanism; by supposedly different attitudes to the nation; and by a great many other factors which I have not considered here. But questions of women and sexuality may have been at the heart of the issue.

7

Catholics versus Freemasons in Late Nineteenth-Century France

Geoffrey Cubitt

'La république n'est que la franc-maçonnerie organisée en gouvernement.'[1] In these words, the Catholic journalist Arthur Loth gave forthright expression to a common Catholic attitude towards the Third Republic. Faced with the anticlerical complexion of Republican politics (both Opportunist and Radical) and with the seemingly inexorable secularizing drift of Republican legislation, many French Catholics in the 1880s and 1890s were understandably disinclined to think of the Republic in constitutional terms, as a framework within and through which their own traditions and aspirations might seek expression. They conceived of it instead as the instrument whereby those traditions and aspirations were systematically denigrated, and those who adhered to them oppressed and excluded from national life. The Republic, as they described it, was the expression, the creation, and the institutionalized hegemony of an alien and sectarian force. In the more abstract sort of political discourse, this force was usually referred to as 'the Revolution'. When Catholics discussed the enemy in more human terms, they tended to call it Freemasonry.[2]

---

[1] *L'Univers* 20 April 1884.
[2] The connection between the two terms is established by Loth: 'La franc-maçonnerie est la révolution agissant et fonctionnant d'elle-même, au moyen d'une multitude d'adeptes réunis dans une même pensée de haine contre la religion et tout ce qui s'y rapporte.' (*Ibid.*)

The purpose of this essay is to explore the vision of Freemasonry that was involved in this rhetorical reaction against the Third Republic (and against the various features of modernity of which the Republic was felt to be the political expression), and to see how this vision of the enemy shaped French Catholics' efforts to fight back. For antimasonic rhetoric did not only provide an outlet for feelings of outrage and alienation; it also purported to describe a target for practical action. In the 1880s, furthermore, Catholics were impelled towards antimasonic action not only by their own local frustrations, but by explicit papal stimulus. The encyclical *Humanum genus*, published in 1884, was scarcely the first official papal condemnation of Freemasonry: a string of them stretched back to Clement XII's *In eminenti* (1738).[3] Yet Leo XIII went further than his predecessors, both in the forcefulness with which he declared the struggle between the church and Freemasonry to be the fundamental issue of modern times, and in the summons he issued to the faithful, both clergy and laity, to engage in that struggle in practical ways – through piety, propaganda, education and social work. In France, at any rate, *Humanum genus* established the antimasonic idiom, for a time, as the quasi-official rhetoric of the Catholic church. Equally importantly, it provoked extensive discussion of the methods of antimasonic struggle and a rash of attempts to respond in practice to the Pope's call for 'a great society of action and prayers' directed against Freemasonry.[4]

In focusing on the French Catholic response to *Humanum genus*, I shall not dwell in any detail on the two features of late nineteenth-century antimasonry that have attracted most attention from historians: its connections with antisemitism,[5] and the embarrassing susceptibility of many of its adherents in the 1890s to Léo Taxil's sustained hoax about Miss Diana Vaughan and the masonic cult of Lucifer.[6] Though Taxil's

[3] For an account of these papal condemnations, see A. Mellor, *Nos frères séparés: les francs-maçons* (Tours, 1961), pp. 161–224, 296–306.

[4] The Latin text of *Humanum genus* is in *Leonis XIII pontificis maximi: acta* (Rome, 1881–1905), iv, 43–70. The English translation used here is in D. Wright, *Roman Catholicism and Freemasonry* (London, 1922), pp. 180–203 (passage quoted on p. 202).

[5] R.F. Byrnes, *Antisemitism in Modern France*, vol. 1, *The Prologue to the Dreyfus Affair* (New Brunswick, 1950), *passim*; P. Pierrard, *Juifs et catholiques français: de Drumont à Jules Isaac* (Paris, 1970), pp. 27–30; S. Wilson, *Ideology and Experience: Antisemitism in France at the Time of the Dreyfus Affair* (London, 1982), *passim*; J. Katz, *Jews and Freemasons in Europe, 1723–1939* (Cambridge, Mass., 1970), chs. x–xii, xv.

[6] E. Weber, *Satan franc-maçon: la mystification de Léo Taxil* (Paris, 1964).

career as an antimasonic publicist began with his supposed conversion in 1885, and he had become one of the dominant figures in French antimasonry by the end of the decade,[7] it was not until the 1890s that his influence was systematically exerted to make Luciferianism one of the central themes of antimasonic literature; even then by no means all Catholics accepted his revelations. Antisemitism, for its part, was certainly a common ingredient in the antimasonic polemics of the 1880s. At least until the appearance of Drumont's *La France Juive* in 1886, however, the Freemason rather than the Jew dominated Catholic political demonology,[8] and even in the 1890s and beyond, antimasonry was by no means always an antisemitic subsidiary. In short, Luciferian fantasies and antisemitic themes were occasional rather than universal elements in late nineteenth-century antimasonry. My concern here will be rather with the broad structures of antimasonic thinking within which these and other elements found a place. These structures are studied here as they are revealed in antimasonic literature from the late 1870s to the early 1890s; many of the same features, however, could be found at a later date.[9]

French Catholics sought to discharge the duty placed upon them by *Humanum genus* in various ways and under assorted auspices.[10] Four different organizational realms of antimasonic activity may be distinguished. The first was that of new and specifically antimasonic initiatives. The most notable of these in the 1880s were the monthly review *La franc-maçonnerie démasquée*, launched by the bishop of Grenoble, Mgr. Fava, in 1884,[11] and two organizations designed to coordinate the antimasonic struggle of

[7] Taxil first acquired a regular influence in the movement through his editorship of the journals *La petite guerre* (1887–89) and *La France chrétienne* (1889 onwards).

[8] Byrnes, *Antisemitism*, p. 155, calculates that works attacking the Freemasons were published in France at an average rate of about nine a year from 1879 to 1886, falling to six in 1887, five in 1888, and one in 1889; works against the Jews ran at an average of less than one a year from 1879 to 1885, then leapt to fifteen in 1886, followed by fourteen in 1887, nine in 1888 and twenty in 1889.

[9] On the antimasonic movement and literature of the twentieth century, see D. Rossignol, *Vichy et les franc-maçons: la liquidation des sociétés secrètes, 1940–1944* (Paris, 1981). R. Mennevée, *L'organisation anti-maçonnique en France (de 1900 à 1928)* is analytically thin and almost entirely concerned with organizational detail.

[10] I intend to publish a more detailed account of the antimasonic organizations and initiatives described in the following paragraphs at a future date.

[11] *La franc-maçonnerie démasquée* (hereafter *F.M.D.*) was published in Paris until 1887, then removed to Grenoble until 1893, when it returned to Paris as the organ of the newly-formed *Comité Antimaçonnique de Paris*.

French Catholics: the *Croisade Franc-Catholique*, also founded by Fava in 1884 (after a seemingly unsuccessful earlier attempt in 1881),[12] and the *Ligue Antimaçonnique*, introduced into France (and other countries) in 1886, whose prime mover was Père Regnault, the director-general of the *Apostolat de la Prière*.[13] *La franc-maçonnerie démasquée* provided the most regular channel of ideas and materials for the French antimasonic movement in the decade after *Humanum genus*; it passed under the control of the Assumptionist *Maison de la Bonne Presse* in 1894, and survived till 1924. Neither the *Croisade* nor the *Ligue*, however, encountered the success their founders had hoped for.[14] The *Croisade* produced one fairly durable offshoot, its *Section des Négociants-Voyageurs* (whose membership rose steadily but unspectacularly to around 500 in the early 1890s),[15] but the national network of antimasonic cells Fava had envisaged showed little sign of developing. The *Ligue*, though it distributed 50,000 copies of its antimasonic manual in France,[16] experienced significant resistance in the world of Catholic *oeuvres*. While its guidelines for antimasonic action were welcomed by the 1887 *Assemblée des Catholiques* (the annual national congress of the *Comités Catholiques*), the same gathering refused to endorse the idea that a new *oeuvre* was needed to coordinate such action.[17]

This should warn us against treating the extent of support for specialist antimasonic organizations as a straightforward index of French antimasonic energies. There were those who believed, as did one participant in the 1887 debate, that 'l'Eglise peut lutter efficacement contre la franc-maçonnerie avec ses oeuvres multiples, agissant chacune dans leur sphère propre'.[18] Seasoned Catholic activists might well feel that their own tried and tested

[12] On Fava's 1881 initiative, see his *Croisade-réparatrice des francs-catholiques* (Grenoble, 1881), and the documents in *Union des associations ouvrières catholiques: congrès d'Autun (1882) compte-rendu. . .*, pp. 318–23. On the organization of 1884, see A. Rastoul, *Souvenirs d'un jubilé épiscopal* (Grenoble, 1896), pp. 149–53, and regular reports in *F.M.D.*

[13] On the *Ligue*, see reports to the *Assemblée des Catholiques: 12e année* (1886), pp. 336–41 and *13e année* (1887), pp. 187–92.

[14] For admissions of this failure, by two leading antimasonic journalists, see G. Soulacroix in *F.M.D.*, x, p. 259, and Rastoul, *Souvenirs*, p. 153.

[15] The *section* claimed 185 members in January 1886, around 315 in July 1887, and around 500 ('répandus dans toutes les provinces de France') in October 1891. In 1881, probably registering a broadening of its professional constituency, it extended its name to *Section des Industriels, Négociants et Voyageurs de Commerce* (*F.M.D.*, ii, p. 516; iv, p. 231; viii, p. 369; v, p. 402).

[16] *Assemblée des catholiques: 16e année* (1887), p. 187.

[17] *Ibid.*, (1887), pp. 187–92 (report), 507–9 (discussion).

[18] *Ibid.*, p. 508.

organizations were better suited to antimasonic struggle than the hasty creations of men whom René de la Tour du Pin dismissed as 'initiateurs plus ardents que façonnés au maniement des hommes'.[19] The pre-existing frameworks of Catholic militancy, then, constituted the second realm within which antimasonic debate and activity took place. Particularly in the aftermath of *Humanum genus* the practicalities of antimasonic struggle were the subject of reports, debates, and resolutions at the annual congresses and in the periodicals of the main groupings of Catholic *oeuvres*: *Comités Catholiques*; *Oeuvre des Cercles*; *Union des Oeuvres Ouvrières Catholiques*.[20] The 1884 *Assemblée des Catholiques*, for example, after hearing a lengthy report by a well-known Catholic authority on secret societies, Claudio Jannet, passed a set of six resolutions on the antimasonic duties of the laity; perhaps the most notable stated that each *Comité Catholique* should establish a sub-committee to study and expose the activity of Freemasonry at the local level.[21] The organizers of *oeuvres* of various sorts hastened, in the years following (and sometimes before) *Humanum genus*, to stress their actual or potential antimasonic virtues. The *Société Bibliographique*, for example, proposed itself for the role of 'Union catholique de propagande anti-maçonnique': 'il s'agit . . . simplement d'amener l'action si efficace de cette Société sur *le terrain maçonnique*'.[22] The Tertiaries of St. Francis awoke, perhaps a trifle sleepily, to the fierce light of expectation which the Pope had focused on their pious confraternity by explicitly commending it in *Humanum genus* as a means of antimasonic struggle.[23] Most significant of all, perhaps, were the claims of the leaders of

[19] *Association catholique*, xix, 9 (January, 1885).

[20] See for example the published *comptes-rendus* of the annual *Assemblées des catholiques* and congresses Of the *Union des Oeuvres Ouvrières Catholiques*; also frequent references to Freemasonry in *Association catholique* (the house journal of the *Oeuvre des Cercles*) and the *Bulletin de l'union des oeuvres ouvrières catholiques*.

[21] *Assemblée des catholiques: 13e année* (1884), pp. 75–101 (Jannet report), pp. 102–3 (resolutions).

[22] *Bulletin de la société bibliographique*, March 1884, p. 76 ('Ligue anti-maçonnique')

[23] The view that the Third Order of St. Francis was the natural antagonist of Freemasonry (and indeed that it alone could rid the world of 'toutes les pieuvres sorties de l'océan de feu') had been expressed by the *gérant* of the *oeuvre franciscaine*, Brion, in a report in 1876 (*Union des oeuvres ouvrières catholiques. Congrès de Bordeaux. Compte rendu* . . ., pp. 342–44). Similar claims were made after *Humanum genus*: see the reports of Nicolaï (*Assemblée des catholiques, 13e année* (1884), pp. 134–44 and Kerval (*ibid., 19e année* (1890), pp. 219–45), and G. Soulacroix (abbé de Bessonies) in *F.M.D.*, x, pp. 257–60 (August 1893). By no means
continued

the *Oeuvre des Cercles*, who seized on *Humanum genus* not as a summons to new forms of antimasonic combat but as an official endorsement of Catholic corporatism. By recognizing the antimasonic efficacy of the programme to which they had been committed for fourteen years, they argued, the Pope surely gave them the right to count on the support from Catholic clergy which had too often been lacking in the past.[24] Their organization, rather than any other, had the discipline and the vision to coordinate the struggle against the masonic forces.[25]

The third realm of antimasonic activity was that of individual lives. Here we are concerned not only with the role of individuals as antimasonic writers or lecturers but also with the regulation of private conduct. The principal short-term purpose of both the *Croisade Franc-Catholique* and the *Ligue Antimaçonnique* was to encourage Catholics to make sets of prescribed *voeux* (promises before God) relating to their own lives.[26] It does not necessarily follow from the relative failure of the *Croisade* and the *Ligue* to establish themselves as organizations that such efforts to build up a capital of moral resolve among believers had no effect. We simply do not know how many Catholics scrupulously said their antimasonic prayers, or avoided masonic shopkeepers, or refrained from voting for Freemasons at elections, or forced their children or servants to swear never to join a secret society.

The fourth realm contained the more or less institutionalized antimasonic action of the Catholic clergy. *Humanum genus* was addressed to bishops: it was to them that the general responsibility of guiding the faithful in antimasonic crusade was entrusted. Several of them devoted Lenten

---

continued

everyone agreed with Soulacroix that the Third Orders were 'providentiellement toute prête pour la lutte contre l'armée maçonnique'. Léon Harmel, for example, regretted that the once militant Franciscan Third Order had become merely a pious confraternity; he urged it to return to its earlier traditions (speech to the Limoges Congress of Franciscan Tertiaries in 1895, reproduced in *F.M.D.*, xii, pp. 253–55).

[24] R.P. Alet, *L'encyclique Humanum genus et l'oeuvre des cercles catholiques d'ouvriers* (Paris, 1884), esp. p. 15 (Alet was the *Oeuvre*'s chaplain). Similar remarks were made by other leaders, for example Marquis d'Auray in *Association catholique* xvii, p. 559 (May 1884). The *Oeuvre*'s value as counterpart and antagonist of Freemasonry had already been stressed before *Humanum genus*; see *Association catholique*, xiii, p. 653 (May, 1882).

[25] See De la Tour du Pin in *Association catholique*, xix, pp. 8–9 (January, 1885).

[26] See Rastoul, *Souvenirs*, pp. 151–52 and *Association catholique*, xxii, p. 92 (July, 1886) for the *voeux* or resolutions of members respectively of the *Société des Porte-Christ* (in which would-be *francs-catholiques* were first enrolled) and of the *Ligue Anti-Maçonnique*.

mandements to the encyclical or issued other official statements on the masonic question.[27] Some bishops issued instructions banning masonic insignia from religious processions;[28] others, like Langénieux at Reims and the tirelessly antimasonic Fava at Grenoble, insisted that children taking their first communion must vow never to enrol as Freemasons.[29] The enforcement of such instructions was, of course, largely the reponsibility of the parish clergy, as was the application of antimasonry in the confessional.[30] At an individual level, also, many curés clearly felt obliged by their cloth to take an active antimasonic role. As one of them wrote, when replying to the appeal in *La Croix* which launched the *Croisade Franc-Catholique* in 1884, 'la Franc-maçonnerie étant l'Eglise de Satan, tout prêtre catholique est son ennemi-né'.[31] *La Croix* received more than 350 messages of support, many of them collective; of the 162 signatories who gave their occupation, sixty-four were curés, and there were 100 clergy all told.[32]

Two things emerge from this necessarily brief survey of antimasonic behaviour in France in the 1880s: first, that the means and forms of antimasonic activity were many, varied and only rather loosely and unsuccessfully coordinated; second, that the efforts of French Catholics to form the 'great society of action and prayers' which the Pope had called

---

[27] In 1885 extracts from numerous episcopal *mandements* and letters against the Freemasons were printed in *F.M.D.*, ii, pp. 26–36, 70–93, 257–63, 289–92. Earlier episcopal attacks on the Freemasons include Mgr. Dupanloup, *Etude sur la franc-maçonnerie* (Paris, 1875); Mgr. Turinaz, *Le grand péril de notre temps, ou la franc-maçonnerie* (Paris, 1879); Mgr. Besson, *Oeuvres pastorales* (Paris, 1879), i, pp. 215–61 (*Instruction pastorale*, 20 February, 1878). The most substantial of Mgr. Fava's numerous antimasonic works was *Le secret de la franc-maçonnerie* (Paris, 1883).

[28] See, for example, Besson, *Oeuvres pastorales*, i, pp. 259–61.

[29] *Assemblée des catholiques: 16e année* (1887), pp. 507–8 (remarks of Abbé Juillet, vicar-general of Reims, on Mgr. Langénieux's measures against Freemasonry); Fava, *Croisade-réparatrice*, p. 214.

[30] Guidance for clergy (especially confessors) in dealing with Freemasonry was provided in *Les conférences diocésaines*, September 1882, pp. 386–92 (*conférence* of Abbé Laurent, diocese of Grenoble); February, 1885, pp. 124–26 (*conférence* of 'Abbé Z.', diocese of Rodez). See also 'Les peines canoniques portées contre la franc-maçonnerie', *F.M.D.*, x, pp. 433–47 (December, 1893).

[31] Abbé Thonnelier of Langres, cited in *La Croix*, 23 June 1884.

[32] This necessarily vague statistic is based on the messages of adherence (to a 'ligue anti-maçonnique', whose final form had yet to be settled) reported in *La Croix* from 1 May to 31 July 1884. Among the collective adherences were ones from a husband and wife and their fifteen children (16 June); from a curé of the Gironde and 120 pious women (2 July); and from 435 inhabitants of Marseille (30 May).

for were hampered by a number of tensions. Some of these were simply tensions endemic in late nineteenth-century French Catholicism: between lay and clerical leadership; between diocesan and national frameworks; between traditionalists and innovators; and so on. But it may be useful also to relate them to differences in the way Freemasonry was perceived. These can best be approached by first reconstructing in broad outline the ideological framework within which Catholic discussions of Freemasonry were usually carried on.

There was no shortage of evidence to support a connection between Freemasonry and the secularizing and Republican currents of the age.[33] French Freemasonry in the later nineteenth century undoubtedly was becoming more anticlerical and more aggressively free-thinking. The symbolic moment in 1877 when the *Grand Orient* voted to suppress the clause affirming the existence of God and the immortality of the soul, which had been inserted into its constitutions in 1849, reflected a powerful drift towards a notion of 'absolute toleration' or neutrality in dogmatic questions which was all too often interpreted in practice in a way which ostracized rather than accommodated religious believers.[34] There was also, undeniably, a striking overlap, both at the national and at the local level, between the personnel of Freemasonry and of Republican politics, in both its Opportunist and its Radical forms. Ferry, Gambetta, Brisson, Flocquet, Bourgeois, Buisson, Méline, Combes merely headed the list of masons prominent in public life. Not all these masonic politicians were assiduous attenders of their lodges, but it was not hard to find men like Frédéric Desmons, who combined masonic and political careers at a high level.[35] Nor, finally, were Freemasons always reticent in affirming the intimate historical and spiritual connection between the masonic and the Republican movements: when antimasonic writers called the Republic the daughter of the *Grand Orient*, or declared that Freemasonry was the Republic in secret, and the Republic Freemasonry in the open, they

[33] See M.J. Headings, *French Freemasonry under the Third Republic* (Baltimore, 1949); D. Ligou, *Frédéric Desmons et la franc-maçonnerie sous la 3e république* (Paris, 1966); P. Chevallier, *Histoire de la franc-maçonnerie française* (3 vols., Paris, 1974–75), vol. 2, ch. vi and vol. 3, *passim*.

[34] See Ligou, *Frédéric Desmons*, ch. 4; P. Chevallier, 'Le frère Thevenot, secrétaire général du Grand Orient devant la suppression des affirmations dogmatiques et la tolérance absolue (1877–1882),' in J.-M. Mayeur (ed.), *Libre pensée et religion laïque en France, de la fin du second empire à la fin de la troisième république* (Strasbourg, 1980).

[35] Ligou, *Frédéric Desmons, passim*.

were quoting textually from speeches reported in the *Bulletin du Grand Orient.*[36]

Catholic polemicists made full use of this material, and in so doing so turned antimasonry into a telling language for the description of Republican corruption and cliquishness, but their use of it served also to relate contemporary politics to a far grander schematic framework for the interpretation of modern history, in which Freemasonry had a significance that was clearly not grounded simply in contemporary observation. Crucial to this framework was an ingrained habit of binary vision which owed much, no doubt, to the traditional Christian opposition of God and the Devil, but which owed its intensity to the profound sense of historical and moral rupture produced by the French Revolution. The modern world appeared as the scene of a desperate struggle between irreducibly antithetical spiritual entities – Christianity and the Revolution – whose vital forces were concentrated respectively in the Catholic church and in the network of secret societies dominated by Freemasonry. This struggle was itself regarded as merely the modern form of a more ancient conflict. The more developed versions of counter-revolutionary historiography, which antimasons derived from late nineteenth-century developers of the ideas of Abbé Barruel, like the Jesuit Deschamps,[37] were arranged telescopically: each stage in the conflict between the church and its successive enemies fitted into the preceding one, and the whole structure was ultimately retractable into the primeval warfare (to which Leo XIII referred in the opening sentences of *Humanum genus*)[38] between the Kingdom of God and the Kingdom of Satan. Freemasonry might be a late arrival on the historical scene but, as the

[36] Quotations of this sort were common in antimasonic literature. These examples were quoted (from texts contained in the *Bulletin du Grand Orient*, August–September 1888, p. 576, and August–September 1894, p. 389) by E. Tavernier, 'Freemasonry in France', *The Nineteenth Century*, April 1910, p. 389.

[37] N. Deschamps, *Les sociétés secrètes et la société, ou philosophie de l'histoire contemporaine*, 5th ed. (Avignon, 1881). The second and subsequent editions contain a lengthy Introduction ('De l'action des sociétés secrètes au XIXe siècle') by Claudio Jannet of the *Institut catholique*.

[38] 'The Human Race, after, by the malice of the devil, it had departed from God . . . divided itself into two different and opposing parties, one of which assiduously combats for truth and virtue, the other for those things which are opposed to virtue and to truth. The one is the Kingdom of God on earth – that is, the Church of Jesus Christ . . . The other is the kingdom of Satan . . .' (Text in Wright, *Roman Catholicism and Freemasonry*, p. 180.)

129

bishop of Saint-Brieuc put it, 'elle résume en elle toutes les hérésies antérieures'.[39]

In the analysis of current affairs, as in that of history, attention was focused less on the particularity of masonic forms than on the supposed pervasiveness of the masonic spirit; this spirit was defined essentially by its opposition to the Christian order. It was this that established a connection, for example, between the cautious bourgeois Freemasons of the Third Republic and the fanatical members of Revolutionary secret societies.[40] It was considered perfectly appropriate, as *La franc-maçonnerie démasquée* explained, to apply the label 'masonic' to any newspaper which, directly or indirectly, consciously or unconsciously, 'travaille à l'exécution du programme maçonnique'. Any protests would be rightly ignored by those who appreciated that the whole of history could be reduced to 'un duel gigantesque entre le catholicisme et l'esprit du mal incarné dans la maçonnerie'.[41]

Freemasonry was considered to embody a spirit that was constant in its essence but complex and elusive in its ramifications. French Catholics who took this view were left, one may suggest, with two basic ways of envisaging Freemasonry as a human organization. At an intellectual level, within the framework of antimasonic conspiracy theory, these were perfectly compatible, but when it came to planning antimasonic action they led in different directions.

The first view saw Freemasonry as the *synagoga Satanae* – the church of Satan.[42] To say that Freemasonry was Satanic meant different things to different people. Allegations of masonic Satan-worship, and even speculations about the physical presence of Lucifer in the lodges, can certainly be found in the antimasonic literature of the 1880s,[43] but it was not until Taxil began his revelations about 'la maçonnerie palladique' in the

---

[39] Mgr. Bouché, quoted in *F.M.D.* ii, p. 84 (April, 1885). There was disagreement among antimasonic writers as to whether the origins of Freemasonry were most accurately described as Templar (e.g. Besson, *Oeuvres pastorales*, i, p. 217) or Socinian (e.g. Fava, *Le secret de la franc-maçonnerie*, p. 16).

[40] See e.g. Jannet's Introduction to Deschamps, *Des sociétés secrètes*, p. cix.

[41] 'Que faut-il entendre par presse maçonnique?' *F.M.D.*, vi, p. 560 (February, 1890).

[42] The Latin term (derived from Revelations, II, 9) was widely used.

[43] E.g. André Dufaut in *F.M.D.*, iii, pp. 64–69, 157–62 (April and June 1886). Having addressed the question of whether the Devil acted in Freemasonry 'par inspiration, par insufflation de ses pensées seulement, ou bien s'il ne préside pas certaines loges sous la figure humaine' (pp. 68–69), Dufaut reported three supposedly authoritative sightings of Satan in human form at masonic gatherings (pp. 159–60).

1890s that they became widespread.[44] More typical of the 1880s were the views of the organizers of an antimasonic committee in Lille in 1884, who described Satan as 'le Grand-Maître occulte' of Freemasonry, but who saw atheism and anarchism, rather than Luciferianism, as its basic doctrine.[45]

Antimasons were often vague about precisely *how* Satan was involved in Freemasonry, but this does not mean that their references to him had no precise significance. Satan might not be a goatish real presence in the *arrière-loges*, but he was not just an abstract figuration of generalized evil either. He had specific characteristics, which Freemasonry was held to reflect.

In the first place Satan was the rebel angel. Here an interesting comparison can be made with Christian antisemitism. For the Christian antisemite, the crucial episode in sacred history was the Crucifixion: the Jews' hostility to the Christian church was a sustained reenactment of this ancestral Deicide.[46] Antimasons concentrated instead on episodes of revolt – the rebellion of Satan and the disobedience induced by Satan in Adam and Eve. René de la Tour du Pin, for example, attacked the masonic belief in human perfectibility in these terms: 'c'est le langage même que la sainte Bible attribue à Satan vis-à-vis de nos premiers parents, et sa conséquence la plus immédiate est la révolte contre la royauté sociale que Jésus-Christ prétend exercer sur son Eglise jusqu'à la fin des siècles: c'est le *non serviam* des anges maudits'.[47] According to this view Freemasonry's war on the church was rooted in theological revolt – in a denial of man's dependence on God for salvation. This led inevitably to a rejection of Christ the redeemer and a deification of human reason.[48] Various words were used to describe masonic doctrine – naturalism, pantheism, paganism, socinianism, materialism, atheism – but its essence, as far as most antimasons was concerned, was as Jannet described it: 'Mettre les *droits de l'homme* à la place de la *loi divine*, établir le

[44] See Weber, *Satan franc-maçon*.

[45] Programme of the *Ligue Antimaçonnique sous le patronage de Saint Michel Archange*, reproduced in *F.M.D.*, i, pp. 282–83 (November 1884).

[46] Thus Vincent de Paul Bailly in *La Croix*, iii, p. 161 (August 1882): 'le bras de Satan qui tue Jésus-Christ sur la terre c'est toujours le juif; car au Calvaire . . . le juif déïcide a dit le premier: tuons-le, c'est l'ennemi, et il a transmis cette parole comme un héritage à ses enfants'.

[47] *Association catholique*, xiv, p. 552 (November 1882).

[48] *Ibid*, pp. 552–53.

règne de l'humanité à la place de celui du Créateur'.[49] The spirit of rebellion was seen as spreading out from the theological to the social and political spheres: secularization, democracy, socialism and anarchism had a common Satanic source. The antimasonic analysis of contemporary evils hinged on the sin of human pride. Where the Catholic antisemite blamed the erosion of the Christian order on the atavistic hostility of outsiders, the antimason blamed it on an internal breakdown of subordination: a Satanically-inspired revolution from within.

Satan was also the ape of God, and Freemasonry, as far as its Catholic critics were concerned, was part of his mimicry: it was the Satanic counterpart, as well as the Satanic enemy, of the Catholic church. Not all antimasons went as far as the writer in *La franc-maçonnerie démasquée* who held that each secret masonic ritual counterfeited and profaned a Christian sacrament, in a systematic programme of mimetic sacrilege which had to be sustained by regular thefts of consecrated hosts from Catholic churches.[50] Most, however, would have agreed with André Dufaut that Freemasonry embodied 'une religion retournée, une contrefaçon religieuse, une piété de l'abîme',[51] and with Jannet that masonic unity 'ne saurait être qu'une contrefaçon grimaçante de l'unité divine de l'Eglise'.[52]

For all its claims to be a purely secular organization, Freemasonry, in the eyes of its Catholic denouncers, could not but be understood in religious terms: both formally and doctrinally it was the negative image and the irreducible antagonist of the one true church. Some Catholics concluded from this that the struggle against Freemasonry ought to be waged above all as a spiritual struggle, using the weapons of piety and devotion. The statistical reports published monthly by *La franc-maçonnerie démasquée* in the 1890s,[53] giving the number of masses heard, prayers recited, and other devotional acts performed for the conversion of the Freemasons and in reparation of masonic outrages against God, bore witness to such a view, as did the efforts to present the Third Orders as the lynchpin of the antimasonic crusade. The *Croisade Franc-Catholique* is another striking example. Conceived by Fava as an *oeuvre de réparation* for

[49] Jannet's Introduction to Deschamps, *Des sociétés secrètes*, p. ci.

[50] A. de Sarachaga, 'La franc-maçonnerie comme régime social', *F.M.D.*, i, pp. 235–36 (October 1884).

[51] *F.M.D.*, iii, p. 66 (April 1886).

[52] *L'église et l'état. La lutte – la doctrine: compte-rendu du congrès de jurisconsultes catholiques* (Grenoble, 1881), p. 34 (report by Jannet).

[53] More or less detailed reports appeared monthly in *F.M.D.*, beginning in mid 1896.

masonic blasphemy and sacrilege, it was launched with a pilgrimage of an estimated 15–20,000 people to La Salette.[54] The initial undertakings of its members were essentially symbolic or devotional – to wear a crucifix, to observe the Sabbath, to recite certain prayers – in effect to be punctilious in the Christian life.[55] Only later were obligations of a more social kind (for example to boycott masonic shopkeepers) added.[56]

This was one conception of antimasonic action, but it was not the only one. Some Catholics, while agreeing that the core of Freemasonry was Satanic, laid greater practical emphasis on its means of action. If Freemasonry's basic aim was universal destruction, Mgr. Besson warned the faithful, its strength was 'd'avoir rallié tant de bras qui travaillent, sans le savoir, à cette oeuvre impie . . .'[57] The second image of Freemasonry, then, saw it as a system of concentric circles, of *meneurs* and *dupes* – in Emmanuel d'Alzon's trenchant phrase, 'un groupe de scélérats se servant de masses incalculables d'imbéciles'.[58] Antimasonic imaginations excelled at adding further levels of occult hierarchy to the masonic system of initiation. The whole masonic machine, in Besson's view, was manipulated by three or four 'scélérats obscurs', whose identities were hidden even from each other.[59] From the numerous variations on this theme emerged a common message, which may be summarized in the terms used by Mgr. de Ségur, when he distinguished between 'la Franc-Maçonnerie qui se voit plus ou moins' and 'la Franc-Maçonnerie qui ne se voit pas du tout'. The latter secretly plotted the destruction of Christianity and of society. The former – 'cette multitude qui boit, qui chante et qui parle de morale' – for the most part 'ne savent pas où on les conduit'.[60]

---

[54] Reports of the pilgrimage, during which a pilgrims' cross, fresh from the Holy Land, was carried to the top of the mountain, are contained in *La Croix* 10 July 1884 (by Joseph Ménard) and in the *Semaine religieuse de Grenoble* 10 July 1884, pp. 579–82. Fava's conception of antimasonry is especially apparent in his *Croisade-réparatrice* (1881).

[55] Rastoul, *Souvenirs*, pp. 151–52.

[56] See articles 8 and 9 of the *Croisade*'s *règlement: F.M.D.*, i, pp. 215–16 (September 1884).

[57] Besson, *Oeuvres pastorales*, i, p. 246, (*Instruction pastorale*, 20 February 1878).

[58] E. D'Alzon, 'Les sociétés secrètes et la société,' *La Croix*, i, p. 460 (October 1880).

[59] Besson, *Oeuvres pastorales*, i, p. 246. In his *mandement* on *Humanum genus*, the bishop of Viviers, Mgr. Bonnet, discerned in Freemasonry 'une double hiérarchie: l'une officielle et purement honorifique; l'autre occulte et agissante qui échappe à toutes les investigations'. (Cited in *F.M.D.*, ii, p. 90.)

[60] Mgr. de Ségur, *Oeuvres* (Paris, 1874), v, pp. 10–12 (*Les Francs-maçons*, originally published in 1868).

Such masonic *dupes* were not be found only in the lodges themselves. Beyond these lay the so-called 'sociétés maçonniques imparfaites': organizations like the *Sociétés de la Libre Pensée*, the *Union des Femmes de France* or (most notoriously) the *Ligue de l'Enseignement*, whose members might well be ignorant of the broader design to which their work contributed.[61] Beyond them, in turn, lay the 'auxiliaires de la franc-maçonnerie', to whom the antimasonic writer Jules des Aperts devoted three articles in *La franc-maçonnerie démasquée*: the three sinister cohorts of schoolteachers, *commis-voyageurs*, and proprietors of *débits de boisson*, who, again without always knowing it, performed the work of Freemasonry in every corner of France.[62] Des Aperts concluded by excusing himself for having discussed the masonic problem in these purely practical (i.e. non-theological) terms: it was essential, he argued, to examine each spring and cog in Freemasonry's social machinery.[63]

To many Catholics it was on this social machinery, rather than on the religious core of Freemasonry, that antimasonic efforts must be concentrated. It was essential to know who served the masonic cause and who didn't: hence the need to publish lists of Freemasons or of masonic businesses,[64] and also of Catholic tradesmen and employers in whom the faithful might safely trust. It was essential also to realize that the masonic rank-and-file were motivated less by Satanic pride than by self-interest:[65] antimasonry should aim to create conditions in which masonic connections

[61] See A. Rastoul, 'Les sociétés maçonniques imparfaites', *F.M.D.*, iv, pp. 193–203 (July 1887), drawing on a work by the Benedictine J.P.A. Benoit, *La cité antichrétienne au XIXe siècle* (Paris, 1887); also Jannet's 1884 report (*Assemblée des catholiques: 13e année*, p. 83). The standard antimasonic work on the *Ligue de l'Enseignement* was J. de Moussac, *La ligue de l'enseignement: histoire, doctrines, oeuvres, résultats, projets* (Paris, 1880). On the 'masonic' connections of the *Union des Femmes de France*, see *F.M.D.*, i, pp. 30–31 (March 1884); ii, p. 237 (July 1885).

[62] *F.M.D..*, v. pp. 539–48 (February 1889); vi, pp. 78–84 (April 1889); pp. 108–15 (May 1889).

[63] *Ibid.*, vi, p. 115 (May 1889).

[64] For example the list of Freemasons published by Taxil, *La France maçonnique, nouvelles divulgations* (Paris, 1888). The need for a centralized antimasonic *bureau de renseignements* was argued in *La Croix*, 26 November and 3 December 1884. The establishment of one was reported in *F.M.D.*, i, p. 320 (December 1884).

[65] On the differing psychologies of masonic *meneurs* and *dupes*, see J. des Aperts, 'Psychologie du franc-maçon', *F.M.D.*, v, pp. 253–63 (August 1888). Des Aperts also stressed that the *dupes* were attracted by the mystery of Freemasonry: 'cette maladie du secret indique un état mental inférieur' (p. 255).

would no longer bring unfair social or commercial advantages, and it could best do this by encouraging Catholics to develop quasi-masonic habits of solidarity in commercial life.[66] One of several efforts to do this was the *Section des Négociants-Voyageurs*, which originated (as already noted) within the *Croisade des Francs-Catholiques*, but which gravitated increasingly towards the *Oeuvre des Cercles*.[67] The *Section* arose from the startling discovery that some of that notorious breed, commercial travellers, were actually Catholic. It set out, as its propaganda put it, to unite such men 'pour la défense de leur foi et le succès de leurs affaires'.[68] Besides defending religion, in second-class railway carriages and at the *table d'hôte*, against the sneers of their masonic counterparts, the *Section's* members were to procure clients and provide hospitality for each other. A bulletin was also briefly published, carrying advertisements and job offers.[69]

French Catholics in the 1880s were fertile in antimasonic projects (and antimasonic redescriptions of earlier activity), but they did not achieve the disciplined antimasonic movement for which the Pope was assumed to have been calling in 1884. This was at least partly because their antimasonic ideology permitted the development of divergent views on what an antimasonic movement should look like. Was antimasonry to be a spiritual resurgence or a new vibration of Social Catholicism? Ought it to issue, under ecclesiastical leadership, in a campaign of militant piety, or to marshal itself in largely lay-led battalions for action in the social field? The later developments in antimasonry may perhaps be seen in the light of these competing visions – the acceptance of Taxil's suggestions as an accentuation of the spiritual emphasis, the longer interbreeding with Drumont-style antisemitism as a drift towards more social concerns. It

[66] See especially *Assemblée des catholiques: 14e année* (1885), pp. 517–26: report of the Capuchin Ludovic de Besse on the need for antimasonic action 'sur le terrain du travail et des intérêts', involving the creation of *bureaux de placement, associations mutuelles* and lists of Catholic businesses. The duties of Catholics to avoid all commercial or social contact with Freemasons were spelt out by the Lille antimasonic committee mentioned above (*F.M.D.*, i, p. 283).

[67] *F.M.D.*, iv, pp. 231–32 (July 1887); vi, p. 455 (December 1889).

[68] Recruiting circular reproduced in *F.M.D*, vi, p. 404 (November 1889).

[69] *Bulletin des négociants-voyageurs (francs-catholique)*, published monthly in 1886; thereafter regular reports and notices on the *Section* appeared in *F.M.D*. On the tasks and duties of the *Section's* members, see especially its *règlement*, published in the *Bulletin* in February 1886 (pp. 21–24), and the speech of its president, Baron Paul d'Allemagne, reproduced in *F.M.D*, ii, p. 522 (January 1886).

seems clear, at any rate, that the question of antimasonic strategy was one which focused, without resolving, a fundamental problem faced by those who saw the social evolutions of the modern world as a spiritual threat: how, in responding to that threat, could one balance social with spiritual commitment, within an efficient framework of crusading action?

8

Socialism and Catholicism in France: Jaurès, Guesde and the Dreyfus Affair[1]

Clive Castaldo

Between the publication of the Communist Manifesto in 1848 and the outbreak of the First World War in 1914, French Socialism was divided over its attitude to Catholicism. In orthodox Marxism it was the bourgeoisie and not Catholicism which was the enemy. Religion was at worst an opiate, but never a deadly poison. Edouard Berth, writing in *La revue socialiste* in 1902, posed the problem concisely:

> Il y a en France, actuellement, trois grandes classes dominantes: les classes précapitalistes, qui restent attachées à la religion Catholique et dont l'idéal sociale est plus ou moins réactionnaire; les classes capitalistes, qui sont au pouvoir et se réclament des principes de '89; enfin la classe ouvrière, dont le socialisme est l'idéologie. Catholiques, Républicains, Libre-penseurs, Socialistes, ce sont les forces du passé, du présent et l'avenir qui se heurtent. Le problème consiste à assurer le triomphe des forces de l'avenir, mais comment?.[2]

Berth, like most other politicians on the Left, held to a Two France

[1] The author would like to acknowledge the receipt of a postdoctoral research award from the British Academy which helped towards the preparation of this essay.

[2] 'La politique anticléricale et le socialisme', *Cahiers de la quinzaine*, onzième cahier de la quatrième série, E. Berth (3 February 1903), pp. 3–59. Citation p. 9. This article was originally printed in *La revue socialiste* 15 November 1902.

thesis, which presented Catholicism as the general portmanteau of the past: Monarchism, Bonapartism, and Counter-Revolution. By contrast, the Republic represented the forces of progress and the French Revolution. While this thesis was convenient for the politicians such as Ferry and Gambetta who made their reputations in the 1870s and 1880s, this interpretation of French history posed dangers for Socialism. Emerging from years of struggle for national recognition, the Socialist Left did not want to be confused with Opportunism or a general Republicanism. The Two France thesis only served to blur distinctions because it put all the enemies on the Right into one camp, thereby diminishing the importance of Socialism which was threatened with absorption, not with persecution.

In 1889 the Socialists were not even a distinct faction within the Chamber, but belonged to a group of one hundred Radical and Socialist deputies. The Socialists even had trouble in achieving distinction when the safety of the Republic was itself an issue. Only in the year 1893, following bitter industrial strikes, did they establish their own group in the Chamber, forty-nine separating from the Radicals to form a distinct association. In the same year, Jean Jaurès became the spokesman for the moderate Socialists. He believed that the Republic and Socialism ought to be one and indivisible – this was *la question sociale*. Men could not be given universal rights and manhood suffrage and yet denied the educational and economic facilities to sustain themselves as voting citizens. When the Catholic church had rallied to the Republic in 1890, no such claim had been made by an important politician on the Left. Yet by 1893 Socialism was claiming to be the authentic brand of Republicanism, the heir of the French Revolution. The long postponed question of anticlericalism's true importance for Socialists was confronted only when Socialism had become distinct from general Republicanism. Now that bourgeois anticlericals had established their authority, Socialists in France were forced to examine the true radicalism of anti-Catholic politics.

The Dreyfus Affair was the crucial turning point in determining the attitude of French Socialism towards Republican anticlericalism, not least because it occurred just as Socialism was emerging from its local federations and dividing into two national tendencies. The present essay explores the different ways in which Socialists confronted this problem. It examines first the approach of reformist Socialists, led by Jaurès, and contrasts this with the attitude of Revolutionary socialists, led by Guesde. Reformist Socialism sought to build on the human rights tradition deriving from the French Revolution by transforming French law into an instrument capable of championing the rights of the working class. The privileged status of the church under the law was, of necessity, to be scrapped. By way of contrast, Guesde believed that anticlericalism was a distraction to the class struggle, merely an opiate administered by the bourgeoisie. The essay ends by looking at the *Ligue des Droits de l'Homme*, an organization which exemplified the human rights ideology on which Jaurès wished to build.

Jaurès, the champion of Reformist Socialism, had initially called for Dreyfus to be shot as a common traitorous soldier, but in 1898 he was forced, following Zola's article *J'accuse*, to examine the facts of the case and set aside class prejudice. Concluding that Dreyfus was innocent, he published a series of articles in *La Petite République* called *Les preuves* outlining the flaws in the army case against Dreyfus. Inspired by the humanist tradition of the French Revolution, Jaurès adopted the language of the rights of man. He claimed that Dreyfus was a representative of suffering humanity, and thus demanded the attention of all Socialists as a symbol of injustice. Furthermore, Jaurès saw in the Affair an opportunity for Socialism. He had never been able to accept the bourgeoisie as the enemy of Socialism per se, due to his interpretation of the French Revolution. After all, the bourgeoisie had brought about the French Revolution, which itself had produced a manifesto for the whole of humanity. The Declaration of the Rights of Man was a permanent conquest for the whole of mankind, and did not belong to a group or class of Frenchmen. The Dreyfus Affair gave to the Left the opportunity to protect what was permanent and humane in the French Revolution. Thus Jaurès believed that the French Socialists should join in the same campaign as the *Ligue des Droits de l'Homme*, a group of bourgeois intellectuals formed in 1898 to vindicate Dreyfus. As Jaurès explained:

Il y a deux parts dans la légalité capitaliste et bourgeoise. Il y a tout un ensemble de lois destinées à protéger l'iniquité fondamentale de notre société. Il y a des lois qui consacrent le privilège de la propriété capitaliste, l'exploitation du salarié par le possédant. Ces lois, nous voulons les rompre, et même par la révolution, s'il le faut, abolir la légalité capitaliste pour faire un ordre nouveau. Mais à côté de ces lois de privilège et de rapine, faites par une classe et pour elle, il en est d'autres qui résument les pauvres progrès de l'humanité, les modestes garanties qu'elle a peu à peu conquises par le long effort des siècles et la longue suite des révolutions . . . nous, socialistes révolutionaires, nous voulons dans la légalité d'aujourd'hui, abolir la portion capitaliste et sauver la portion humaine.[3]

---

[3] J. Jaurès, *Les preuves: l'affaire Dreyfus* (Paris 1898), pp. 11–12.

This statement reveals the extent to which Jaurès and the Republican anticlericals shared a common ground. Both possessed a belief in human progress, and it is also clear that Jaurès considered that a social revolution might not be necessary. The bourgeoisie was not simply a class to be defeated by revolution, and capitalism was not simply a system to be dismissed out of hand.

Jaurès was trying to adapt the Two France thesis to Socialism by dividing the bourgeoisie into two groups, the one progressive and the other regressive. The progressive section was to inaugurate Socialism and therefore Socialists could not stand aside in the conflict between bourgeois republicans and the church. Jaurès was rewriting the ideology of the 1880s to fit the emergence of Socialism in the 1890s.

Jaurès' attitude to the *Ligue des Droits de l'Homme* can be understood in this context. The rights of man were the platform for a Socialist future and the bourgeois who espoused them were, unconsciously, conserving something of use to the emerging Socialism which would replace capitalism. Yet if Socialism was prefigured in the capitalist system, its final emergence was threatened by the clericalism of the past. By extending the rights of man to the regime of private property, humanist values could be adapted to Socialism. Even so, these secular values were not totally secure. As Jaurès explained in *Les preuves* '. . . le parti clerical, ayant perdu pendant la periode républicaine de la république la direction des administrations publiques, des services civils, s'était réfugié dans l'armée. Là, les anciennes classes dirigeantes, les descendants de l'armée de Condé se groupaient en une caste hautaine et fermée'.[4] Jaurès believed that the church and the army were not only a threat to the Republic and to human rights, but also to the type of Socialism which would emerge from the Affair.

For Jaurès, as he examined the Dreyfus case, past, present and future could all be delineated in the France of 1898. To bring about the material transformation of France it was necessary to support the progressive humanist elements of the bourgeoisie against the decadent elements of the distant past. He believed it important that the Socialist movement engage itself in what he perceived as the linear progress of humanity: as a consequence, he was prepared to champion secular humanism, state education and the separation of church and state.

[4] *Ibid.*, p. vii.

A very different approach was taken by Jules Guesde, the orthodox Marxist. Initially he had admired Zola's action in publishing *J'accuse*, as a brave protest against injustice. He quickly changed his position as he realized the implications which the Affair had for French Socialism, both in theory and in practice. From an idealogical standpoint the proletariat should stand aside from what was, in his eyes, merely an internal struggle waged amongst elements of the bourgeoisie. Dreyfus's emerging reputation as a millionaire and the descriptions in the press of his family's wealth served to reinforce this view. As the Dreyfus Affair unfolded Guesde was also concerned that a single individual had come to stand as the symbol for all oppressed humanity, affronting traditional Marxist ideology with its stress upon class struggle. This contrasted markedly with Jaurès' approach. As we have seen, he was concerned to stress the inalienability of human rights which were common to all individuals. Socialism thus represented the fulfilment of these rights.

For practical reasons also, Guesde felt that Socialists should refuse to become involved in the Affair. In 1899 the new Prime Minister Waldeck-Rousseau had formed a broad-based coalition government, which was intended to resolve the Affair. It included General Galliffet, notorious for his bloody repression of the Commune, and Alexandre Millerand, a moderate Socialist who had advocated collaboration with bourgeois governments. Both men, for different reasons, were wholly unacceptable to Guesde, who refused to allow involvement in the Dreyfus matter to draw him and his colleagues into supporting any ministry in which they were included.

In the event Guesde was outmanoeuvred by the crafty Waldeck-Rousseau. In 1900 the Prime Minister made the speech which was to be the keynote of his administration.[5] He avoided the rhetoric of army against the nation, but argued instead that the Dreyfus Affair could only have happened in a France divided into *les deux jeunesses* by its educational system. The rivalry between Catholic congregational schools and the *écoles publiques* perpetuated the ideological and political divisions amongst the nation's youth. Those raised within the Catholic system were suspected of an uncritical acceptance of authority, whereas those educated by the

---

5 For a full discussion see C.V.J. Castaldo, 'La Foi Laïque and its Critics: Secular Humanism after the Dreyfus Affair' (unpublished Ph.D. thesis, Cambridge University, 1985), pp. 88–90. Waldeck-Rousseau's speech of 28 October 1900 stated: 'Les deux jeunesses: celle qui sort de l'école laïque et celle qui vient des éstablissements congrégationistes; "deux jeunesses" moins séparée encore par leur condition sociale que par l'éducation qu'elles reçoivent grandissent sans se connaître jusqu'au jour où elles se rencontrent si dissemblables qu'elles risqueront de ne plus se comprendre'.

state could be expected to have regard for the fundamental values of the Republic which of necessity included protection for an individual's human rights. In so doing Waldeck-Rousseau steered the Dreyfus case into the familiar territory of the church against the Republic by connecting it to an educational theme. The speech paved the way for a new Law of Associations which was introduced in July 1901. Religious schools would now need to apply for authorisation. Thus Waldeck-Rousseau skilfully united the broad Left behind a coalition based on anticlericalism. He carried with him all the intellectuals who had supported Zola in January 1898 and the burgeoning *Ligue des Droits de l'Homme,* whilst carrying a portion of the Left into the *Bloc des Gauches*. This tactic of turning the Dreyfus Affair into an attack on the church worsened the schism between Jaurès and Guesde.

The Dreyfus Affair asked fundamental questions of the Socialist Left concerning cooperation with non-Socialists and support for anticlericalism. Caught in a dilemma Socialists found it impossible to unite. From 1899 to 1901, a series of congresses failed to produce a unified Socialist party. The question was how far would it advance Socialism actively to side with the Ministry of Republican Defence. Jaurès believed that anticlericalism was part of the continuing development of the bourgeoisie's relationship with Socialism. Guesde replied that all intimate collaboration was a betrayal of Socialist principles. In 1902 two major tendencies emerged amongst Socialists, the *Parti Socialiste Française* (P.S.F.) under Jaurès, and the *Parti Socialiste de France* (P.S.d.F.) under Guesde. Ironically the Dreyfus Affair was more divisive for the French socialists than it was for the French nation as a whole.

Jaurès adopted the reference points of the Waldeck-Rousseau admin-istration, arguing that the Republic was threatened by the clerico-military coalition of the Right. The clear passion Jaurès demonstrated on the subject of anticlericalism and human rights opened him to the charge of compromising reformism. It was claimed that his position was impossible to reconcile with Marxism and that, as a distinguished commentator has put it, he was irredeemably compromised by the original sin of bourgeois idealism.[6]

---

[6] Madeleine Réberioux 'presentation' in J. Jaurès, *La classe ouvrière* (Paris, 1976), p. 10. For Jaurès' relationship to Marxism see the remarks by Labrousse in A. Soboul, (ed.), *Histoire socialiste de la révolution française* (Paris, 1968), vol. 1, pp. 1–35, where he argues that Jaurès had an orthodox link between economics and class mentality. For Jaurès' championship of the Dreyfus case and his aspiration that Socialism might be the outcome see C. Rappoport, *Jean Jaurès: l'homme, le penseur, le socialiste* (Paris, 1915), pp. 35–52.

At Lille in 1900 Guesde and Jaurès debated their alternate methods for achieving the Socialist future. The public dispute ranged widely over the affair and the question of bourgeois reformism. Jaurès located himself in the Marxist tradition with a quotation which justified the interpretation he had given in *Les preuves*. In the heat of debate he exclaimed:

Je suis étonné, vraiment, d'avoir à rappeler ces vérités élémentaires qui devraient être le patrimoine et la règle de tous les socialistes. C'est Marx lui-même qui a écrit cette parole admirable de netteté: 'Nous, socialistes révolutionnaires, nous sommes avec le prolétariat contre la bourgeoisie et avec la bourgeoisie contre les hobereaux et les prêtres.'[7]

Thus Jaurès claimed to be in the mainstream of Marxism and he went on to argue that there was a qualitative moral and political difference between different bourgeois governments, some of which justified proletarian support:

La société d'aujourd'hui est divisée entre capitalistes et prolétaires; mais, en même temps, elle est menacée par le retour offensif de toutes les forces du passé, par le retour offensif de la barbarie féodale, de la toute-puissance de l'église, et c'est le devoir des socialistes, quand la liberté républicaine est en jeu, quand la liberté de conscience est menacée, quand les vieux préjugés qui ressuscitent les haines de races et les atroces querelles religieuses des siècles passés paraissent renaître, c'est le devoir du prolétariat socialiste de marcher avec celle des fractions bourgeoises qui ne veut pas revenir en arrière.[8]

For Jaurès, the *Ligue des Droits de l'Homme* was the very paradigm of the progressive bourgeoisie which merited cooperation.

In his response to Jaurès, Guesdes made clear that his own method rejected cooperation with the *Ligue*. In defence of this position he pointed to the antisocialist elements in the *Ligue* who were opposed to strikes and unions. For Guesde, the bourgeoisie had no advanced guard; behind the reformist bourgeoisie were the hard-faced men who had put down the Commune. No reconciliation between Jaurès and Guesde was possible. At the Amsterdam International Jaurès was forced to defend himself. His speech in defence of cooperation fell on deaf ears, and when a new united socialist party of France, the S.F.I.O., was formed in 1905 it accepted the

---

[7] *Les deux méthodes: conférence par Jean Jaurès et Jules Guesde* (Paris, 1945, Editions de la liberté), p. 10.

[8] *Ibid.*

143

Guesdist line.[9] Even so Jaurès subsequently used his far from negligible political and rhetorical skills to draw the S.F.I.O. back to his own reformist policy, seeking to redefine the conflict of Republicanism against Catholicism as the coming of Socialism.

There were definite limits to Jaures' achievements in this respect as a study of the history of the *Ligue des Droits de l'Homme* from 1898–1914 indicates. We have seen that the league, formed in February 1898, quickly became committed to anticlericalism. Its subsequent growth was phenomenal: 269 members on 29 March 1898 and about 1,000 by May 1898. The following month if formed its first central committee and held its first annual general meeting. By December 1898 it boasted 4,580 members and growth was maintained throughout the *Bloc des Gauches* of 1899–1906: 25,017 members in December 1901 and 63,659 members in 1905, peaking at 82,619 members in December 1907, after which the league became shy about its adherents.[10] The estimate for 1910 was 80,000 falling to 50,000 in 1913. The league did not sustain the momentum of the *Bloc* and its declining numbers suggest that after the separation of church and state (1905–6) it could not find a policy to rally its supporters. Thus the membership figures do not support Jaurès' contention that a mass movement would carry the momentum of anticlericalism into Socialism.[11]

Personnel and finance are other indicators with which to measure the success of Jaurès' efforts to link anticlericalism and socialism. The *Ligue*'s personnel included a central committee which between 1901 and 1905 was composed of fifty-three men, thirty of whom could be described as academics or men of letters. Financial solvency of the organization was guaranteed only by gifts from the predominantly bourgeois membership.[12]

In June 1902, the *Ligue* held a banquet to celebrate the election results of April and May 1902. We have the names of the fifty-six deputies attending who had given their adhesion to the *Ligue*; an analysis of this group provides

[9]   On the Amsterdam International see M. Réberioux, 'Jaurès, homme politique', *Europe*, October-November, 1958, p. 10.

[10]   For all the above figures, see 'Récapitulation, 4 Juin 1898 – 4 Juin 1908', *Bulletin officiel de la Ligue des Droits de l'Homme*, viii (1908), p. 1303. For estimates after 1907, see the figures cited in H. Sée, *Histoire de la Ligue des Droits de l'Homme* (Paris, 1927), pp. 106, 163, 215.

[11]   Castaldo, 'La Foi Laïque', pp. 48–49.

[12]   J. et M. Charlot, 'Un rassemblement d'intellectuels: la Ligue des Droits de l'Homme', *Revue française de science politique*, ix (1959), p. 997. The authors claimed that only fifty-three deputies attended, but omitted to include the three who hosted the banquet.

us with the best guide to its political complexion.[13] If we correlate the banquet names with the *Annuaire de parlement* we find that the *Ligue* was supported by fifteen Socialists, twenty-two Radical-Socialists and nineteen Radicals. The Socialist presence in the *Ligue* cannot be denied but it was a minority one. If we analyse further the fifteen Socialists, the most striking finding is that ten of them belonged to Jaurès' P.S.F., only one to Guesde's P.S.d.F., he being Walter from St. Denis, the Paris suburb which contained the burial ground of the French kings. Orthodox Marxists found it impossible to associate with militant anticlericalists.

An analysis of the election manifestoes of the fifty-six deputies who supported the league in April/May 1902 is also revealing. Only twenty-nine out of fifty-six deputies called for the separation of church and state; twenty-four wanted the rigorous application of the Law of Associations; and twenty-two demanded the abolition of the *Loi Falloux*. A mere fifteen mentioned free instruction at every level of the educational system.[14] Jaurès had hoped that anticlericalism would blur the distinction between Republican anticlericals and Socialists but these figures reveal that it did not. The deputies had a keen sense of electoral priorities and knew where to draw the line. There were more votes in attacking church schools than in proposing an upset of the social bias in education. Thus when it came to practical politics militant anticlericalism did not easily confuse itself with Socialism.

Jaurès also postulated the development of human rights and the gradual application of equality to property rights. Once again we can test his success by an examination of the *Ligue des Droits de l'Homme*. In 1907 the *Ligue* set up working parties to study twelve issues. The subjects which concerned the *Ligue* are a guide to its development subsequent to the separation of church and state.[15] Only three of the twelve issues might be termed Socialist: the union rights of civil servants; the abolition of the conspiracy laws governing terrorism; and old age pensions. Nine other issues concerned civil rights abuses and educational problems. It is possible to connect these tangentially to Socialism but in essence they were issues concerning individual liberty rather than issues involving collective and community rights. The educational issues were the state monopoly of education, the payment of fees and compulsory schooling. The

---

[13] 'Banquet offert le 1er Juin 1902', *Bulletin officiel de La Ligue des Droits de l'Homme*, ii (1902), 501–18. Here the deputies are listed on an unnumbered page which introduces a series of speeches at the banquet.

[14] Castaldo, 'La Foi Laïque', pp. 168–78.

[15] For the 1907 Working Parties, see *ibid.*, pp. 67–73.

education monopoly was an old anticlerical chestnut which dated back to the Revolution. The civil rights issues were reform of the judiciary; reform of the law on the mentally ill; the abolition of court martials; the disbanding of the vice squad; wider legal education; and international arbitration and progressive disarmament.

A study of the *Ligue des Droits de l'Homme* proves that militant anticlericalism divided Socialists more than it advanced the cause of Socialism. The *Ligue* members behaved far more like Lenin's bourgeois radical democrats than like Jaurès' embryonic Socialists. The Republican anticlerical could draw a line between civil liberties and Socialism. The history of the *Ligue des Droits de l'Homme* illustrates this distinction precisely. Jaurès tacitly admitted his disappointment, increasingly seeing pacifism as the bridge between Socialism and Radicalism. After the end of the *Bloc* in 1906, Jaurès devoted more time to the struggle against European war.

It is commonplace to remark that the Dreyfus Affairs cleansed French Socialism of antisemitism, but less attention has been paid to the way in which it affected Socialism's perception of Catholicism. The Affair was the first crisis met by the emerging Socialist Left; it served to divide the Left and it stamped the character of French socialism as it broke from Communism. French Socialism remained reformist, anticlerical, and indifferent to orthodox Marxism.[16] The Dreyfus Affair also proved that the Two France thesis could not be adapted or defeated; where Jaurès failed Guesde did even not attempt to try. Capitalists against proletarians was a dramatic rewriting of Catholics against Republicans but there were still only two sides. The two France theory cast its long shadow over the Dreyfus Affair and over the development of socialism and Catholicism.

Doubtless the Two France thesis – *l'eglise et la république* –was a clichéd description of French antagonisms but it monopolized French political expression. The majority of Socialists, at the beginning of the twentieth century, chose not to depart from convention. They became the victims of a language and a tradition which they were unable to adapt. By 1904 Anatole France could summarize all political strife in these two terms.[17]

[16] For discussion of the relationship of Socialism to Communism and anticlericalism see D. Bell and T. Criddle, *The French Socialist Party* (London, 1984), pp. 10–12, 15–20.

[17] See his *L'église et la république* (Paris, 1904), esp. pp. 17, 32–44 and the references in footnotes 5 and 6.

The Dreyfus Affair proved that France was unable to escape from the strait-jacket of two France politics. Socialism adopted anticlericalism because Socialism was a Republican ideology and traditionally Republicans were anticlerical. Paradoxically dialogue between Socialists and Catholics was more likely through the language of the extreme Left. The Guesdists had attached a lower priority to anticlerical politics in the decades before the formation of the French Communist Party. Guesde claimed that anticlericalism might be just another opiate for the masses, administered by the radical politicians of the *Belle époque*. Anticlericalism was therefore a bourgeois ruse rather than the appropriate political tactic of a burgeoning Socialism. Jaurès tried to attach Socialism to the Two Frances, as the third force of the future. The Guesdists were critical about a smooth transition from bourgeois anticlericalism to future Socialism, hence the Guesdists were able to assess Catholicism without preconceived tactical hostility. Eventually a genuine dialogue could be opened between Marxists and Catholics.

9

The Politics of Legality: The Religious Orders in France, 1901–45

Nicholas Atkin

The political history of religious orders in France in the first half of the twentieth century has been largely ignored by historians. Although considerable attention has been paid to the law of 1901 on associations and the law of 1904 prohibiting congregational teaching,[1] far less has been said about the orders in the post-1914 period. Broadly speaking, the reasons for this neglect are twofold. Firstly, any study of the orders poses considerable logistical problems to the historian. Congregational archives are scattered throughout much of France and Europe and several of these remain officially closed to researchers. Secondly, and more importantly, it is widely assumed that, after the initial round of *Combiste* expulsions had ended, the legal position of the orders was no longer a major political issue. Members of the regular clergy were allowed to continue their duties undisturbed by the state. Catholics, however, viewed matters differently. They believed that the orders had been denied fundamental human freedoms and repeatedly called for the revision of all discriminatory legislation.

In view of Catholic concern, this essay explores how the church

---

[1] See P. Sorlin, *Waldeck-Rousseau* (Paris, 1966) and M.O. Partin, *Waldeck-Rousseau, Combes and the Church: The Politics of Anticlericalism, 1899–1905.* (Durham, N.C., 1969).

attempted to win back the lost liberties of the congregations. It begins with an examination of the origins and impact of the laws of 1901 and 1904. These measures were far more damaging than has previously been recognized and were important in drawing up the legal and ideological battlelines for the next forty years. Next, the essay considers the inter war period. Following the *Union Sacrée* of 1914 there appeared to be a real possibility that the state would rescind the secular laws; yet this hope came to naught. The period from 1918 to 1940 was one of uneasy compromise. It was left to the Vichy regime to attempt to resolve the issue. Anxious to win the support of the church, Vichy made several changes to the laws controlling the orders; yet these amendments fell far short of Catholic expectations. At the Liberation the new government had little choice but to revert to the *status quo ante* of 1940.

The failure to resolve the legal position of the orders was a major source of religious and political friction in France in the first half of the twentieth century. The responsibility for this deadlock is usually accredited to the intransigence of Republican deputies. There is a large measure of truth in this argument; but it should also be noted that the church itself could not agree on the most suitable approach to the problem. Meanwhile, members of the orders became accustomed to living outside of the law. Largely unconcerned about the irregularity of their status, they continued to play a vital role in the intellectual, educational and social life of the church.

Until the advent of the Third Republic, the orders in France enjoyed considerable freedom. Although the Revolutionary and Napoleonic regimes questioned the usefulness of monks and nuns, successive governments generally welcomed the charitable and educational work performed by congregations. Close watch was kept only on politically suspect male orders such as the Jesuits. Little official hostility was expressed towards female congregations which, in the mid nineteenth century, enjoyed an impressive boost in membership. All this was to change with the creation of the Third Republic. Determined to place the new regime on a secure footing, Republicans sought to weaken the considerable influence which the orders exercized over education. Otherwise, it was argued, there was a danger that church and state schools, operating independently and in competition with one another, would produce, in the memorable phrase of René Waldeck-Rousseau, 'deux jeunesses' which would divide France into two hostile camps thus threatening civil war. Moreover, official hostility towards the orders was rooted in Republican ideology. As Ralph Gibson has remarked, the Jacobin tradition in France was nationalist, individualist and statist whereas the congregations appeared to be foreign, unpatriotic and corporatist.[2] The vows of chastity, poverty and obedience were all regarded as a fundamental denial of human personality and a challenge to the values which Republicans held so dear.

Given these concerns, the Republic was quick to take the offensive; decrees of March 1880 dissolved the Jesuits within France, confiscated their property, and expelled other unauthorized male orders. More important was the Loi Goblet of 30 October 1886, which prohibited the regular clergy from teaching in state schools. Even this measure was not as damaging as was originally feared: it was some while before it could take effect, and this gave members of the orders a breathing space in which they were able to find jobs in Catholic schools. Far more destructive were the laws of 1901 and 1904 – the so-called *lois d'exception* – which struck at the very heart of congregational activities.

The first of these measures, introduced by the centrist Prime Minister Waldeck-Rousseau, came into force on 1 July 1901.[3] This established the right of association, but drew a distinction between congregations and other bodies. The latter were allowed the freedom of formation, a right denied to the orders. The law stipulated that the orders were to seek authorization from parliament and banned members of non-authorized orders from teaching. The penalties for contravention of these rules were severe. Any non-authorized order was illegal and individual membership of it could be punished by either a fine or a jail sentence, or both. Those orders whose demands for recognition were rejected, or those *congrégations réfractaires* which did not seek authorization, were to be dissolved and their wealth confiscated.

Naturally Catholics bitterly resented these dispositions. They believed that the orders should be subject to common law and allowed freedom of association like any other citizen. According to an eminent Catholic jurist, Auguste Rivet, the purpose of the law had been to submit the orders to a draconian police regime.[4] Yet this had not been the intention of Waldeck-Rousseau. He believed that in submitting the orders to a legislative authorization, they would thereby possess the security of a

---

[2] R. Gibson, *A Social History of French Catholicism, 1789–1914* (London, 1989), p. 131.

[3] Full details of the association law are to be found in P. Sauret, *Répertoire des congrégations légalement reconnues et de leurs établissements autorisés* (Paris, 1939), pp. 156–58.

[4] A. Rivet, *Traité des congrégations religieuses, 1789–1943* (Paris, 1943) p. 29.

legal existence. Thus he had no intention of using the legislation against all of the 3,216 different orders which existed in France at that time. Instead the law was aimed principally at controlling politically suspect orders such as the Assumptionists. Important teaching congregations like the *Frères des Ecoles Chrétiennes*, which already possessed authorization, were to remain unaffected.

Different concerns motivated Emiles Combes who succeeded Waldeck-Rousseau in June 1902. A provincial Radical and hardened anticlerical, Combes sought to reduce significantly clerical influence within education. Consequently, he applied the above legislation far more vigorously than his predecessor.[5] By October 1903 he had closed down some 10,000 congregational schools. Yet even this was not enough and on 7 July 1904 a further law was introduced which prevented the regular clergy from teaching altogether. Only a small handful of missionary orders were exempt from this restriction.

Despite the severity of the above measure, there were a number of ways by which congregations could escape the full impact of the law. Robert Gildea has shown how in some municipalities Republican deputies were so worried about their slender majorities that they guaranteed a stay of execution for church schools.[6] Elsewhere, Gildea continues, there were problems with property rights. Although schools owned by the orders were forfeit, they might be taken over by a *société civile* which harboured a congregation. Nor was it always easy to identify teaching congregations. For example, few female orders were exclusively concerned with education. Instead, they carried out a whole range of duties, including looking after hospitals and orphanages. Thus many nuns were able to teach clandestinely. Other orders took the more drastic step of going into exile, often setting up schools just over the French border. Most orders circumvented the law by abandoning their religious robes and by continuing to teach in civilian dress. As *Le Temps* of 7 September 1940 put it, 'Une soutane noire remplaçait le blanc vêtement'.[7]

Given the ingenuity of Catholic resistance, historians have been quick to

[5] For Combes' application of the 1901 law in the Finistère, see C. Ford, 'Religion and the Politics of Cultural Change in Provincial France: The Resistance of 1902 in Lower Brittany', *Journal of Contemporary History*, 62, no. 1 (1990), pp. 1–33.

[6] R.D. Gildea, *Education in Provincial France, 1800–1914: A Study of Three Departments* (Oxford, 1983), p. 114. The present study has relied heavily on the insights provided by this work into the operation of the 1904 law.

[7] *Le Temps* 7 September 1940.

underline the ineffectiveness of the *Combiste* expulsions. Between 1904 and 1911 the Republic closed only 1,843 of the 8,200 schools run by the orders.[8] Nevertheless, the laws of 1901 and 1904 were more damaging than is sometimes acknowledged. Firstly, they made the job of recruitment extremely difficult. Now that the educational influence of the church had been weakened, it was no longer as easy for monks and nuns to cultivate pious children and encourage them to take holy vows. As a result the regular clergy was unable to maintain the impressive growth in membership that it had enjoyed in the nineteenth century. In 1848 there had been 3,000 monks; in 1901 this figure stood at 37,000; in 1945 the number had dropped to 29,500.[9] Clearly this decrease cannot be blamed solely on the *lois d'exception*, yet it cannot be denied that these measures were an important obstacle to the further growth of the regular clergy. Secondly, and more importantly, this legislation left a bitter political legacy. Catholics did not understand why the orders should be denied basic human freedoms and were taken aback by the brutality of the anticlerical assault. For many these laws were the most hated feature of Republican *laïcité*. The level of this contempt may be illustrated by the clerical reaction to Vichy's law of 3 September 1940 which restored the right to teach to congregations. Although *La Croix*, regarded by many as the official daily newspaper of the church, welcomed this new-found freedom as a gesture of reconciliation,[10] for much of the local Catholic press this was a time for revenge. *La semaine religieuse de Nîmes*, the weekly bulletin for the diocese, commented that it had never known a law more hypocritical or more cynical than that of 1904.[11] For *La semaine religieuse de Valence*, this was the opportunity to recite a long list of orders and their schools which had been banished from the Drôme.[12] Obviously, evidence from 1940 must be treated with some caution. In the aftermath of the defeat, the church was in a vengeful mood and was disinclined to forgive and forget. Even so, there is little doubting the intense hatred which many Catholics still felt towards the *lois d'exception*. That distaste had been intensified by the failure of successive governments in the interwar years to discover a solution to the problem.

[8] M. Larkin, *Church and State after the Dreyfus Affair: The Separation Issue in France* (London, 1974), p. 100.

[9] Figures taken from T. Zeldin, *France, 1848–1945* (2 vols., Oxford, 1973–77), vol. 1, p. 1010.

[10] *La Croix* 6 September 1940.

[11] *La semaine religieuse de Nîmes* 8 September 1940, no. 34, p. 368.

[12] *La semaine religieuse de Valence* 21 September 1940, no. 37, p. 455.

In the years immediately following the First World War, it seemed to many that the anticlerical squabbles of the early 1900s had come to an end. The *Union Sacrée* of 1914 had helped promote a spirit of reconciliation and had given rise to hopes that the orders might recover their former liberties. The *Union Sacrée* brought with it the *Circulaire Malvy* of 2 August, 1914, which instructed prefects to suspend the closure of schools run by congregations.[13] In the course of the war members of the orders had distinguished themselves in battle; no longer could it be maintained, as it was in 1870, that the orders were antipatriotic. For example, in 1914 1,896 of the *Frères des Ecoles Chrétiennes* were mobilized. Of this number, 280 were killed, 185 wounded and 397 decorated for bravery.[14] In return for their unswerving devotion to their country, the brothers believed their reward should be nothing less than the abolition of the *lois d'exception*. Accordingly Catholics placed great hopes in the election of the right-wing *Bloc National* in 1919. The new government promised a reversal of the hardened laicism of the past and was instrumental in reestablishing the French embassy at the Vatican. Likewise the church itself appeared more favourably disposed towards the Republic. The new Pope, Pius XI, was concerned to place church-state relations on a new footing and in 1926, in a gesture of reconciliation, condemned the extremist movement, the *Action Française*.

Viewed together, these moves seemed to herald a new *ralliement* between church and state in France.[15] Yet this was never to take root. Catholics and Republicans continued to distrust one another. To a large extent the roots of this distrust may be dated back to the secular legislation of the 1880s and early 1900s, in particular to the measures governing the orders.[16] In a famous article of 1 August 1939 for the right-wing journal *La revue des deux mondes*, the influential priest, Ferdinand Renaud, argued that religious peace in France could be attained only if the government amended the *lois d'exception*.[17]

[13] *Circulaire Malvy* of 2 August 1914 cited in Rivet, *Traité des congrégations*, p. 41.

[14] A.N. 2 AG 82 SP10 E, Note relative à l'Institut des Frères des Ecoles Chrétiennes et à sa demande de reconaissance légale (no date, early 1944?).

[15] This question is considered in H.W. Paul, *The Second Ralliement: The Rapprochement between Church and State in France in the Twentieth Century* (Washington, 1967).

[16] S. Bernstein, *La France des années 30* (Paris, 1988), p. 22.

[17] Abbé F. Renaud, 'Pour une politique religieuse', in *Revue des deux mondes* 1 August 1939, 639–63.

During the interwar years Catholics continued to oppose the laws of 1901 and 1904 on a number of grounds. From a legal point of view these measures were regarded as an affront to the liberties of the church. There was also the worry that the Republic might revert to the militant anticlerical policies pursued by Combes. It was not enough that the orders could continue their duties outside of the law. As long as the *lois d'exception* remained on the statue books, there was always the possibility that they might be re-enforced. These fears were heightened in 1924 when the Radical *Cartel des Gauches* threatened to extend the secular legislation to Alsace-Lorraine where, of course, it had never been in force. Finally Catholics considered the law of 1904 as a stranglehold on Catholic teaching. Although the church continued to hold its own in primary education, instructing around one fifth of the school population, there was little chance of expansion as long as the orders were banned from teaching. Desperately short of money, Catholic schools became increasingly reliant on the services of lay personnel. Yet lay teachers were not easy to recruit and were put off by poor pay and long working hours.[18]

These concerns led the church to make several attempts to revise the *lois d'exception*. However, these efforts did not always win the unanimous approval of Catholics. Between the wars it is possible to discern a certain ambiguity in the attitude of the church towards the orders. Although evidence remains impressionistic, it appears that disagreement centred on means rather than ends. The hierarchy tended to favour a moderate path. Aware of Republican sensibilities, the episcopate contented itself with demands for the abrogation of the law of 1904 and a gradual relaxation of that of 1901. Militant Catholics were more daring and called for the total and immediate abolition of all discriminatory legislation.

Militant views were expressed most forcibly by the *Ligue des Droits des Religieux des Anciens Combattants* (D.R.A.C.). Founded on 4 August 1924 by two relatively unknown war heroes – Dom Moreau, a Benedictine monk, and Daniel-Michel Bergey, a priest from St. Emilion – the original purpose of D.R.A.C. had been to mobilize support among war veterans of the regular clergy against the possibility of the *Cartel des Gauches* reenforcing the *lois d'exception*.[19] Having fought for their country, D.R.A.C. believed

---

[18] The study of Catholic schoolteachers in the interwar period has been neglected by historians. Some insights into the world of the *professeurs libres* may be found in P. Guiral and G. Thuiller, *La vie quotidienne des professeurs de 1870 à 1940* (Paris, 1983).

[19] Mgr. Théas, *Livre d'or des congrégations françaises, 1939–1945* (Paris, 1948), p. 13.

that the congregations should be subject to common law and be permitted to associate freely without authorization from the state. This belief was embodied in the motto: 'Egaux comme au front'. After the threat of the Herriot government had passed, D.R.A.C. continued its struggle, holding regular reunions of superiors from a wide range of orders, among them the Dominicans, Jesuits, *Oblats de Marie Immaculée* and *Frères de Saint Vincent de Paul.* To mobilize public support for its campaign, D.R.A.C. encouraged lay membership and founded a youth movement, *Jeunes D.R.A.C.* which under Vichy became part of the *Equipes et Cadres de la France Nouvelle.*[20] Yet D.R.A.C. did not believe freedom of association should be permitted solely to monks who were war veterans, but to all members of the regular clergy. This led D.R.A.C. to be deeply critical of those orders which sought to exist within the letter of the law. 'Les quatre plaies de l'église' was how D.R.A.C. described the four missionary orders – the *Sulpiciens, Lazaristes, Pères de Saint Esprit* and *Missions Etrangères* – which had conformed to earlier legislation on authorization.[21]

In view of the differing approaches of the hierarchy and D.R.A.C., it is perhaps no surprise that the church made little headway in its attempts to modify the *lois d'exception.* Yet far more obstructive was the opposition of the National Assembly. If a majority of deputies had no desire to implement this legislation, neither did they wish to modify it. The *lois d'exception* had become *lois intangibles,* touchstones of *laïcité.*[22] The extent to which deputies were committed to them was clearly demonstrated in 1928 when not even the authority of Poincaré could secure the legal authorization of a handful of missionary orders.[23] Similarly, in spring 1939 two separate attempts to modify the laws governing the orders met with failure, despite Daladier's attempts to improve church-state

[20] Details of this change may be found in the journal of the *Equipes et Cadres de la France Nouvelle, bulletin no. 1 d'information et de critique,* Spring 1941, contained in A.N.2 AG 79 SP6 no. 11.

[21] A.N.2 AG 492 CC73 E, Note à propos des revendications de la D.R.A.C., 8 August 1941.

[22] The attitude of the deputies to *laïcité* is discussed in R. Rémond, *The Right in France from Dreyfus to de Gaulle* (Philadelphia, 1966), p. 264.

[23] P. Bouthillier, *Le drame de Vichy* (2 vols., Paris, 1951), vol. 1, p. 355. For a list of non-authorized orders which existed in France in the interwar years, see 'Documents relatifs à la rentrée des congrégations', in *Europe Nouvelle* 30 juin 1923, and 'Une liste des congrégations d'hommes rentrées en France sans autorisation', in *Europe Nouvelle* 10 November 1928. Details of applications for authorization in this period are to be found in A.N. F19 8051 and A.N. F19 8052.

relations.[24] The first, and more ambitious, of these proposals was that of Eugène Pébellier, a deputy from the Haute-Loire. This advocated the abolition of the law of 1904 and a relaxation of that of 1901 in the interests of French missionary orders whose numbers were steadily dwindling. The second proposal – backed by Edmond Miellet, a deputy from Belfort, and Abbé Polimann, deputy for the Meuse – had the more limited aim of lifting teaching restrictions on those individual monks who had fought in the last war. Yet neither proposal commanded majority support especially among deputies of the centre right, many of whom remained committed to the ideals of *laïcité*. This failure came as no surprise to the church. Earlier, in January 1939, Cardinal Verdier of Paris had gloomily reflected, 'La France n'a pas changé un iota de sa législation anticléricale et laïque . . . ses dirigeants n'osent pas prononcer le nom de Dieu'.[25]

The coming of the war quickly reopened the issue of the orders, on two fronts. Firstly, there was an influx of refugee orders from Alsace-Lorraine, where Republican secularist legislation had never been enforced. Secondly, the call up of several Catholic lay teachers led to their places being filled by members of the regular clergy, many of whom had come out of retirement, having rummaged through their wardrobes for their religious dress. This soon led to friction. For instance, in April 1940 *L'Ecole Libératrice*, the newspaper of the *Syndicat National des Instituers* (S.N.I.), reported the case of a Catholic school in the Sarthe where the place of the mobilized teacher had been filled by three old brothers of the *Frères de la Doctrine Chrétienne*.[26] The academy inspector had duly intervened only to provoke a storm of criticism in the Catholic press. Similarly in the neighbouring department of the Maine-et-Loire the prefect had prevented the *Frères des Ecole Chrétiennes* from reopening a school at Teloche but, after Catholic protests, was forced to back down.[27]

Petty incidents like these called for a clear ruling. Secularists hoped that the government would reinforce the 1904 legislation. The S.N.I. saw no

[24] See J.-M. Mayeur, 'La politique religieuse', in Fondation Nationale des Sciences Politiques, *Edouard Daladier: chef de gouvernement avril 1938-septembre 1939* (Paris, 1977), p. 250 ff.

[25] Verdier quoted in J. Marteaux, *L'église de France devant la révolution marxiste* (2 vols., Paris, 1968), vol. 2, p. 108.

[26] A.N. F17 13390, press cutting from *L'Ecole Libératrice* 13 April 1940.

[27] Abbé J. Desgranges, *Journal d'un prêtre-député, 1936–1940* (Paris and Geneva, 1960), p. 367.

reason why the law should be flouted in time of war. Conversely Catholics hoped for a relaxation of teaching restrictions. This was the aim of a memorandum of Cardinal Verdier submitted in January 1940 to the Quai d'Orsay.[28] Yet no such resolution was forthcoming. A report of 4 April 1940 by the *Directeur de l'enseignement du premier degré* claimed that the problem was not his to solve; instead, it was the responsibility of the Minister of Education in consultation with the government.[29] A fortnight later a memorandum for the minister admitted that the problem was *délicate*, but confessed that in the circumstances there were insufficient texts to make a clear ruling.[30] Stranded on the sandbanks of legal niceties, the Republic soon found itself washed over by the tide of events.

The establishment of the Vichy government marks another step in the troubled history of the congregations. Given the pro-clerical nature of the early Vichy cabinets, Catholics were hopeful of a reversal of the past sixty years of institutionalized secularism. Pétain himself was especially well-disposed towards church demands. Although he was not a fervent believer, he regarded religion as the most effective of social cements and was an open admirer of the hierarchical structure of the church.[31] He was particularly sympathetic towards the congregations. After all, as the Catholic press was forever recalling, Pétain had been a pupil of the Dominicans. What better proof was there, it was enquired, of the worth of congregational teaching? In February 1941 *La semaine religieuse de Belley* recalled the words of one of Pétain's former teachers, who in May 1917 had modestly remarked, 'Si je n'avais grondé Philippe, nous n'avions peut-être

[28] Verdier's memorandum is referred to in a document of 20 October 1940 entitled 'Mémoire à consulter pour une politique religieuse de l'état', contained in A.N. 2 AG 492 CC72 A. The October paper had been drawn up by Pierre Sauret, *Directeur des cultes* at the Ministry of Interior. For Verdier's demands, also see J.P. Cointet, 'L'église catholique et le gouvernement de Vichy', in *Eglises et chrétiens dans la IIe guerre mondiale: la France. Actes du colloque de Lyon 1978 publiés sous la direction de Xavier de Montclos* (Lyon, 1982), p. 437.

[29] A.N. F17 13390, note of 4 April 1940 from *Directeur de l'enseignement du premier degré* to the Minister of Education.

[30] A.N. F17 13390, Aide-mémoire pour M. le Président Sarraut sur les relations avec l'enseignement privé (premier degré), 17 April 1940.

[31] For Pétain's religious beliefs see H. Bequart, *Au temps du silence: de Bordeaux à Vichy. Souvenirs et réflexions* (Paris, 1945), pp. 196–97; R. Gillouin, *J'étais l'ami du Maréchal Pétain* (Paris, 1966), pp. 87–88; and H. du Moulin de Labarthète, *Le temps des illusions: souvenirs juillet 1940 – avril 1942* (Geneva, 1946), p. 95.

pas Pétain'.[32] Another evocation of the value of congregational teaching came from Albert Rivaud, the first of Vichy's six Ministers of Education. In two articles for the *Revue des deux mondes* he recounted the educative role of orders such as the Jesuits and the *Frères des Ecole Chrétiennes*.[33] It was they, not the 'écoles officielles' of the state which had laid the foundations of 'la civilisation française'.

But although Vichy was favourably disposed towards the orders, what policy was envisaged in their regard? The church hierarchy wanted to see the abrogation of the law of 1904 and a revision of that of 1901. This was made clear by the cardinals meeting together in July 1940 at Paris. For Vichy this was moving too fast. The defeat had come too quickly to resurrect relics of the *Union Sacrée*. Instead the regime preferred to bide its time by offering more gradual concessions. The most important of these was to return to the orders the right to teach. This would not only restore a basic human right, but would also regularize the position of all those orders which had returned during the *drôle de guerre*. At the same time Vichy did not wish to relinquish all form of state control. While the question of authorization would require revision, it should not be abandoned completely. Like every other government since 1789 Vichy wanted to retain some form of regulatory supervision.

The outcome was the law of 3 September 1940 which abolished the legislation of 1904 prohibiting congregational teaching. At the same time article 14 of the law of 1901, which prevented non-authorized orders from teaching, was annulled. This returned to congregations the right to teach in the same conditions as any other French citizen, something which the orders had been doing since 1914. What it did not do was release them from the need for authorization. Thus those orders such as the *Frères des Ecoles Chrétiennes*, which had lost their legal existence in 1904, still had to seek authorization if they wanted to remain within the law.

As has already been remarked, the law of 3 September 1940 received a warm welcome in the Catholic press. Yet, not all elements within the church were as enthusiastic. Catholic lay teachers, mindful of protecting their jobs, were not always pleased to see their colleagues in the regular clergy resume their teaching duties. A government report of 20 May 1943

---

[32] *La semaine religieuse de Belley* 13 February 1941, no. 7, p. 47.

[33] A. Rivaud, 'Vers une école nouvelle', in *Revue des deux mondes* 1 September 1940, p. 227, and 'L'avenir de l'enseignement libre', in *Revue des deux mondes* 15 November 1941, 129–47.

cited incidents in regions as varied as the Isère, Orne, Seine-Inférieure, Alpes-Maritimes and Paris where lay teachers had been put out of work following the return of a congregation.[34] The same report was astonished at the insensitivity of certain superiors. As soon as they had recovered their right to teach, they had 'congédié sans aucun égard les malheureux instituteurs et institutrices libres qui, depuis 1904, se sont dévoués, en général pour un salaire de famine, à maintenir l'enseignement chrétien'.

Nor were the militants of D.R.A.C. satisfied with Vichy's concessions. They were concerned that the orders still required state authorization. In a letter of February 1941, published in the organization's newspaper, Moreau told his members that while their efforts were beginning to be rewarded, much remained to be done.[35] 'Malgré leur volonté,' he declared, 'le Maréchal ni son Ministre n'ont pu encore publier l'abrogation officielle du Titre III de la loi du 1er juillet 1901 pour nous rendre le droit de nous associer, d'hériter, de posséder comme tous les français.' It was still necessary, concluded Moreau, for D.R.A.C. to remain on its guard in order to ensure that all its good work was not undone by those who opposed the 'vrai renouveau de la France'.

The issue of authorization was further highlighted by the unusual case of the contemplative order of the Chartreux. On 21 February 1941 they became the first male order in nearly forty years to have gained legal recognition. Usually this move is cited as evidence of Vichy's clericalism, yet, as André Latreille has shown, the law was as much a matter of legal expediency as it was a gesture of reconciliation.[36] When in 1903 the Chartreux were banished from France, the majority of the monks took refuge at Farnetta in Italy. This caused them some embarrassment in 1940 when Mussolini declared war on France. Refusing loyalty to the *Duce*, they returned to French territory. On 8 June 1940 their *procureur-général* asked the Ministry of the Interior for permission to reopen their old monastery of the Grande-Chartreuse in the Isère. After some initial hesitation, the Ministry granted their request and on 21 June the Chartreux were allowed to reinstal themselves at their former home. This decision

[34] A.N. 2 AG 496 CC78 A, report of Jardel, Secrétaire général du Chef de l'Etat, to Mgr. Chappoulie, the church hierarchy's representative at Vichy, 20 May 1943.

[35] Letter of Moreau in *D.R.A.C.* February–March 1941 contained in A.N. 2 AG 79 SP6 no. 11. DRAC's concerns are clearly documented in a report it submitted to Vichy – 'Histoire succincte de la question des congrégations depuis l'armistice', 18 July 1941, to be found in A.N. 2 AG 493 CC75 B.

[36] A. Latreille, *De Gaulle, la libération et l'église catholique* (Paris, 1978), pp. 82–84.

was, however, highly irregular. Not possessing a legal existence, the order was not entitled to occupy national property. Thus it was left to Vichy to regularize their position through the law of 21 February 1941.

Ultimately Vichy grasped the nettle of authorization. After months of intense negotiations,[37] a law of 8 April 1942 ruled that it was no longer an offence for a congregation to exist as a non-authorized order. Even so, a congregation was still able to obtain legal recognition which would be granted by a unamimous decision of the Conseil d'Etat. Those that were successful in their demand would enjoy much the same rights as any other association considered to be of a *utilité publique*. Likewise, the dissolution of an order or one of its establishments could be decided by the Conseil d'Etat. Finally, those orders which had not previously been recognized and which subsequently obtained recognition would be able to reclaim their former property which had not since been liquidated. In this way Vichy believed it could meet Catholic requests without relinquishing all form of state control.

The above measure did not provoke the same kind of excitement in the Catholic press as the law of 3 September 1940. This was largely because few people were interested, or in a position to understand, the legal complexities involved.[38] The fact that the orders were teaching once more and, in the popular phrase, allowed to *rhabiller*, was enough to satisfy even the most devout. Similarly the hierarchy welcomed the solution, at least as a temporary expedient. By 1942 the episcopate was wary of Vichy and was concerned not to compromise itself too much with the regime. It understood that a definitive solution to the question of the orders would require consultation with the papacy and that any precipitate moves might damage negotiations for a future concordat between church and state.[39] Such concerns did not trouble D.R.A.C. which had long been campaigning for a more radical solution. It believed that the new legislation left uncertain the fate of those orders which had not sought authorization.[40] These would still be outside of the law and would stand little chance with

[37] These negotiations are analysed in N.J. Atkin, 'Catholics and Schools in Vichy France, 1940–44', unpublished London Ph.D. thesis, 1988, pp. 190–232.

[38] Latreille, *De Gaulle, la libération et l'église*, p. 86.

[39] The question of a concordat is discussed in Atkin, 'Catholics and Schools', pp. 68–74, and F. Delpech, 'Le projet de concordat de l'été 1940', in *Eglises et chrétiens*, pp. 185–88. Cf. also J. Duquesne, *Les catholiques français sous l'occupation* (Paris, 1966), *passim*.

[40] A.N. 2 AG 492 CC73 E, letter of *Supérieur général de la Société de Marie* to Mgr. Rastouil, bishop of Limoges, 15 October 1942, gives details of D.R.A.C.'s response to the law of April 1942.

the Conseil d'Etat which, it was alleged, was 'pénétrée des idées de '89'. D.R.A.C. therefore argued that a congregation should enjoy all the benefits of association without having to request recognition. If a congregation was to be dissolved, then this should be decided by the courts and not by a 'political' vote in the Conseil d'Etat.

These arguments carried little weight with Vichy, which was intensely suspicious of D.R.A.C. Coercion, it was argued, was the only way in which D.R.A.C. managed to obtain the support of so many Superiors.[41] Nevertheless, the law of 8 April 1942 did not work in the way in which the regime had hoped. In several areas congregations ignored the law and continued their duties as before. Elsewhere it created confusion. In spite of detailed circulars from the Ministry of the Interior, many state officials did not grasp the full implications of the change. For instance, in January 1944 it was reported that in the strongly Catholic department of the Mayenne nearly all the *institutrices libres* had readopted religious dress, although none of them belonged to an authorized order.[42] The academy inspector wondered, therefore, whether their schools were allowed to receive state subsidies (granted by legislation of 2 November 1941) since not one of the nuns belonged to a recognized congregation. In his reply of 28 April 1944 Abel Bonnard, the Minister of Education, pointed out that they were eligible for subventions because it was no longer an offence to be part of a non-authorized order.[43] Yet it may be that some officials deliberately feigned misunderstanding of the law in order to use it as a stick with which to beat the congregations.

Only a small number of orders considered applying, under the provisions of the law of 8 April 1942, for legal recognition. Why this was so remains unclear, but there are three possible explanations. Firstly, it may be that the orders, like the church in general, wanted to distance themselves from Vichy and not be seen courting favours from a politically suspect regime. A second possibility is that some orders feared the scorn of their more militant brothers if they sought recognition. Thirdly, it may have been that most orders believed that they enjoyed sufficient freedoms and did not want to take their chance with the Conseil d'Etat. The fact that the Chartreux were the

[41] A.N. 2 AG 492 CC73 E, Note à propos des revendications de la D.R.A.C., 8 August 1941.

[42] A.N. F17 13390, letter of academy inspector of the Mayenne to Abel Bonnard, Minister of Education, 18 January 1944.

[43] A.N. F17 13390, letter of Bonnard to academy inspector of the Mayenne, 28 April 1944.

only male order since 1901 to have received recognition – and then in the most unusual of circumstances – must have been an important factor in this regard.

These reasons did not prevent three female congregations from seeking and obtaining recognition. Among their male colleagues it is known that at least three orders – the Dominicans, the *Frères de St-Jean-de-Dieu* and the *Frères des Ecoles Chrétienne* – were in October 1942 seriously considering the move, despite earning the censure of D.R.A.C.[44] Of these, only the *Frères des Ecoles Chrétiennes* took the plunge. Not only did they wish to recover lost property and reassert their educational standing, they also wanted to preserve the French character of the order. In 1940 only 4,000 of the 14,500 brothers were French.[45]

The strength of these arguments had already led the order to make two unsuccessful bids for authorization in 1922 and 1928.[46] The brothers were so disappointed at the failure of their second attempt that it was decided to transfer the *maison mère* from its temporary home in Belgium to Rome. Nevertheless, the Superior General had delayed this move until 1936 hoping for a change of heart on the part of government. The election of the Popular Front had, therefore, come as a particularly crushing blow. Vichy proved just as obdurate as Republican governments beforehand. When in August 1944 the order's demand for authorization came to the attention of the Conseil d'Etat, it was rejected on a number of grounds.[47] Although the *conseillers* agreed in principle to the desirability of recognition, they were concerned that only one-third of the order was French and that the *maison mère* was no longer in France. To recognize an order whose seat was in Rome, they objected, was to place 'en mauvaise posture devant la papauté les congrégations françaises qui lui ont refusé de s'installer à Rome'. Before recognition could be granted they demanded that the *maison mère* be returned to France and insisted that in future the post of Superior General should be filled only by a Frenchman. Such Gallican scruples ended any realistic hope of the brothers gaining recognition.

The failure of the *Frères des Ecoles Chrétiennes* to obtain authorization sharply underlined the limitations of the law of 8 April 1942 and did little to

[44] A.N. 2 AG 492 CC73 E, letter of D.R.A.C. to Mgr. Rastouil, 15 October 1942.

[45] A.N. F17 13365, note from *Secrétaire général* of the *Frères des Ecoles Chrétiennes* to Bonnard, 26 November 1943.

[46] A.N. 2 AG 82 SP10 E, Note relative à l'Institut Frères des Ecoles Chrétiennes et à sa demande de reconnaissance légale (no date, early 1944?).

[47] A.N. F17 13365, report of St. Jolly, *Directeur de l'enseignement du premier degré*, 1 August 1944.

endear the orders to the regime. Not that their support had been very great in the first place. It is noticeable that, in the immediate aftermath of the defeat, the regular clergy were one of the most restrained sections of the church in their support for Vichy. This attitude is not difficult to explain. As male orders were directly responsible to Rome they enjoyed far greater independence in their internal affairs than their secular colleagues. Freedom of action quickly led to freedom of thought. This was the concern of the Dominican *Prieur provincial de la province de Lyon*. In August 1941 he urged his fellow brothers to cast away their doubts about Vichy and practise 'un loyalisme sincère, complet envers les pouvoirs publics'. [48] He vigorously denied claims that a majority of male orders, in particular the Jesuits and Dominicans, were Gaullist in sympathy. While it is difficult to substantiate such allegations, it cannot be denied that the orders were well placed to become part of the Resistance. Given the closed world of several congregations, they were able to carry out many resistance acts unnoticed by either the German or Vichy authorities. In 1944 many orders came out into the open and played a prominent role in the Liberation. [49]

The occupation was a key episode in the history of the orders. It brought to a head several of the debates which had simmered for the past forty years. Yet these arguments proved as intractable as in the past. Small wonder, then, that the Fourth Republic shied away from the issue. Although Vichy legislation was rescinded, the orders had no reason to fear state interference. [50] The new government preferred to revert to the status quo which had existed before 1940.

Why did it prove so difficult to resolve the issue of the legal status of the orders? To a large extent the problems lie in the ambiguities created by the legislation of 1901 and 1904. On the one hand, Waldeck-Rousseau wanted to control but conciliate the orders. On the other, Combes wished to eliminate them altogether. Given these different approaches, Republicans were uncertain in their attitude towards the congregations. Many preferred to leave the legislation on the statute books without actually implementing it. In this way they were able to remain loyal to the traditions of *laïcité* and

[48] A.N. 2 AG 492 CC72 A, letter of *Prieur provincial de la province de Lyon* to *Prieur des Dominicains*, St. Alban-en-Leysse (Savoie), 23 August 1941. This letter had been intercepted on 26 August by the Vichy authorities.

[49] Latreille, *De Gaulle, la libération et l'église catholique*, p. 87. Also see B. Sécret, *Les Frères des Écoles Chrétiennes en Savoie, 1810–1844–1944* (Chambéry, 1944), pp. vii–viii.

[50] Latreille, *De Gaulle, la libération et l'église catholique*, p. 145.

maintain the illusion of state control. Accordingly the compromise reached in the 1920s and 1930s appeared as the best solution. Catholics were less satisfied; the images of nuns being forcibly thrown out of their convents by armed soldiers remained in the memories of many. Militants argued that the orders should enjoy full liberties and be allowed to associate freely without any need for authorization. Moderate Catholics, particularly among the hierarchy, adopted a more subtle line. They wished to see the abrogation of the law of 1904; yet conscious of Republican traditions, were prepared to concede that orders, if they so chose, should have the opportunity to seek recognition. If an order was to take this path, then the state should always guarantee authorization. Thus Vichy's law of 8 April 1942, which perhaps came closer to the intention of Waldeck-Rousseau than some Republicans cared to admit, remained deficient in that it did not provide any certainty of recognition.

In view of the complex arguments involved it is no surprise that, whenever a government attempted to resolve the legal status of the orders, the old wounds of the early 1900s reappeared. These arguments retained much of their vitality and were a sticking point in church-state relations. Yet the history of the regular clergy does not end here. This essay has concentrated exclusively on political matters and serves largely as a *point de départ*. Much work remains to be done on social history of the orders in the twentieth century. If historians pursue this path, then they may well find that congregations have played a much greater role in the contemporary life of French Catholicism than has previously been acknowledged.

10

Church and State: Prelates, Theologians and the Vichy Regime

W.D. Halls

Various aspects of the network of relationships that emerged between church and state in France from 1940 to 1944 may be regarded as unusual. The Vichy regime was above all one of *personalities* – the institutions of the Third Republic, from the chambers of the National Assembly to the trade unions, were all dissolved. Discussion is here restricted to only two groups, the bishops and theologians of the Catholic church. Their Protestant counterparts followed a different path. The emphasis was also on *continuities*. The goals pursued by the prelates were those they had sought between the wars, and even earlier. The doctrinal questions were those that had preoccupied Catholic thinkers from time immemorial.

The extreme loyalty of the bishops of Marshal Pétain, and to a lesser extent, to the administration, is first examined in detail, because it is the most striking phenomenon and conditions all else. How far the initial Vichy programme of *redressement national* coincided with the ideas of the bishops is then evaluated. The positive gains registered by the church are briefly summarized, as is the failure to achieve a concordat, an agreement which in the end all parties involved agreed would have to await the end of the war. The evolution of theological views on the relationship between church and state, which first accepted the provisional status quo of the regime, then came out positively in favour of its legitimacy, only later to argue fiercely that its enslavement to the Germans robbed it of validity, demonstrates that at the Liberation the church of France was split on basic issues. This illustrates a passive aspect of the Resistance which has only recently been highlighted.

The situation in 1940, after the French collapse, bears some resemblance to the Restoration in 1815. As young priests many of the higher clergy had experienced the separation of church and state. They had survived periods of extreme anticlericalism under the Third Republic and bitterly resented the advent of the *Front Populaire* in the 1930s. They, who had been *émigrés de l'intérieur*, found themselves in an analogous position to the returning *émigrés* after Waterloo. Their defeated country had become missionary territory. Their goal was clear: 'Nous referons Chrétiens nos frères', in the words of the song of the *Jeunesse Ouvrière Chrétienne*. Maurras' 'divine surprise', in the form of Philippe Pétain, sat in the seat of absolute power. The possibility existed of a new alliance between 'throne and altar'. As in 1815, there was a *Chambre introuvable*. Some, ecclesiastics and Maurrassians alike, would even have liked to revert to a veritable *ancien régime*. Though falling short of this questionable ideal, those who initially took power at Vichy were favourable to church aspirations.

There the resemblance with 1815 ends. The Nazis who occupied two-thirds of French territory for four years were more ruthless than the Prussian troops who withdrew from France in 1818 to the derisory cry of 'Bon voyage, Messieurs les Prussiens, n'y revenez plus'. The new 'Chief of State' was no Louis XVIII, certainly no 'Bishop-King' like Charles X, but an octagenarian lacking any deeply held religious convictions.

One cannot understand church and state relations during the Vichy period without first considering the personal nature of the relationship between the bishops and the new *Chef de l'État français*. The hero of Verdun, deemed twice saviour of his country, was held in almost religious idolatry by the bishops, whose faith in him scarcely wavered to the end. 'Venerated' was the epithet they most frequently applied to the Marshal. Mgr. Martin, bishop of Le Puy, even submitted for his approval the words, written by one of his flock, for a 'Marseillaise des Temps Nouveaux', sung to the original tune:

> Chef glorieux de la Patrie,
> Père au grand coeur, va, nous t'aimons,
> Tes enfants ont l'âme meutrie,
> Mais, commande, et nous te suivrons (bis).[1]

---

[1] A.N. 2 AG 76, Correspondence Ménétrel. Letter from Mgr. Martin to Dr. Ménétrel, private secretary to Pétain, Le Puy, 21 March 1941.

(Glorious leader of our country,
Father great of heart, we love you,
Your childrens' soul has been shattered,
Yet only command, and we will follow you).

Such adulation was perhaps comprehensible in 1940, when '40 millions de Pétainistes' lauded the Marshal for rescuing France from the fate of occupied Poland.

Subsequent events did indeed stir the conscience of not a few prelates, but they appeared able to divorce their misgivings from their loyalism to Pétain, whom, as the conflict wore on, they continued to consider as God's gift to France, 'l'homme providentiel', as they commonly spoke of him. Thus Mgr. Mennechet, bishop of Soissons, thought fit to inform the Marshal in October 1941 that his congregation had prayed for 'le chef admirable que la Providence a donné à la France dans votre auguste personne'. He reported that, to close the mass in his basilica the choir had intoned a special anthem: 'Fortissima Galliae duci Philippo valetudo et fides intrepida', ('Health in abundance and faith intrepid be given to Philip, leader of France').[2] At the height of the uproar against the round-ups of Jews the archbishop of Aix and bishops of South-East France sent Pétain a telegram supporting his task of 'renewing' France. Some days later Mgr. Suhard, the cardinal-archbishop of Paris, and thirteen bishops from the occupied zone, despatched a message couched in similar terms.[3] Pétain replied from Vichy on 24 October 1942, 'C'est avec une satisfaction toute spéciale que je sens l'église de France me garder sa confiance'. Mgr. Delay, bishop of Marseille, who had vigorously condemned the Jewish deportations only a few weeks before – by then it was generally realized that Pétain planned to stay put after the North African landings – declared: 'Dieu veuille nous conserver le Maréchal'.[4] Such episcopal loyalty continued even in 1943, when it was apparent that Pétain was no longer in control. Mgr. Suhard nevertheless wrote to the Marshal: 'Je veux vous dire que plus que jamais la France a besoin de votre

[2] A.N. 2 AG 493, letter from Mgr. Mennechet to Pétain, Soissons, 24 October 1941.

[3] A.N. 2 AG 492, telegram sent from Aix, 20 September 1942; telegram sent from Châlons, 2 October 1942 by Mgr. Tissier, bishop of Châlons, on behalf of Mgr. Suhard and his fellow-bishops: they pray for the rebuilding of France, 'auquel vous vous consacrez si généreusement'.

[4] A.N. 2 AG 493, letter from Mgr. Delay to M. Lavagne, *cabinet civil* of Pétain, Marseille, 28 November 1942.

personne'.[5] Even after the Liberation, in March 1945, the director of Catholic education in Mende wrote to his bishop, Mgr. Auvity, who was in danger of being forcibly deposed from his see by the Gaullists, recounting a meeting in Paris with Mgrs. Suhard and Roncalli, the new papal nuncio – and future pope John XXIII – at which both had shown 'la même bienveillance et la même compréhension à l'endroit de notre chef vénéré', the same who a few weeks later was under lock and key in the fort of Montrouge, facing charges of collusion with the enemy.[6]

Loyalty, therefore, even adulation, and limitless faith was put in Pétain throughout. It would seem that no bishop – not even the rebellious Mgr. Saliège, archbishop of Toulouse – ever disavowed the Marshal. Their attitude exasperated many less illustrious Catholics. In 1942 it motivated a few of them anonymously to address a 'Mémoire aux evêques de France' which declared, 'Que cessent de retentir dans la chaire chrétienne ces éloges hyperboliques et permanents de la personne du Maréchal'.[7] Père Dillard, a prominent Jesuit figure at Vichy who was later to die in Dachau in 1943, publicly criticized 'la fausse idolâtrie Pétain': 'It is insulting to him to seek to admire him as one would a wily diplomat or to venerate him as one would a stupid Buddha'.[8] But this was not the way the hierarchy felt.

In October 1941 a slightly bizarre note was struck in church-state relations. The proposal, most likely emanating from a ecclesiastical source, was made that an act of intercession for the Head of State should appear in the mass. A similar prayer – but for the Republic – 'Domine, salvam fac Rempublicam' ('O Lord, make safe the Republic'), a relic of the 1801 Concordat, had survived in part and had continued between the wars in a few dioceses. (The second part of the prayer, 'Domine, salvos fac consules', – 'O Lord, save the Consuls' – had been abandoned, for obvious reasons.) The suggestion was now made to put in 'Domine, salvum fac Phillipum, ducem nostrum' ('O Lord, save Philip our Leader'). The *Conseil d'État*, duly consulted, gave as its opinion that the Vatican would not favour the word 'Philip' because the Marshal's power was personal and not dynastic. Moreover, the insertion of the word *ducem* would be little appreciated by the

[5] A.N. 2 AG 493, letter from Mgr. Suhard to Pétain, Paris, 24 June 1943.

[6] A.N. Fla 3351, intercept of letter from Mgr. Bouniol, *vicaire-général, directeur de l'enseignement*, Mende, dated 21 March 1945, to Mgr. Auvity, at Bonnecombe, Aveyron where he had gone at the Liberation.

[7] A.N. 2 AG 492, unsigned 'Mémoire aux Evêques de France', 30 June 1942.

[8] 'Le Mystere du Maréchal', *Nouvelles de Versailles* 11 March 1943.

Holy See, because it would constitute a precedent for other formulas: not only *Duce*, but *Führer*, and even (for Romania) *Conducator*. The advice was to wait until the concordat; the proposal was dropped.[9] Other suggestions, such as those that Joan of Arc should become officially the patron saint of France, that the nation should be formally dedicated to the Sacred Heart of Jesus, and that the emblem of the Sacred Heart appear on the French flag, 'as a symbol of love', were likewise rejected.

A special personal regard for Pétain existed among the many bishops who had served in the First World War. They respected him as a soldier. Mgr. Liénart, cardinal-bishop of Lille, for example, had been decorated by him in 1917. The same esteem was not felt for Pétain's two main chief ministers. Towards Darlan, rather indifferent to religion, they felt lukewarm, particularly after his dismissal of Chevalier, the very Catholic minister of education, who had secured temporary privileges for Catholic schools and for a while had reintroduced religion into state schools. Towards Laval, who headed the government from July–December 1940 and again from April 1942 to the end of the Vichy regime, although grateful for new laws and subsidies that favoured the church, they felt no particular goodwill, especially after he had publicly wished for a German victory and acquiesced in so many German demands. Politically the episcopacy felt pushed into a corner. They could not accept *la dissidence* – the Gaullists in London and the Resistance – indeed they dubbed many of the maquis *terroristes*. Save for one prelate, Mgr. Dutoit of Arras, collaboration with the Germans was equally abhorrent to them; in any case they were aware of the fate that awaited Christianity in the event of a Nazi victory. It was the kind of church-state relationship they hoped to avoid. They therefore clung to the Marshal, always trusting that in the end, when the time was ripe, and a compromise peace emerged (they were sceptical of an out-and-out Allied victory), he would prove an acceptable intermediary to the Americans and thus prevent France from falling into the hands of the 'Bolsheviks'.

Meanwhile, the relationship showed substantial gains for Catholics. The bishops looked forward to the new era for both positive and negative reasons. They were hopeful – and they were not disappointed – that Catholic education would receive permanent aid and recognition. Pétain's rural policy was commended: the return to the land – because 'la terre ne ment pas' – represented the reinstatement of the Frenchman in his

[9] A.N. 2 AG 492, letter of Lavagne, head of Pétain's Private Office, to Louis Canet, Conseil d'État, Vichy, n.d. (October, 1941).

natural environment. The encouragement of family life and the pursuit of an active population policy also chimed with Catholic thinking. They accepted that a strong authoritarian government was needed. They condemned the Third Republic because it was associated with an aggressive secularism (*le laïcisme*, as opposed to *la laïcité*), which they held to be 'the great sin of France'.[10] It signified: a democracy that had become a 'demagogy', a party system that tore the country apart, electoral procedures that 'elected atheists'[11], the C.G.T that had promoted the class struggle and placed the Popular Front in power in 1936, 'the year of our internal defeat'.[12]

The doubts that slowly began to beset the man in the street, as well as the Catholic in the pew, arose from a succession of events. The two Statutes on the Jews, and their subsequent persecution, the Syrian war that saw de Gaulle emerge from the shadows, the German shootings of hostages, the curb on free speech and condemnation for so-called 'délits d'opinion', the deportation of French youth for forced labour in the Reich, the spider's web of collaboration with the Nazis from which increasing numbers of patriots could only free themselves by joining the Resistance: these phenomena made the average Frenchmen, Catholics included, revise their judgement.

Nevertheless, from July 1940 to April 1942 and even beyond, the hierarchy lived through a honeymoon period. Whilst the laws of 1901 and 1905 that had so disadvantaged the church were not repealed, they were progressively modified. Already in July 1940 – a symbolic act – the monks had been allowed to return to their monastery in the Dauphiné, the Grande Chartreuse, from which they had been expelled earlier in the century. In September the ban on teaching by members of religious orders had been lifted. The situation of chaplains in state schools was considerably improved in February 1941 and further modified in December 1942. By a law of November 1941 Catholic primary schools were to receive subsidies. In April 1942 the procedure for the authorization of religious orders was simplified. In December 1942 subsidies were also given to Catholic higher education. At the same time the powers of the diocesan associations that administered Church property were enlarged so as to allow them to receive gifts and legacies. The state was empowered to fund the physical upkeep of all churches. Such substantial concessions, which effectively reversed the

[10] C. Langlois, 'Le régime de Vichy et le clergé d'après les 'Semaines religieuses' des diocèses de la zone libre', *Revue française de science politique*, 4 (1972), p. 760, quoting, *Semaine religieuse*, Nîmes, 1940: 'Voilà le grand péché de la France'.

[11] *Ibid.*

[12] Bishop of Dax's Lenten letter, *Semaine religieuse*, Dax, 28 February 1941: 'l'année de notre défaite intérieure'.

tide of Republican discrimination against Catholics, were welcomed, but were held to be insufficient by the bishops, who, for example, wanted a comprehensive statute for their denominational schools.

The first two years of the Occupation were also marked by episcopal enthusiasm for the 'regeneration' of France, a campaign for the so-called *Révolution Nationale*. 'The Principles of the Community' was a document that set out Vichy's official aims; these accorded well with the aspirations of social Catholicism. The various Catholic movements before the war had all promoted an ethic related to work, the family and patriotism. The new youth organizations that Vichy set up owed much to the style, methods and ideas of the Catholic *Scouts de France*, as well as to the *Action Catholique de la Jeunesse Française* (A.C.J.F.) and its federated movements. The ideal that capital and labour must unite to rebuild France, as expressed in Vichy's labour settlement, the *Charte du Travail*, went back to such Catholic thinkers as de Mun, although bishops such as Cardinal Liénart had misgivings about such measures as the abolition of the C.F.T.C, the Catholic trade union. The episcopacy not only viewed with approval the initial participation of Catholics such as Baudouin, Alibert and Chevalier in the government, but also the appointment of Catholics as mayors and municipal councillors to replace elected Socialists and Communists. Catholics were also well to the fore in such institutions as the *Corporation Paysanne*, which organized rural workers, the *Secours National* (Garric) and the *Légion des Anciens Combattants* (Valentin), the monolithic ex-servicemen's organization that replaced the diversity of pre-war institutions. In the organization of youth, Catholics such as Lamirand, secretary-general for Youth, and General De La Porte du Theil, the head of the *Chantiers de la Jeunesse*, as well as countless regional youth delegates and subordinate workers were likewise prominent.

However, the bishops felt that they might have taken on or encouraged too political a role, and drew back. In April 1941, clarifying its attitude to the regime, the Assembly of Cardinals and Archbishops (A.C.A.) had defined its policy as 'loyalisme sans inféodation'. They did not want to be seen to be politically too closely identified with the regime. Thus in September 1941 the A.C.A ordered priests to refrain from active participation in the *Légion*.[13] The sombre events of 1942 – the deportation of the Jews, the departure of workers for Germany in the so-called *Relève*, the loss of Empire and

[13] G. Cholvy and Y.-M. Hilaire, *Histoire religieuse de la France contemporaine, 1930–1988* (3 vols., Toulouse, 1985–88), vol. 3, p. 83.

the sabotage of the fleet – cast a blight on the *Révolution Nationale*. A diehard such as Père Doncoeur, the chaplain of the Rover scouts and a very influential cleric at Vichy, complained: 'You know . . . that many Frenchmen think and say that the *Révolution Nationale* is a farce. I am among those Frenchmen who do not accept that serious matters should be made fun of'.[14] By this time his was a minority voice. Incidentally, and typical of the prevailing climate of moralism, Doncoeur mentioned this when writing on an ethical issue: to advocate that the *Loterie Nationale* should be abolished or privatized. The pro-German Abbé Catry wrote to Pétain asserting that the *Révolution Nationale* was dead, 'sabotaged by the Jews [*sic*] and other degenerates'.[15] Yet Mgr. Valerio Valeri, the papal nuncio, in a speech in November 1943, could still declare:' . . . the programme of the Holy Father . . . is close to that of the magnificent Head of the French State . . . Family, Work and Country'.[16] By then all hope of a cosy relationship between church and state had disappeared.

One aspiration of the episcopate had long been the conclusion of a concordat. Indeed, the *Union Sacrée* achieved in the First World War had led in 1918 to an unsuccessful bid for a new agreement. In the autumn of 1940, however, all such plans were premature and in November Pétain, on Laval's advice, dismissed them.[17] Nevertheless, one step was immediately taken: Bérard, who had been Minister of Education in the *Bloc National* government, and was a committed Catholic, was appointed ambassador to the Holy See and serious attempts were made to formulate a religious policy. The head of Pétain's private office later took over this responsibility, and worked in close liaison with Sauret, the head of ecclesiastical affairs in the Ministry of the Interior. The former also had oversight of affairs relating to Alsace-Lorraine, where the original Concordat of 1801 had, by a freak of history, remained in existence.

In some Vichy circles Franco's Spain was regarded as a potential model for the new French state. This was particularly the case in June 1941, when a concordat with Spain was close to completion. (In fact it was not formally signed until 1942, when Catholicism was formally recognized as the state

[14] A.N. 2 AG 75, letter of R.P. Paul Doncoeur to Dr. Ménétrel, Pétain's private secretary, Lyon 31 August 1942.

[15] A.N. 2 AG 487, letter of 12 October 1942.

[16] A.N. 2 AG 494, speech at an official reception at the Prefecture of Tarn, 20 November 1943.

[17] A.N. 2 AG 492, report of Bérard, ambassador to Holy See, to Laval, as Minister of Foreign Affairs, Vatican, 8 June 1942.

religion). Scrupulous of their Gallican rights, the French followed closely the new Spanish procedure for the selection of bishops. The papal nuncio, after consulting the government, would submit six names for a post to the Vatican, which would then choose three. From these three the Franco government would make the final appointment. The Spanish agreement provided a useful precedent. In a policy document dated August 1941, Pétain's Private Office set out its views.[18] Catholicism should become the most favoured religion, since it was the faith of the majority. Prudence should be the watchword since it would not do to upset public opinion – the abortive measures Chevalier had taken in January 1941 to reintroduce religious instruction into state schools provided a bad example, because they had aroused a storm of protest. Any negotiations with the Holy See should be on the principle of *do ut des* – no concessions should be made without reciprocity. At the time it was hoped that a concordat could be negotiated 'in the near future'.

By June 1942 such an expectation had faded. In the previous month the *Journal des Débats* (2 May 1942) reported that strong rumours of negotiations already in progress were completely without foundation. Bérard, the ambassador to the Vatican, however, continued to show a keen interest in the form that any concordat should take. He prepared a detailed comparative study of the fourteen concordats that had been concluded from the papacy of Benedict XV in 1928 to that of Pius XII in 1942, of which that between Franco and the Pope was the most recent.[19] He forwarded the document to Vichy but insisted that it had no immediate application. Rather was it a guide for those who might eventually negotiate such an agreement. He struck a note of Gallican caution: past concordats with France had paradoxically resulted in an increase of papal powers and prerogatives, placing certain tenets of public law in jeopardy. On the other hand, sticking to a secularist policy had merely increased Catholics' dependence on Rome in religious matters.

From his comparative study Bérard noted that over the past fourteen years no government had retained an absolute right to nominate bishops, a privilege that previously popes had granted more liberally, although the possible model for France would be Spain. In another document the ambassador spelt out what he surmised might be some of the Vatican's

[18] A.N. 2 AG, 'Note sur une politique religieuse de l'Etat français', 4 August 1941.
[19] A.N. 2 AG 543 CC142, Divers, 'Dépêche de M. Bérard', 8 June 1942.

conditions for an agreement:[20] subsidies for Catholic education on a permanent basis – the law put through by Carcopino only guaranteed them for the duration of the war; religious instruction on the timetable in the state school; with regard to marriage, canon law to take precedence over civil law; a preponderant say in the appointment of bishops, as previously mentioned; perhaps a state contribution to the salary of the clergy. Although in April 1942 laws regularizing the activities of the religious orders had already been passed, he thought one matter for negotiation would be the position of those religious orders and institutions expelled from France in the early years of the century and which had moved to Rome. There they were strictly supervised and removed from French control. The Superior-General of the Christian Brothers, for example, was even 'mis en résidence canoniquement surveillée'. Sometimes a foreigner had been appointed as their head: thus the vicar-general of the *Soeurs de St. Joseph de Cluny* was a Portuguese. One notes again a certain Gallican and nationalist approach to questions.

Bérard's conclusions were optimistic. If and when the question were reopened:

> Our representatives will be able to treat in the name of a refurbished state that has proved by its actions that it intends to attribute a fair share to spiritual values and religious sentiments and to Catholic influence in the task of renewal that it has undertaken.[21]

The North African invasion in November 1942, the hinge on which the war turned, finally put paid to any expectation of a concordat before the conclusion of peace. The bishops, who had always been lukewarm in their advocacy of an agreement, the Vatican authorities and the Germans (who had already torn up the agreement they had made with the Pope in 1933 and were busy dismantling in Alsace-Lorraine the nineteenth-century concordat that had had a continued existence in that province ever since the days when it had formed part of the Wilhelmine Empire) – all the interested parties in fact – were agreed that the time was not opportune.

In January 1943 Mgr. Suhard, the cardinal-archbishop of Paris, paid a visit to the Pope, which restimulated interest. However, Mgr. Courbe, secretary-general of *Action Catholique*, who accompanied Suhard, explained

[20] See n. 17.
[21] See n. 19.

that although the question of a concordat had been raised, it was agreed that its realization was along way off. [22] In February 1943 a new element intervened: Doriot's collaborationist *Parti Populaire Français* began to woo the clergy. It published a brochure, 'Vers une politique religieuse', which was sent out to a number of priests, advocating a concordat. [23] Dr Ménétrel, Pétain's private secretary, noted that the P.P.F propaganda had achieved little effect on the clerical rank and file, but such an agreement remained inappropriate at the present time, 'although it might improve [their] material conditions', because the state might contribute to their salaries. [24]

Nevertheless Pétain's staff continued to work out what should be the guidelines for the state in its dealings with the church. In a document dated 9 May 1943 the Private Office set these out. [25] Negotiations should always be on a diplomatic plane and conducted as between equals. The church, 'having eternity on its side', had a long memory both for favours granted and for acts committed against it. It could not be threatened, coerced or bought. It was always ready to sacrifice any debt of gratitude to a higher duty. It had a doctrine, even if the state had none. It tended to move the boundaries between the temporal and the spiritual according to the circumstances. It was ready to disown those who negotiated on its behalf at any time, if the situation justified it. This was especially true if subordinates dealt on behalf of their superiors. Having expounded precepts for a religious policy not unworthy of Machiavelli, the authors of the document concluded that so long as there was no concordat, actions based on expediency alone were possible. Somewhat ruefully, they added that 'democratic opinions' were as likely to be found within the church as elsewhere.

By July 1943 other collaborationist elements were concerned, in view of the independent stance then being taken by some prelates, to place the church more firmly under state authority, through the conclusion of a concordat. If this were impossible the church should simply be eliminated from public life because, as Drieu la Rochelle insisted in *Révolution Nationale* (10 July 1943), ultimately religion and politics did not mix. In *L'Oeuvre* (15 May 1943, 'L'Eglise et la Révolution') Déat, a secularist and collaborationist, declared that the church must decide where

22 A.N. 2 AG 492, 'Note' (Secret), 21 January 1943.
23 A.N. 2 AG 492, 'Note' (Secret) 10 February 1943.
24 A.N. 2 AG 75, Correspondence et documents de Ménétrel. 'Note' (Secret) 26 March 1943.
25 A.N. 2 AG 82, 'Règles à suivre en matière de politique religieuse', *Cabinet civil*, Vichy, 19 May 1943.

it stood and opt firmly for the new European order under Germany. There the matter of a concordat and a religious policy rested. Nearer than it had been for over a century, the possibility of a formal treaty with the Holy See has since been remote. The constitutions of the successor Republics have both proclaimed that France is a secular state. The Vichy regime therefore marks a phase when relations between church and state came closest to a formal accord.

Paradoxically, despite the enthusiasm shown for the new state, its validity became increasingly questioned as the war proceeded. There arose a violent dispute between the bishops and theologians. Yet for Catholics, as indeed for the vast majority of Frenchmen, the legitimacy of the Vichy regime in 1940 was beyond question. Looking back in 1945, François Mauriac clearly supported this view: 'A Catholic, and particularly a priest, and even more so a bishop, and above all a cardinal, would be ungracious if he did not consider to be legitimate a government to which an apostolic nuncio was accredited . . . For the Catholic hierarchy the presence of the nuncio clinched the argument'.[26] Traditionally the church does not query the authority of the civil power, whether *de facto* or *de jure*. Indeed it was unthinkable for the bishops to deny the authority of a government whose newly-appointed ambassador to the Vatican, Léon Bérard, had been warmly received in Rome, and which had been recognized by almost every major power, with the notable exception of Britain. The church proceeded cautiously in its approach to full recognition: when the Assembly of Cardinals and Archbishops met in Paris on 15 January 1941 they were careful to speak of the *pouvoir établi* rather than the *autorité légitime*, although some bishops showed themselves more ready than others to accord full status to the new regime.[27] As time passed a majority of their number preached absolute obedience to what they now termed the *pouvoir légitime*.[28] The very fact that Valerio Valeri, the papal nuncio, stood by Pétain to the end was a constant justification for them of the Marshal's legitimate claim to govern.[29] In January 1941 a typical pastoral letter by Mgr. Chollet, archbishop of Cambrai, had spelt out the situation as most Catholics then saw it:

[26] F. Mauriac, *Le baîllon dénoué* (Paris, 1945), p. 105, quoted in R. Bédarida, *Les armes de l'ésprit: Témoignage Chrétien, 1941–1944* (Paris, 1977), p. 16.

[27] A. Deroo, *L'épiscopat français dans la mêlée de son temps, 1930–1954* (Paris, 1955), p. 78.

[28] A. Latreille, *De Gaulle, la libération et l'église catholique* (Paris, 1978), p. 19.

[29] *Ibid.*, p. 44.

Marshal Pétain is the head of the French state. He became so in the most regular and most constitutional manner by a vote of the National Assembly. Marshal Pétain is our legitimate leader. We owe him our respect, our obedience and our prayers.[30]

The A.C.A, meeting on 24 July 1941, continued to speak of the *pouvoir établi*, but in enthusiastic terms: 'We want there to be pursued, without anyone being held in thrall, a sincere and utter loyalty to the established authority'.[31] If there were any qualification to this it was the belief that the civil authority was nevertheless dependent ultimately upon God.[32]

This last caveat became uppermost in the minds of a few Catholic theologians by the end of 1941. Already in 1931 Vialatoux, 'le philosophe des Semaines Sociales' (an organization that fostered a socially-oriented Catholicism), had stated that a Christian could not accept his own preservation from a state that bore its citizens away into slavery.[33] In 1941 the Abbé Lesaunier published, with the imprimatur of the archbishopric of Paris, a brochure entitled, *La conscience catholique en face du devoir civique actuel: lettre à un Français*.[34] In it he went farther than most Catholics were prepared to go. Not only did he insist on the need for obedience to Pétain, but he added, 'I submit myself without recrimination to the occupying authorities (the Germans)', for 'he who refuses to obey the legitimate authority refuses to obey God himself and deserves punishment'. As for de Gaulle, he also deserved punishment because he was 'a rebel who is opposing the very order that is the will of God'.[35] Amazed that none of the bishops reacted adversely to Lesaunier's ideas, another theologian, Père Fessard, who had been responsible for the challenge in the first number of the clandestine Catholic Resistance publication *Témoignage Chrétien* 'France, prends garde de perdre ton

[30] Quoted in Bédarida, *Les armes de l'esprit*, p. 15.

[31] A. Mallet, *Pierre Laval* (2 vols., Paris, 1955), vol. 1, p. 162. See also: Mgr. Guerry, *L'église catholique en France sous l'occupation* (Paris, 1947), p. 156, who coined the phrase, 'loyalisme sans inféodation'.

[32] A.N. 2 AG 492, 'Vues sur les questions actuelles' cites the Abbé Marc Lallier, on 16 June 1941, who stated that, although in 1939 a just war had been declared, loyalty to Vichy was required, because the regime was 'legitimate', albeit dependent upon God.

[33] X. de Montclos et al. (eds.), *Eglises et chrétiens dans la IIè guerre mondiale: région Rhône-Alpes. Actes du colloque de Grenoble* (Lyon, 1978), p. 34.

[34] P. Bolle and J. Godel (eds.), *Spiritualité, théologie et résistance. Actes du colloque de Biviers* (Grenoble, 1987). (Henceforth: *Colloque de Biviers*). For comments on the brochure cf. pp. 116 ff.

[35] *Ibid.*

âme', took up the cudgels. He approached Cardinal Suhard and was invited to write a report on the theological position as he saw it. This was ready by the end of summer 1942. Originally entitled, *La conscience catholique devant la défaite et la révolution*, the document acquired the dramatic title, *Le prince esclave*, and was to play a key role in theological thinking about this time. It was written with the help of a much older theologian, the Jesuit Père Lebreton, a professor at the Institut Catholique de Paris. Lebreton himself wrote a tract entitled *Consultation sur quelques cas de conscience posés aux catholiques de France par l'occupation allemande*. It is convenient to deal with this latter document first.

Within the Institut Catholique, (where Lebreton was also dean), there were at the time violent disagreements. The collaborationism of its rector, Cardinal Baudrillart, was notorious. The Abbé Lesaunier, the author of the original brochure that had stirred up controversy, sided with the rector. Lebreton, on the other hand, was supported by another Jesuit, Père de Montcheuil, also a theologian, who later met his death at the hands of the Gestapo. Lebreton set out clearly the position of France as he saw it. The state must be assisted, insofar as it seeks the common good. However, the occupying power was certainly not a state, since it had installed itself on territory that was French. With that power, therefore, there was no duty of alliance. Nor could there be any identification with its cause. Between France and Germany there was only an armistice and not peace. Thus France was not neutral. Since it was not, the *Légion des Volontaires Français* (L.V.F.), the mercenaries fighting for the Germans on the Russian front, the *Phalange Africaine*, the force raised to aid the Germans in North Africa, and any conscription of French labour to aid the war machine in Germany itself, were violations of international law. Not only was the illegality of collaboration proven, but also its immorality, because the war declared in 1939 was just and remained so.[36] Lebreton's document circulated in both the occupied and unoccupied zones, and was reissued in a more precise form as it applied to forced labour in Germany in the spring of 1943.[37]

As well as the documents by Lebreton and Fessard, there would appear to have been an even more radical document drawn up. Headed 'Consultation

[36] A.N. 2 AG 609, gives the text. It was discovered in a postal intercept dated 15 April 1943.

[37] H. de Lubac (ed.), *Correspondence G. Marcel and G. Fessard, 1934–1971* (Paris, 1985), p. 299, n. 2.

donnée par un groupe de juristes et théologiens: notes sur quelques observations techniques concernant de problème du gouvernement', [38] this stated that the France of Vichy, divided into three parts, – the two zones and the empire – did not constitute a state. No sovereign power was being exercised over the national community as a whole. Hence no legitimate government existed. Men such as de Brinon, the Vichy delegate in the occupied zone who functioned in Paris, and Laval (who since April 1942 had become once more head of government), no less than Abetz, the German 'ambassador' in the capital, were creatures of the Nazis. The regime itself was subordinate to the occupying forces. Resistance to them was the only response to any demand for collaboration. As for the Vichy government, it should only be obeyed insofar as obedience was required for it to deal with day-to-day business.

We return now to Fessard's memoir, *Le prince esclave*, which set out a much more detailed philosophical argument. Unfortunately there is no complete copy available of the original document and it has had to be reconstituted from various sources. The most reliable version is the reconstitution that Fessard himself made of it after the Liberation in the Jesuit periodical *Etudes*. [39] What follows below is an attempt to combine the latter with other texts so as to give the full flavour of his theological thinking at the time.

Fessard begins with the question of the legitimacy of Vichy. In 1940 there was no other possible government – de Gaulle was too weak to constitute one. Thus, 'speaking in the name of the Christian conscience, the Holy See and the Episcopate had recognized it'.

His theoretical argument proceeds from two pronouncements of Leo XII. On 16 February 1892 the then pope had stated: 'the common good, after God, is in a society the first and last law'. On 3 May 1892 he had also pronounced: 'the common good is the creative principle and the conservative element in human society; hence it follows that every true citizen must desire it and obtain it at any price'. For Fessard the corollary to this was: a government is legitimate if it ensures the common good. Externally, since the common good is the basis of any international

[38] A.N. 2 AG 609, gives the text. It is undated.

[39] Père Fessard, 'Journal de la conscience française', *Etudes* (January and February 1945). A.N. 2 AG 609 contains an abbreviated version of the *Prince esclave* given in a postal intercept made between August and September 1942. Another version, with a commentary, is given in *Colloque de Biviers*, pp. 118, 122–23, 124–29.

community, the declaration of war in 1939 may be viewed as an act to assist a third party attacked unjustly by an aggressor. But the common good also means, as regards internal matters, the ensuring of the existence and security of its citizens. In 1940 Vichy had undoubtedly accomplished this. Yet it also requires a government to remain the guardian of national values. This Vichy had not done, because after the defeat it had renounced a just cause and the mission of France in the world. Thus it became a 'slave prince' (*Prince esclave*) subject to the will of another. Not being free, it can therefore only require a limited obedience. The citizen must judge every order coming from the authorities on the yardstick of the common good, in order to decide whether it emanates from the government or from the enemy.

This judgement is a matter of conscience. The principles that govern the conscience are dual. 'Lex affirmativa semper obligat sed non pro semper; lex negativa semper obligat et pro semper.' In effect, if one should always do good and shun evil, when one should perform a good action depends on time and opportuneness; but evil actions are always forbidden. Likewise, 'Lex positiva non obligat cum nimio incommodo': a law prescribing an action need not be observed if a greater evil (than disobeying it) will result. It follows that 'the more the action he (the citizen) was ordered to perform had an immediate and direct relationship to the unjust ends of the enemy, the more resistance was justified for him'. Thus resistance to forced labour in Germany, for example, was admissible. The reverse of the medal was 'the more (the action) had a direct and immediate relationship to the national interest, the more obedience was necessary'.[40] Examples of the latter might be food rationing, charitable works connected with social assistance, measures to promote the family, or education, or better cooperation between employers and employed. Legitimacy may therefore be defined as what is in conformity with law, justice and morality. Writing with hindsight, Fessard declares that from 1942, after the total occupation of France, this legitimacy of the government diminished. In any case the distinction has to be drawn between *constitutional legality* and *legitimacy*.

A practical question that Fessard raised was: What should be the attitude of a Frenchman towards the war in Russia? Was it an anti-Bolshevist crusade, as the Nazis made it out to be? The appeal made to the French bourgeoisie was that it was a question of saving European civilization from atheistic Communism, of which Pius XI, the previous pope, had denounced the 'intrinsic perversion'. But, then, who began the dispute? Since the

---

[40] Fessard, *Etudes* (January 1945), p. 94.

answer to the last question was clear, it could be argued that the Soviet Union was exercizing the right of legitimate defence, and the ordinary citizen was defending his homeland and not atheistic Communism. Pius XII himself had hinted as much in his message to the Portuguese on New Year's Eve 1942, the twenty-fifth anniversary of the appearance of Fatima. In a prayer he had asked that 'God's Holy Church obtain peace and complete liberty; that the invading deluge of neo-paganism be halted'.[41] For Fessard this was a clear reference to Nazism.

Reverting to the question of forced labour in Germany, Fessard argued that it represented active collaboration with the enemy and therefore raised serious issues of conscience. Industry and young people were to be mobilized in fulfilment of a policy that had external ramifications. But, it could be argued, was Vichy, by requiring Frenchmen to work in Germany, doing anything more than would a state that mobilized its soldiers to fight a foreign war? However, for Fessard, there were enormous differences between the two situations. In the first case the workers were not serving the common good, whereas troops fighting the enemy on foreign soil were. The situation was compounded because, so long as France had signed only an armistice, Germany remained the enemy. For those called up to work in Germany 'the duty cannot lie in obedience, but in resistance'. If the workers cannot resist this form of conscription, their duty is to sabotage the work they are called upon to perform. 'In the face of the wishes of an unfair master he (the Frenchman) may nod his assent, but defends himself by resistance and patience.'

Fessard concluded that so long as the world was embroiled in the turmoil of war, 'the citizens of the conquered people can in all security of conscience pass from resignation to passive and active resistance, either within the country, or with the external Resistance, if their resolve is based on generous service to the national cause and the values of the international common good'.[42]

What was the impact of this closely reasoned document? The evidence would seem to be that it was not widely read or circulated, but was nevertheless influential. It would appear that Cardinal Suhard, to whom it

[41] This message was given also at a time when the Catholic world was asked to dedicate itself to the Sacred Heart of the Virgin Mary. The Germans sought in vain to halt the publication of the papal message in the form of tracts. Finally, on 25 March 1943, it was read in its entirety from French pulpits.

[42] *Colloque de Biviers*, p. 122–23.

was sent, may have been induced by it to make a fresh protest, in February 1943, against the deportation of Jews.[43] It was also discussed in meetings of branches of the J.O.C. in early 1943. A copy of the document eventually reached London and Raymond Aron published an article on it in *La France Libre* on 15 October, 1943.[44] At least for one bishop, Fessard's reasoned argument made no difference. On 21 November 1942 Mgr. Béguin, bishop of Auch, persisted in declaring that Catholics owed respect and obedience to 'legitimate authority'; and the occupying forces also had a right to respect and to correct behaviour.[45]

That the theological controversy was not over is evinced in a document produced about Christmas 1942 by 'a theologian', which is perhaps more open-ended than the *Prince esclave*. In a reference to the total occupation of France and the invasion of North Africa in November, the author declared that in spite of 'recent events' Catholics should continue to support the authorities. Their attitude to the Germans should be one of neither allowing themselves to be allied to them nor engulfed by them. So far this was the bishops' position. The war had been just in 1939. Was the war now being waged by the Germans just or unjust? The question was left open. Certainly a French declaration of war against its former allies would be unjust. On the other hand, if the war waged by the Germans was unjust the French must avoid all collaboration with them, if only because a 'spiritual vassaldom' – the phrase is reminiscent of Père Lebreton's document previously mentioned – that the Germans sought to impose not only endangered national independence but also 'our Christian faith'.[46]

Finally, the A.C.A pronounced upon the welter of theological arguments that were being put forward. In moderate terms it deplored the dissemination of clandestine statements whose 'conclusions are normally opposed to the authority and legitimacy of the regime.'[47] Some bishops went farther, attacking what they termed anonymous self-styled theologians and jurists who had neither a mandate nor exercised any responsibility. *Témoignage Chrétien*, which felt itself particularly under fire, responded by saying that the ordinaries of the priests involved were perfectly aware of their names.[48]

[43] *Ibid.*, p. 118.
[44] R. Aron, *De l'armistice à l'insurrection nationale* (Paris, 1945), pp. 320–21.
[45] *Semaine religieuse*, Auch, 21 November 1942.
[46] A.N. 2 AG 492, unsigned document, dated 'Christmas 1942', by 'a theologian'.
[47] *La Croix* 4 October 1943.
[48] Cf. n. 37 Joseph Barthélemy, *Mémoires: Vichy, 1941–1943* (Paris, 1989), p. 614 ff.

After the introduction of the S.T.O the legitimacy of the Vichy regime even became a matter for general public debate. Joseph-Barthélemy, as Minister of Justice, gave his legal opinion in an interview published in *Le Petit Parisien* (20 March 1943). As a good Catholic also, he quoted St. Thomas Aquinas who had decreed that obedience was due to the legitimate authority of a country, asserting that Vichy represented just such a duly constituted government. The minister claimed that his pronouncement sparked off a number of supporting declarations from Catholics and others. As a jurist Barthélemy argued that power springs from the will of the people, but when the people is unable to express that will then it springs from its elected representatives. Certainly the people could not be consulted in July 1940, because millions were either in German hands or under German occupation at the time. In his memoirs he alludes also to another theological declaration on legitimacy, this one circulating in July 1943, written by 'a priest who wishes to remain anonymous' ('un prêtre qui veut garder l'incognito'), which stated that Vichy was a mere de facto government; the young man called up for forced labour in Germany had thus the right to evade the draft and even to join the Resistance. [49]

The novelty of all such discussions on the theological, political and legal aspects of Vichy legitimacy is that, despite such official intervention, decisions on practical consequences were left to the individual Catholic. For the first time conscience was to be practically the sole arbiter. Criteria were set up for the individual to judge the rights and wrongs of his actions for himself. The individual Catholic, and not the ecclesiastical authorities, would determine for himself his relationship to the state. This potential disobedience to the church when it had pronounced upon the government of the day was in part because the bishops had ended up either by refusing to give a clear lead, or gave one that to many appeared hostile to real French interests. As the war continued the bishops indeed lapsed more and more into silence, with only isolated voices speaking out for or against specific actions.

The vicissitudes of war, rather than abstract principles, in the final analysis determined the nature of the relationships between church and state. The high hopes with which ecclesiastical leaders had greeted the advent of the new regime, including a state agreement with the Vatican, the support they gave to Vichy, the benefits that accrued from it (most of which in fact did not survive the Liberation), finally achieved nothing. On the other

[49] *Ibid.*

hand Catholic thinkers, who had usually toed the official line, encouraged a ground swell of revolt and of rejection of Vichy; the passage from passive obedience to active resistance. For the first time the lower clergy and the Catholic laity disregarded the exhortations of their superiors. A precedent had been created. Meanwhile any alliance of 'le sabre et le goupillon' had collapsed.

11

Catholics and Communism in Liberation France, 1944–47

Michael Kelly

Liberation France was an intellectual melting pot. The richness of the 'French Ideology' which was formed in these years around the existentialist and neo-Hegelian movements is well known. Less well appreciated are the changes which took place during the period in the intellectual framework of French Catholicism, whose representatives have for a long time played a leading role in the international development of their church. Many of these changes occurred in the process of conceptualizing relations with the strong French Communist movement which exercized such a powerful attraction on Catholics in the Liberation period. The forms which this process took in France subsequently provided patterns and frameworks which continue to shape political and philosophical dialogue between the two movements throughout the world. The purpose of this essay is to examine both the historical context and the conceptual forms in which French Catholics defined their relations with Communism between the summer of 1944 and the spring of 1947.

The brief intermission between the end of the Second World War and the beginning of the Cold War was a period of rapid historical change and deep uncertainty for Europe. Far reaching changes in frontiers, in alliances and in economic and political structures were the inescapable horizon of awareness at all levels of social intercourse, from casual private conversations to formal public declarations. They were echoed in equally far reaching shifts in the field of beliefs, values and representations, which became the context of intellectual activity at all levels from practical policy formation to philosophical reflection.

The period of the Liberation was therefore an exceptional moment, when a dizzying range of possible futures briefly opened up and when the crucial decisions were made which defined the contours of France and the postwar world as we now know it. Though the chill winds of Cold War began to blow after Churchill's Fulton speech in early 1946, it was only during 1947 that the doors finally closed on the once high hopes of a new and different future for France in the world. The liberation of Paris in late August 1944 marked the symbolic beginning of the postwar era for France. The country was still at war and French ports remained under German control until the surrender of May 1945, but in the intervening nine months many of the key features of postwar France were laid down, in outline if not in detail. The main political forces which drew their legitimacy from the Resistance, Communists, Socialists and Christian Democrats, established a working relationship which lasted as a basis for government until the middle of 1947, initially in tandem with the conservative nationalists led by General de Gaulle, then without them, and eventually against them.

The anchor of this tripartite arrangement was the relationship of cooperation which had evolved in the difficult conditions of secrecy, especially between Catholics and the Communists. The practical importance of working together against the occupying enemy had taken precedence over deep-seated reservations on both sides. The bonds forged in this experience, the recognition by each of the other's dedication, and the discovery of each other's ideals and aspirations contributed a new and original dimension to French political life.

Working relationships between Communists and Catholics were not invented in 1944, but the articulation of them in terms of a political partnership and an intellectual encounter was one of the genuine originalities of the Liberation period in Europe. The rapid postwar changes, following hard on the experience of war and occupation, accelerated fundamental reappraisals which were already in train among French Catholics. A large measure of reappraisal was conditioned by their perception of Communism, from which there seemed both much to learn and much to fear. There was no inevitability about the process. On the contrary, Catholics were familiar with Pius XI's declaration of

March 1937 against the 'Satanic scourge' of atheistic Communism, [1] and the theme was a commonplace of Catholic discourse. Yet for a time many of the obstacles which might have prevented the close relationship from surviving the German defeat were set in abeyance by the ideological conditions of Liberation. The massive involvement of Communists in the Resistance had to be acknowledged and, temporarily at least, it earned them readmission into the nation in the eyes of many former opponents. The deep complicity of the Catholic hierarchy in the collaborationist policies of the Vichy regime muted the most conservative voices for the time being. Catholics who could lay claim to any sort of Resistance credentials were propelled into prominence, even though they were for the most part politically of the Left.

At the level of political commitment, it is clear that a significant number of Catholics took the almost unprecedented step of joining the Communist party. It was not uncommon for class-conscious Catholic workers to take out a party card as a logical concomitant of their trade union card. It was especially widespread among young Catholic workers of the *Jeunesse Ouvrière Chrétienne* (J.O.C). This branch of the Catholic Action movement, founded in 1927, had encouraged young workers to take their faith actively into their working life. There they found themselves drawn into practical activity on behalf of their fellows, often struggling shoulder to shoulder with Communist militants. Their chaplains, like the Abbé Joseph Folliet, recognized the sincerity and commitment of Communists, but tried, not always successfully, to convince their own members that the notion of class struggle was a doctrinal error. [2] A comparable development, though more limited in scope, was taking place among the lower clergy. The wartime call to missionary work among the proletariat, [3] and the apparent vacuum left by the proscribed Communist leadership, had led to a growing number of worker priests, particularly in the working-class districts in and around Paris. These priests, who became full-time employees in factories and elsewhere, frequently found themselves taking the same path as their

---

[1] Pius XI, *Divini Redemptoris*, encyclical of 19 March 1937, reproduced in *Seven Great Encyclicals* (New York, 1963), pp. 177–206.

[2] See Abbé Joseph Folliet, 'Comment je les ai vus', *Temoignage Chrétien*, 11 November 1944, p. 1; 18 November 1944, p. 2. Folliet also recounts his experience in prison with Italian communists.

[3] Much of the impetus came from the report of two Parisian priests, H. Godin and Y. Daniel, *La France, pays de mission?* (Paris, 1943), which was much commended and reprinted after the war.

comrades. It was a logical step in their acceptance of the working class condition that they should join a trade union and then, because of their education, accept positions of responsibility in it. The next step was often to accept the class analysis and political leadership of the Communist party, which some of them even joined.

More surprising, the *Parti Communiste Français* (P.C.F) was making definite headway among middle-class Catholics, and especially among the young intelligentsia. The poet Loÿs Masson was a highly public example, combining a robust and unorthodox Catholic faith with an equally energetic and unconventional Communist fervour. In early 1946 the Catholic review *Esprit* published an extensive enquiry on young intellectuals in Paris and whether and why they were intending to join the Communist party.[4] The choice of questions, respondents and responses was evidently designed to harden the reservations of those who were tempted but wavering. Nonetheless it revealed that roughly a quarter of the sixty twenty-to-thirty-year-olds asked had already joined, with as many again seriously considering it. The strong and cohesive P.C.F group in the *Ecole Normale Supérieure*, France's prestigious training ground for its intellectual élite, maintained close links with the Catholic group.[5] Two of the better known intellectuals of this generation to move from the Catholic student movement to the Communist party were Maurice Caveing, who later played a leading role in Catholic-Communist dialogue, and Louis Althusser, whose theory of ideology became a major element in Marxist analyses of religion.

An English observer, Robert Speaight, felt that the appeal of Communism should be attributed to the pervasive spirit of defeatism in France and the lack of a credible alternative.[6] At least there was no doubt that attraction was strong, and leading clerics expressed their concern publicly about what they variously called the temptation,[7] or the seduction,[8] of Communism.

Among both workers and intellectuals the traffic was all one-way. Though many Catholics joined the party, there is no evidence that Communists felt drawn to Catholicism. For its part, the P.C.F. emphasized

[4] 'Ceux qui en étaient, ceux qui n'en étaient pas: enquête sur le communisme et les jeunes', *Esprit* (February 1946), 191–260.

[5] See J.-F. Sirinelli, 'Les normaliens de la rue d'Ulm après 1945: une génération communiste?', *Revue d'histoire moderne et contemporaine*, 33 (1986), 569–88.

[6] R. Speaight, 'Letter from Paris', *Time and Tide* 27 April 1946, 389–90.

[7] See J. Daniélou, 'Tentation du communisme', *Etudes* (April 1946), 116–17.

[8] See E. Rideau, *Séduction communiste et réflexion chrétienne* (Paris, 1947).

its commitment to political unity with Catholics in the context of the C.N.R. charter, jointly adopted by the Resistance movements. In a widely publicized interview in the Catholic paper *Temps Présent* Maurice Thorez, secretary of the party and a government minister, roundly declared:

> We are in favour of freedom of conscience. That is not new. As for myself, like Engels, I have always thought that declaring war on religion was stupid.[9]

Cooperation with Catholics on practical and political issues raised few problems, provided that doctrinal matters were not invoked. And though there were still strong currents of anticlerical feeling inherited from decades of mutual hostility, Communists were for the most part content enough to leave religion as a matter of private conscience. From their point of view, it need not intrude into the public arena.

For the church and for leading Catholics, on the other hand, cooperation with Communism posed serious problems. There was wide agreement among them that the question dominated the political and intellectual scene. Speaking for the Catholic Left, Jean Lacroix declared in December 1944 that:

> The political problem for France, and even for the world, is governed by the attitude of the Communists and by attitudes towards the Communists.[10]

While at the other end of the political spectrum, Jesuit Father Gaston Fessard was fulminating a few months later that:

> Today, one year after the Liberation, we have to point out the new peril which, under the cover of the Resistance, threatens France, it is *Communism*.[11]

---

[9] M.P. Hamelot, 'M. Maurice Thorez nous précise la position du parti communiste', *Temps Présent* (2 February 1945), p. 1; reprinted in M. Thorez, *Oeuvres choisies* (Paris, 1966), vol. 2, pp. 302–7, under the title 'Union française et démocratique'.

[10] J. Lacroix, 'Dépassement du communisme', *Esprit* (December 1944), 56–64.

[11] G. Fessard, *France, prends garde de perdre ta liberté* (Paris, 1945), p. 1. This was published in October 1945 by *Editions du témoignage chrétien*; the title is a reference to Fessard's well-known Resistance pamphlet, *France prends garde de perdre ton âme*, which appeared in the clandestine *Témoignage Chrétien* series.

Perhaps the most surprising point is that the problem of Communism should be seen as somehow new. Certainly both Lacroix and Fessard were repeating positions they had amply elaborated before the war. What *was* new was the urgency with which the problem was posed in the postwar political climate of France.

The prewar anathema placed on communism in Pius XI's encyclical *Divini redemptoris* though technically still in force, was in practice put in abeyance. Pope Pius XII, though more conservative than most of his predecessors, was constrained to some discretion by questions over his own wartime role, by the political situation in postwar Italy, where communists were also in government, and by delicate diplomatic negotiations between the Vatican and the Soviet Union. The French Catholic hierarchy was similarly constrained to discretion, notwithstanding the careful defence of its wartime record which its secretary, Mgr. Emile Guerry, published in 1947.[12]

Hence relations with Communists tended to be worked out on an ad hoc basis at local level, revolving around whether or not a priest like the Carmelite provincial, Père Philippe, could act as representative of the Communist-led *Front National* movement,[13] or whether the bishop of Montauban was right to refuse to let young Communists use a parish hall for meetings.[14] The sense of exploring uncharted territory was widespread, especially during the heady months when it seemed possible that some form of organic unity might be achieved, bonding together the three currents which had emerged from the Resistance. Jean Lacroix stated the problem from the perspective of the Catholic Left:

> With the communists – we have never hidden the fact – the risks are great; without them, it is the vacuum or else the reaction of economic interests, however they are disguised, and the return to interparty wrangling.[15]

Lacroix and the *Esprit* team eagerly grasped the opportunity to break new, albeit dangerous, ground. Others, like the *Témoignage Chrétien* group,

---

[12] Mgr. E. Guerry, *Léglise catholique en France sous l'occupation* (Paris, 1947).

[13] See the short pamphlet by le Père Phillipe, *Les catholiques et le front national* (Paris, n.d., probably late 1944). The F.N. was a Left-wing Resistance-based movement, not to be confused with later organizations bearing the same name.

[14] See P. Théas (bishop of Montauban), 'Christianisme et communisme', *Temps Présent* (November 1944), p. 8.

[15] J. Lacroix, 'L'esprit du mois', *Esprit* (February 1945), pp. 440–43, 443.

were prepared to travel some way with them, though there were plenty of Catholics who, privately at least, fell back on well-established hostilities. In the event, the interparty wrangling reasserted itself, expressed in the tripartite coalition government. However, the experience of tripartism also provided a framework, albeit a more clearly structured one, in which new relationships were explored and new conceptions of Catholic intervention in the world were developed. Although many, but by no means all, Catholics subsequently seemed content to embrace the reassuring polarities of Cold War politics, this experience of exploration provided significant conclusions which were taken up at other times and in other places.

The political manoeuverings of the postwar period have been extensively studied. Less well-known are the intellectual debates which invariably accompany reflexion on politics in France, and which are commonly pared away by Anglo-Saxon commentators as the inessential wrappings for a more tangible essence, such as the pursuit of power. Though it would be a mistake to counterpose an inflated view of the role of ideological factors to this undue neglect, it is clear that issues of ideas, beliefs and values play a major role in the day-to-day conduct of postwar French politics, especially where Catholicism and Communism are concerned. It is also important to remember that issues in the battle of ideas have a more readily transferable significance in time and place than most of the particular events they accompany. It is worth spending some time examining the work of Catholic intellectuals who attempted to theorize their relationship with Marxism.

Jean Jaurès, who led the unified Socialist party in France before the First World War, was noted for his belief that 'la pratique unit, la théorie divise'. He concluded that he should eschew theory and built a broad practical unity among French Socialists. The price he paid was to condemn his movement to conceptual poverty for many years. Taking Jaurès' presupposition and reversing his conclusions, those Catholics in post-Liberation France who most feared the unity of the Left and Centre were quick to focus on doctrinal questions which might serve as wedges between Catholics and Communists. The price *they* paid was to initiate far-reaching reappraisals of Catholic doctrine in the light of Marxism, which strengthened the church's politically progressive wing in the years to come.

The objections levelled against Communism and its theoretical expression in Marxism shifted dramatically in emphasis after the war. In the prewar period, Pius XI had anathematized its determination to curtail the rights of private property and overthrow the Christian social order. Yet the 'Christian social order' could not be mentioned without evoking the ambition for a confessional state embodied in the Vichy regime. And the rights of private property had emerged from the war under a moral and political cloud. On both these counts the Communist position was demonstrably exercizing a powerful attraction on Catholic workers and intellectuals. Hence, in the postwar period, theologians who attacked Marxism did so rather on more ostensibly philosophical issues of doctrine, and in particular on the dangers of atheism inherent in it. Conversely the Catholic intellectuals who had most sympathy with Marxism were led to explore the significance of Marxist social and political theory, in terms of a concept of man from which they could learn. Taken together, atheism and humanism became the two principal grounds on which Catholics defined their relations with Communism.

I have shown elsewhere the way in which atheism can be seen as having acted as a kind of ideological bodyguard to Marxist theory.[16] In comparable fashion, the denunciation of atheism served as a doctrinal starch for Catholic traditionalists, who saw heresy-hunting as the best defence of orthodoxy. Communist atheism was therefore an obvious target for criticism from more conservative Catholic quarters, such as those represented by the Jesuit theologians and their house journal, *Etudes*.

One of the most influential accounts was given by the Jesuit pastoral theologian, Henri de Lubac. His much-reprinted study, *Le drame de l'humanisme athée* (Paris, 1944), examined Feuerbachian, Nietzschean and positivistic forms of atheistic humanism. Written during the Occupation, when Marxism was proscribed and strenuously suppressed, it concentrated most heavily on the legacy of Nietzsche and Comte, considering Marx as essentially a disciple of Feuerbach.[17] When it finally reached the bookshops in the early weeks after the Liberation, this minor theme became its major point of relevance, with all the distortions of perspective that implied.[18]

Lubac's argument was simple: Feuerbach's central position was that the supreme qualities attributed generally to God were nothing other than an illusory and alienated projection of human qualities. This notion struck educated Europe with the force of a revelation in the 1840s and Marx took it as the basis for his own work, completing Feuerbach's philosophical positions with his own economic analysis. Taking up a well-worn pun on Feuerbach's name, he concluded that, 'au seuil du paradis marxiste, il y a

[16] M. Kelly, 'Marxism and Faith', M. Cornick (ed.), *Beliefs and Identity in Modern France* (Loughborough, 1990), 179–193.

[17] Most of the discussion of Marx is confined to the first chapter, entitled 'Feuerbach et Nietzsche'.

[18] See the extensive review by J. Lacroix in *Esprit* (April 1945), pp. 732–34.

le "purgatoire" de Feuerbach'.[19] The import of this argument is summed up by a comment quoted from fellow-Catholic Marcel Moré:

> Marxism, springing form Feuerbach's religious criticism, cannot by virtue of its origins be other than antireligious. It is on this point of transition that any intelligent criticism of Marxist atheism must therefore concentrate.[20]

The view that Marxism is dependent on and inseparable from the critique of religion, and is therefore necessarily antireligious, was perhaps the strongest polemical position for the church to adopt in resisting the advance of Communism. The basic assumption that the most important feature of a body of thought is its attitude to God, was one which could be expected to appeal to Catholics. The further assumption that atheism necessarily means hostility to religion in any or all of its forms was quite unwarranted. The example, at the other end of the political spectrum, of Charles Maurras, atheist leader of the mainly Catholic *Action Française* movement, might have given pause for thought. It was not surprising that de Lubac should base his analysis almost entirely on Marx's writings of 1843–44, which address the philosophical issues relevant to religious doctrine. Yet it is perhaps surprising that he saw no difficulty in subsuming the entire Marxism position into these early works, despite the debates which had taken place after their first publication in French in the late 1920s and early 1930s.[21]

De Lubac's approach was initially supported by fellow Jesuit Jean Daniélou, who later became a cardinal and played a leading role in the Second Vatican Council.[22] Early in 1945 Daniélou was emphasizing

[19] H. de Lubac, *Le drame de l'humanisme athée*, 4th edition (Paris, 1950, 4th ed.), p. 39. In German Feuerbach means 'brook of fire', an image associated with the traditional Catholic notion of Purgatory.

[20] Lubac, *Le drame*, p. 39, quoting from an article by M. Moré, 'Les années d'apprentissage de Karl Marx', *Esprit* (April 1935), 25–26.

[21] The Moré article cited was one of a series published in *Esprit* in 1935–36, discussing Auguste Cornu's doctoral thesis on the early Marx, *Les années d'apprentissage de Karl Marx* (Paris, 1934). The question had also been extensively aired by Henri Lefebvre in several publications of the same period, including his very well-known text *Le matérialisme dialectique* (Paris, 1939).

[22] See his warm review of Lubac's book in *Etudes* (May 1945), pp. 275–76, and the vigorous endorsement of it in his article 'Humanisme athée?', *Témoignage Chrétien* 27 April 1945, pp. 1–2.

the primacy of doctrine and warning that: 'It is precisely the essence of Marxism to set truth in parentheses and to make temporal efficacity into the only reality.'[23] It was true that Communists were setting practical cooperation above doctrinal discussion in their relations with Catholics, though hardly accurate to tax them with neglect of truth in the sense of developing Marxist theory. But then Daniélou's purpose was primarily to stem the tide of Catholics who were impressed by the Communists' commitment to practical action, and drawn to examine the ideas they professed. On closer examination, however, he discerned several different currents of Marxism. In an important review of contemporary intellectual life, published the following autumn, he suggested that writers like Marcel Prenant, Georges Friedmann and Henri Lefebvre might be studied with profit:

> Beside a Communism which is often no more than a political Machiavellianism at the service of a party, we find here in contrast a genuine attempt to deepen Marxist thought: it would be desirable for Christians to participate in this attempt and to demonstrate how the Marxist dialectic of nature and history is independent of the vulgar atheism which Marx inherited from his own day, and how on the contrary it can be naturally extended, as Father Fessard has shown, into a religious dialectic like the one whose principles can be found in Saint Paul.[24]

The shift of emphasis is considerable, from a rejection of Marxism on grounds of atheism to an assimilation of Marxism purged of its atheism, though the hostility to Communism remains constant. Daniélou's new position brought him closer to the Left Catholics, and enabled him subsequently to act as a bridge between them and more conservative tendencies.

Further to the Left, atheism was perceived more as a challenge than a threat. For André Mandouze, a leading *progressiste*, atheism was an inconvenience which got in the way of Christian cooperation with Communists and only helped the *bien-pensants de tout poil*.[25] While he did not object to atheism as a methodological stance in analysis, he found it quite unhelpful as a fundamental dogma, since it made Catholics jumpy and tended to polarize attitudes along the old lines of 'voilà les troupes de

---

[23] Jean Daniélou, 'Tentation du communisme', *Etudes* (April 1946), pp. 116–17.

[24] J. Daniélou, 'La vie intellectuelle en France: communisme, existentialisme, christianisme', *Etudes* (September 1945), pp. 241–54.

[25] André Mandouze, 'Chrétiens et communistes: le jeu de cache-cache', *Temps Présent* 21 December 1945, pp. 1,6.

choc des trusts lancées contre les légions de l'Antéchrist'.

Among the left-wing Catholics at *Esprit*, atheism was regarded as part of the crisis of European civilization, of which Brice Parain wrote, 'elle est essentiellement la crise d'une civilisation qui a rejeté Dieu de sa pensée.'[26] The atheism professed in principle by Communists and others was seen primarily as the reflection or symptom of a godless and self-seeking social system build on the principle of greed: that of capitalism. The Communists, in working against capitalism were therefore helping to destroy the worldly basis of their own atheism. *Témoignage Chrétien* echoed the same sentiment that, in the words of Alexandre Marc, 'le capitalisme est une forme du matérialisme' and 'le capitalisme, voilà l'ennemi'.[27] Aragon's wartime poem 'La rose et le réséda' therefore caught the mood of the Catholic Left in celebrating the common purpose of 'Celui qui croyait au ciel, celui qui n'y croyait pas'.[28]

The Catholic pastoral tradition has several possible approaches for dealing with atheism, of which anathematizing is only one and not necessarily the most prevalent. The approach which prevailed in France of the mid-1940s was a more conciliatory one, which sought to understand and if possible win over the atheists. Such a view was encouraged by the sharp realization that, as Godin and Daniel pointed out, France was virtually a mission field, with the mass of its working class living entirely outside the Christian fold.[29] The lack of atheistic militancy among the Communists was a further factor since, under the leadership of Thorez, they were not for their part keen to make a bone of contention out of a matter of private conscience. Consequently, if the question of atheism was an easy target for right-wing Catholic polemics, it was not necessarily effective in setting obstacles in the way of cooperation with communism. It was certainly not an issue on which Catholics could hope to make common cause with non-Catholic conservative groups.

More crucial in the battle for the minds in liberated France was the issue of humanism. I have argued elsewhere that humanism, the dominant ideological tendency of the immediate postwar period in France, was developed as

[26] B. Parain, 'De la crise européenne et de la nécessité actuelle du communisme', *Esprit* (August 1945), p. 367.

[27] A. Marc, 'La révolution en marche: le capitalisme, voilà l'ennemi', *Témoignage Chrétien* 24 August 1945, p. 4.

[28] See A. Mandouze, 'Celui qui croyait au ciel, celui qui n'y croyait pas', *Témoignage Chrétien* 28 September 1945, pp. 1, 4; B. Voyenne, 'Les communistes et nous', *Témoignage Chrétien* 14 September 1945, p. 1.

[29] Godin and Daniel, *La France, pays de mission?*

a framework within which to reconstruct the shattered political unity of the French nation.[30] As a result the language of humanism became the discourse within which the struggle for control of France's postwar destiny was conducted. Much of the Catholic discussion of Communism was couched in terms of whether it was authentically humanist and had an acceptable conception of man.

Unlike the simple issue of atheism, there was a prior question to be resolved: what was an acceptable Catholic conception of man? In particular, the church had traditionally denounced humanism as an error; it was only in the 1930s that avant-garde Catholic intellectuals had begun to rehabilitate the notion of Christian humanism as against the more traditional emphasis on spiritualism. The most successful was Emmanuel Mounier's Personalism. Elaborated in the mid-1930s as means of combining spiritual imperatives with a humanistic philosophy and a realistic purchase on political development, it rapidly became the basis for modern Catholic pastoral philosophy, in which the *human person* has replaced the *soul* as the main object of concern. Such developments were at first fiercely resisted by conservative circles; and Mounier's *Esprit* was more than once in danger of denunciation from Rome. Yet in liberated France Mounier's views represented a degree of consensus among Catholic thinkers, even when they did not share his Leftist politics.

The Jesuits at *Etudes* had to struggle to adapt. In May 1946 Xavier Tilliette was denouncing Loÿs Masson for his obsession with Man, 'car c'est bien le mythe marxiste de "l'homme nouveau" qui marche derrière ses phrases pathétiques'.[31] His position was consistent with that of Henri de Lubac's attack on atheistic humanism, already quoted, which had treated atheism and humanism as largely synomymous. However, de Lubac's own view was shifting and a year later he began a major study of the issue by admitting: 'It is a good question whether there is such a thing as Christian humanism. More than one person disagrees, for reasons which are not without substance.'[32] He outlined his view of the dual origin of man in God and nature, and argued that the 'new man' would be a product of divine Grace, but stopped short of subscribing to a Christian humanism. However serious the reservations might be, they were outweighed by the church's need to

[30] M. Kelly, 'Humanism and National Unity: The Ideological Reconstruction of France', in N. Hewitt, (ed.), *The Culture of Reconstruction* (London, 1989), pp. 103–19.

[31] X. Tilliette, 'Loÿs Massson et nous', *Etudes* (May 1946), pp. 237–8.

[32] H. de Lubac, 'L'idée chrétienne de l'homme et la recherche d'un homme nouveau', *Etudes* (October 1947), 'p. 1; a second part followed, (November 1947), pp. 145–69.

restore confidence in what *Etudes*' editor Louis Beirnaert called 'son aptitude à penser et à promouvoir l'ordre humain.'[33] The church's proven record was not sufficiently secure to compel confidence that human affairs would benefit from an aggressively spiritualist message. The Thomists weighed in to similar effect with their notion of *une politique humaniste*, elaborated by Jacques Maritain during his wartime exile in New York, and propagated by their journal, *La revue thomiste*.[34] Since the Christian Democrats of the *Mouvement Républicain Populaire* (M.R.P.) had adopted Maritain and Mounier as somewhat reluctant *directeurs de conscience*, the effect of their intervention was a massive political endorsement of humanism. The official seal on the new line was set by Cardinal Suhard, archbishop of Paris, in a pastoral letter in the spring of 1947, which spoke of 'un humanisme mondial' and argued that 'l'humanisme nouveau doit être un humanisme de la croix.'[35]

The different varieties of Catholic humanism each had a slightly different attitude to the Communist, or Marxist, conception of man. The more conservative found it hard to argue that Marxism was not genuinely humanistic, when their real criticism was that it was too humanistic. De Lubac was caught in this dilemma and responded by developing the notion that man was part natural, part divine in origin and criticized the communists for rejecting the spiritual part. In so doing he took up a point from fellow Jesuit Teilhard de Chardin, who in an earlier article had argued that:

> The true name of Communism should be 'earthism'. A real seduction emanates from this enthusiasm for the resources and future of the earth . . . Communism manages to virtually eliminate the human person and to make man into a termite.[36]

[33] L. Beirnaert, 'Fidélité à l'église, fidélité à l'homme', *Etudes* (October 1946), p. 3.

[34] See L. Gardet, 'Principes d'une politique humaniste', *La revue thomiste* (September-December 1946), pp. 613–23. The works by Maritain included notably *Les droits de l'homme et la loi naturelle* (1943), *Christianisme et démocratie* (1943) and *Principes d'une politique humaniste* (1944), all published by the Maison française de New York and republished in Paris by Hartmann in 1945.

[35] See L. Beirnaert, 'Essor ou déclin de l'église: une lettre pastorale de S. Em. le Cardinal Suhard', *Etudes* (April 1947), pp. 105–11.

[36] P. Teilhard de Chardin, 'La crise présente: réflexions d'un naturaliste', *Etudes* (October 1937), 145–65; the article is referred to in H. de Lubac, 'L'idée chrétienne de l'homme . . .', p. 20.

Teilhard's idea of Communist man as a soulless termite became a commonplace of polemic, even though Teilhard's vitalist alternative was also unacceptable to the church, and he himself forbidden to contribute further to the discussion.

In one sense the underlying criticism was still that Communism was atheistic, but more broadly de Lubac articulated the shared Catholic view that what Communist conceptions of man lacked was a dimension of transcendence. To the extent that it could be couched in such broad terms, it was evidently a criticism they shared with existentialists and with agnostic Socialists like André Ulmann, a regular contributor to *Esprit* who argued that 'pour s'accomplir, l'humanisme ne peut être qu'une passion'.[37]

The precise contours of the transcendence needed to transform Marxism into a true humanism were a matter of some disagreement. The maximalist position was stated by Louis Beirnaert: 'En dehors de l'eglise, il n'est pas de fidélité parfaite à l'homme',[38] no salvation outside the church. Jean Daniélou, who had fewer reservations about espousing humanism, took up de Lubac's point to argue that: 'Atheistic humanism destroys itself. There is no true humanism which is not founded in something beyond man.'[39] This interpretation was apparently much wider than Beirnaert's, though the overtones of the something beyond, *un au-delà de l'homme*, strongly suggested that not all forms of transcendence would meet his conditions. It unambiguously excluded Marx's materialist humanism as fallacious.

On the left of the Catholic spectrum, Jean Lacroix argued for a Socialist humanism which was more broadly defined as 'un souci d'universalisme et de spiritualisme à la fois', in which the humanist element was seen as participation in a common national culture.[40] In this perspective, although there was the echo of Léon Blum's criticism of the P.C.F as 'un parti nationaliste étranger', much repeated in Jesuit circles, there was also recognition for the party's efforts to bring together culture and the people, and there was scope for individual Communists and especially the less dogmatic intellectuals among them to be accepted within the humanist family. Lacroix was supported by Mounier in seeing

[37] A. Ulmann, *L'humanisme de XXe siècle* (Paris, 1946), p. 33. The comment occurs in the preliminary essay which introduces an anthology of texts by a variety of European writers since the eighteenth century.

[38] Beirnaert, 'Fidélité à l'eglise, fidélité à l'homme', p. 14.

[39] J. Daniélou, 'Henri de Lubac, "Le drame de l'humanisme athée"', *Etudes* (May 1945), pp. 275–76.

[40] J. Lacroix, *Socialisme?* (Paris, 1945).

the possibility of a Communist branch of Personalism to add to the plurality of other personalisms:

> You do not become a Personalist by abandoning your former loyalties or the practical points of view you have chosen about how to solve practical problems. You can be a Christian and a Personalist, a Socialist and a Personalist, and why not a Communist and a Personalist, if you are a Communist in a way which does not contradict the fundamental values set out here. [41]

Naturally, Mounier's inclusion of Communists was suitably hedged around with safeguards, especially on the matter of fundamental values, but it held the door open for dialogue and above all for the recognition of authentic human values embodied in individual Communists. On this last point there was general agreement even from the bishop of Montauban, who declared, 'J'aime les communistes', [42] and from *Etudes*, where Jean Liéven acknowledged in them 'une capacité de dévouement, un sens de la misère, une volonté de libération humaine, qui font notre admiration'. [43]

Once a minimum of common humanist ground was established between Catholics and Communists it became possible for Catholics to assimilate many aspects of Marxist thought and Communist practice which would otherwise have been a closed book. In principle the process could work in both directions, but it was not until the late 1950s that Communist intellectuals began to declare openly that they had anything to learn from Catholics on this count. [44] Perhaps the most complete statement of the lessons of Communist humanism for a Catholic at this period was given by Jean Lacroix. His essay, 'L'homme marxiste', [45] identified a number of key insights contained in the Marxist conception of man. Above all, these were the inseparability of theory and practice, expressed in the notion of praxis; the Revolutionary commitment to active struggle in history; and the Promethean primacy given to productive work, with the awareness

---

[41] E. Mounier, *Qu'est-ce que le personnalisme?* (Paris, 1947); reprinted in *Oeuvres de Mounier* (Paris, 1962), pp. 177–245, quote p. 177. It is interesting to note that the reference to Communism here was deleted from the translation into English.

[42] P. Théas, 'Christianisme et communisme', *Temps présent* 10 November 1944, p. 8.

[43] Jean Liéven, 'Le communisme, a-t-il changé?', *Etudes* (September 1945), p. 190.

[44] See the work of R. Garaudy, and particularly *Les perspectives de l'homme* (Paris, 1959).

[45] J. Lacroix, *Marxisme, existentialisme, personnalisme; présence de l'éternité dans le temps* (Paris, 1949), pp. 5–48.

of collective values which it entails. Lacroix accepted that this conception contained a dialectic of transcendence, though no external absolute towards which it might be directed. The major criticism he offered was therefore that Marxist humanism offered no opening on to a notion of eternity, without which it was always in danger of falling short of its own basic intentions. The logic of his position was to propose an expansion of the Marxist perspective with the *supplément d'âme* which never failed to irritate Communists, even though it rarely posed a serious threat.

Whereas in Catholic responses to Communism the issue of atheism was primarily a focus for division, to the point of sectarianism, the question of humanism was a focus for unification, to the point of integration. The anti-Communist Catholic Right emphasised the former, while the Communist sympathizers on the Catholic Left emphasized the latter. Yet within Catholic circles themselves, the process was the reverse. The question of atheism united, since all agreed that it was fundamentally unacceptable, even though they might differ in what to do about it. On the contrary, the question of humanism divided, since there was little agreement as to what it might entail, or indeed whether it was ultimately acceptable at all.

In historical practice, it was humanism that became the dominant form of thought in postwar France. Although atheism became a point of division within it, the wide embrace of humanist discourse ensured that Catholics remained in a common humanist frame with Communists. Whatever the political vicissitudes, the circulation of ideas was sustained, albeit mostly on a one-way circuit for the next decade. This contact survived the end of tripartism, the onset of the Cold War and even the Vatican decree of 14 July 1949, which prohibited Catholics from belonging to Communist parties and from most forms of cooperation with them. When the thaw broke out in the early sixties in France it was the enduring basis of many points of contact between the 'deux grandes maisons d'en face'. It informed the thinking of many Catholics throughout Europe, Latin-America and other parts of the world, who at the same period found themselves speaking a common language of humanity with Communist allies. It may well be the most surprising legacy of the brief episode of *le tripartisme*.

12

Christian Democracy in France, 1965–90: Death and Resurrection?[1]

David Hanley

'Christian Democracy appears to be a spent force in France'.

R. Irving

'Les centristes? Ce sont des M.R.P. qui ne songent qu'à aller avec Mitterrand'.

J. Chirac

'Je veux faire une grande C.D.U. à la française'.

C. Millon

Since the defeat of the Right in the presidential and legislative elections of 1988, it has become commonplace to say that this wing of French politics is in something of a crisis.[2] Perhaps the most obvious manifestation of this crisis is the growing challenge to the hegemony of Jacques Chirac within the *Rassemblement pour la République* (R.P.R.), but there are other symptoms as well, such as the *rénovateurs* movement of 1989 which aimed explicitly to span all the parties of the Right, or the *ad hominem* feuding within the coalition of the *Union pour la Democratie Française* (U.D.F.). But the most significant development of all is arguably the attempts by the *Centre des Démocrates*

---

[1] I am particularly grateful to M. Philippe Trolliet of the C.D.S. for providing me with documentation and information. Needless to say the contents of this essay are entirely the author's responsibility.

[2] J.-L. Bourlanges, *La droite année zéro* (Paris, 1989).

Sociaux (C.D.S.) to leave the embrace of the Centre-Right alliance of the U.D.F., where it has languished for over a decade. C.D.S. discomfort at being associated with the Right, albeit the moderate, liberal Right, is nothing new; but this discomfort has found new and stronger forms of expression during the past two years. From mutterings in early 1988 about a possible realignment of French politics, to furtive negotiations with Mitterrand and Rocard between the two presidential ballots, through the whole concept of *ouverture* after May 1988, these Centrists gradually began to gather steam to embark on the reconquest of a lost autonomy. A separate parliamentary group was set up for C.D.S. deputies, the *Union du Centre* (U.D.C.), though the party still remained in U.D.F.; its style of opposition to the new Socialist government became visibly less antagonistic. Attention then focused on the two series of upcoming elections, municipal in March 1989 and European in June. Although there was never much chance of separate C.D.S. lists for the first of these contests, described below, demands grew for such lists in the European poll. In April the leadership duly took the plunge. It can hardly have been encouraged by the result, a bare 8.5 per cent for Simone Weil's list. Indeed many commentators believe that this was the end of any serious attempt to seek autonomy by the C.D.S. and that it could henceforth only crawl back humiliated into a modest place within the U.D.F., rather in the manner of a runaway child driven back home by starvation. This remains to be seen.

This episode, which at first sight seems like just another everyday crisis within the troubled *ménage* of the Right, in fact conceals a deeper drama. The C.D.S. is not just another party of the Right; it comes from a distinct tradition which it is often afraid to acknowledge, for reasons that we shall try to unravel. It is, of course, beneath the anodyne and misleading label of Centrist, which it likes to use as a figleaf, the surviving representative of organized Christian Democracy in France. As such its recent turmoil raises a number of questions of interest to historian and political scientist alike. To what extent was the drive for autonomy by the C.D.S. an attempt to reestablish an authentic Christian Democrat voice in French politics? If, as seems to be the case, this attempt was a failure, to what factors can this failure be attributed? And, finally, what are the implications of this failure for those parts of the French electorate which, if not explicitly Christian Democrat, at least have a strong association in their minds between religious affiliation and political behaviour?

Activists and commentators are often perplexed by the seemingly scrappy historical record of Christian Democracy in France. Compared with its sisters in Italy, Germany and the Benelux countries, it seems to have taken longer to take off; to have held office for much less time; probably to have accomplished much less in terms of policy output; and finally, to have collapsed rapidly and ignominiously. This is not a proud record for the eldest daughter of the church, and there is no doubt that this failure weighs heavily on the minds of activists, sometimes provoking an inferiority complex. Yet Christian Democracy has undoubtedly existed as an organized political form in France and left an indelible mark on the political system.[3] If we accept the conventional view that nineteenth- and early twentieth-century attempts by Catholics to become involved in Republican politics belong to the tradition of paternalistic 'social Catholicism',[4] there is no doubt that the twentieth century saw the growth of a recognizable Christian Democrat doctrine and practice, mediated initially through the Catholic Action groups of the interwar period and afterwards the postwar *Mouvement Républicain Populaire* (M.R.P.).[5] Even hostile critics such as Dreyfus admit that this movement was an authentically French version of the current then becoming hegemonic in much of Western Europe. Certainly the M.R.P. corresponds to Seiler's criteria for such parties.[6] It had a recognizable project (not merely to defend Catholic interests in a secular state, but also to promote actively social and economic justice – 'la révolution par la loi'). It had the structures which such mass parties command (a network of voluntary Catholic associations to back up its work and provide it with *cadres*). It had the catch-all type of electorate (albeit skewed slightly to the Right and with some very marked geographical zones of support) which religious parties inevitably assume, given that their *raison d'être* is to represent an ideological community rather than a particular class. It even had the achievements after its period in office; much of the welfare infrastructure created by the tripartite governments after 1944 owes a great deal to the M.R.P.,[7] and in a less visible but equally important way it eased the participation of Catholics in political life helping

[3] R. Irving, *Christian Democracy in France* (London, 1973); F.-G. Dreyfus, *Histoire de la démocratie chrétienne en France: de Chateaubriand à Raymond Barre* (Paris, 1988); J.-M. Mayeur, *Des partis catholiques à la démocratie chrétienne* (Paris, 1980); P. Letamendia, *La démocratie chrétienne*, (Paris, 1977); D. Zeraffa, 'La démocratie chrétienne en France: éléments historiques', *Esprit*, 143 (October 1988), 65–75.

[4] J.-B. Duroselle, *Les débuts du catholicisme social* (Paris, 1951); G. Cholvy and Y.-M. Hilaire, *Histoire religieuse de la France contemporaine* (3 vols., Toulouse, 1985–88), vol. 1.

[5] Cholvy and Hilaire, *Histoire religieuse*, vol. 2, pp. 13–163.

[6] D.-L. Seiler, *Partis et familles politiques* (Paris, 1980), pp. 305–35.

[7] Dreyfus, *Histoire*, chs. 7 and 9; Irving, *Christian Democracy*, ch. 4.

to destroy the myth (at least in many parts of the population) that a Catholic was necessarily suspect as, a democrat.

Like all parties the M.R.P. had its internal divisions and made many mistakes when in office, and almost from its inception it began losing support to Gaullism. Nonetheless it is fair to say that until the end of the Fourth Republic the M.R.P. performed effectively the function of a Christian Democrat party. When that Republic foundered the effects were bound to be felt by the party which by then had come to symbolize it. The experience of the Fifth Republic has been crucial in shaping the destiny of Christian Democracy, principally because since 1958 the movement has had to take its hardest decisions not as a member of the majority but more often than not in opposition. Some brief recapitulation is necessary here.

Once the M.R.P. had broken with de Gaulle in 1962 over the questions of Europe (the 'Volapük' speech) and of the mode of electing the President, it had to cope with the new position of being in opposition. Its new leadership tandem of Fontanet and Lecanuet soon realized the implications of electing Presidents by universal suffrage with a straight fight on the second ballot between two contestants. These were briefly what has come to be called bipolarization; in other words if the majority had a clear leader in de Gaulle then the opposition should logically try to imitate it. Unfortunately this had implications for the nebula of non-Gaullist parties. Leaving aside the *Parti Communiste Français* (P.C.F.) with its 20 per cent of the vote, which was anathema to the M.R.P., there still remained the socialist *Section Française de l'Internationale Ouvrière* (S.F.I.O.), the Radicals and the various 'independents' of the traditional Right, some grouped in the *Centre National des Indépendants* (C.N.I.) and some soon to be organized by Giscard in the *Républicains Indépendants* (R.I.). With which of these was the M.R.P. supposed to ally? None was a natural partner even if most of them had done business at different times with M.R.P. during various pre-1958 governments. The Jacobin secularism of both the S.F.I.O., and to a lesser extent the Radicals, was a far from negligible cultural barrier. Many on the moderate Right were old-fashioned conservatives of ultra-liberal persuasion in economic matters who at bottom had little in common with Christian Democracy anyway. Yet some combination had to be attempted, whether a short-term alliance or some more ambitious bid at federation or merger.

Lecanuet's instincts went more towards the second option and he was prepared to inflict considerable change on his party in order to achieve it. The lengthy tractations between the M.R.P., Radicals and S.F.I.O. over the abortive presidential candidacy of Gaston Defferre are well known.[8] In the end loyalty to existing principles and party structures proved strongest on every side, so that men who had toyed with the idea of merging their parties into some bigger *ensemble* gave up the idea. As a result, Lecanuet stood as a candidate alongside the official Left representative, Mitterrand. Although he was perceived largely as an M.R.P. figure (and indeed he scored best in traditional Catholic M.R.P. territory),[9] he had tried to define his campaign as Centrist; it is from this period that the term really enters contemporary vocabulary in its modern sense, denoting a form of Christian Democracy that is trying to disguise itself as something more. Encouraged by his fair showing of 15.9 per cent Lecanuet then set up the *Centre Démocrate* (C.D.) with a view to superseding the M.R.P. It aimed to draw in new members from non-Christian Democrat backgrounds on the basis of a modernizing appeal. Its doctrine seemed to water down some of the main messages of Christian Democracy; there was rather less emphasis on social justice but more on economic modernization, while European integration and obsession with the Atlantic Alliance (a measure of the traditional anti-Communism of this political family) bulked large.[10] In fact the movement does not seem to have expanded much. Radicals were discouraged by their own party and both they and the Socialists were now moving into the *Fédération de la Gauche Démocrate et Socialiste* (F.G.D.S.), a forerunner of the Common Programme alliance of the seventies. Giscard was mopping up much of the anti-Gaullian Right.

It is probably the feeling of growing Left/Right polarization which determined the next phase of Lecanuet's strategy. This was basically to try and seek a home within the Right and influence it from inside. In other words, twenty years of confronting Gaullism were abandoned, and modernizing Centrists urged to seek an accommodation with it against the greater evil of the soon-to-be-united Left. Lecanuet's declarations in the 1967 elections gave a hint of this, but the process was really accelerated by the aftermath of the May events. When de Gaulle resigned after the 1969 referendum and Pompidou stood for the presidency, he managed

---

[8] F. Wilson, *The French Democratic Left, 1963–69* (Stanford, 1971); H. Simmons, *French Socialists in Search of a Role* (Ithaca, 1970).

[9] C. Leleu, *Géographie des élections françaises depuis 1936* (Paris, 1972), pp. 140, 310.

[10] Centre Démocrate, *Texte de la charte du centre démocrate* (special number of *Courrier des Démocrates*), 1966, 32 pp. Whereas the socio-economic parts of this text are generous and indeed quite social-democratic in tone, there is not a single reference, even implicit, to the Christian Democrat tradition. This contrasts remarkably with M.R.P. or even future C.D.S. statements.

in his campaign to secure the support of some half of the Centrist parlementarians, the Centre Démocrate et Progrès (C.D.P.) group following J. Duhamel. Lecanuet hung on in opposition and attempted to make up the loss by increased collaboration with the Radicals in the *Mouvement des Réformateurs*; but the Radicals under Servan-Schreiber were highly divided and not that numerous. Meanwhile the unity and growth of the Left continued apace; it took the death of Pompidou and the 1974 election for Giscard to repeat his predecessor's move and bring the remaining Centrists into his majority. By now Lecanuet thought that bipolarization was complete and therefore the only place for his movement to be was on the Right, albeit on the Left thereof.

This gradual drift had changed the face of the Christian Democrat party; indeed many people now doubted whether it could still be called one. Dreyfus claims that only one third of the C.D. parliamentary candidates in 1967 and only fourteen of the eventual forty-one deputies came from an M.R.P. background.[11] This was merely a symptom of a deeper malaise. What Lecanuet did was to weaken the identity of his movement to a point where it became a ragbag. His anxiety for numbers was such that he was quite happy to contemplate not just collaboration but merger with an institution such as the Radical party, with its masonic, anticlerical and rationalistic traditions. Such an institution is completely the antipodes of Catholic traditions, and cultural gaps like this cannot be bridged simply in the name of electoral expediency or because both partners have run out of ideas. Similar criticisms could be made of Centrist appeals to the old Right, in that from a Christian Democrat point of view worship of the market is just as idolatrous as the cult of science-and-progress. In short Lecanuet, in his anxiety to create an presidential *rassemblement* tampered with the doctrine and identity of his movement to the point where it was in danger of losing its soul. His tactic is hard to justify. In the end ministers from his group sat in government (but often, as Dreyfus remarks, to sign laws which they disliked, such as the abortion and divorce legislation of 1974), as a result of his alliance choices. But the electoral audience of his current did not grow; rather it declined.[12] The C.D. vote continued to stand up best where it had always done, in the Catholic areas – Brittany,

[11] Dreyfus, *Histoire*, p. 352.

[12] If in 1962 the Christian Democrat vote was worth 12.2 per cent, then by 1978 it had, according to Dreyfus (p. 387), fallen to 5.4 per cent. It is of course difficult to be categoric given the changing labels and also alliance constraints, which affect candidatures.

Savoy, parts of the North, below the Massif Central – this despite the virtual dechristianization of the movement and its decline into the sands of 'Centrism'. Even more significantly, the actual membership of the movement remained overwhelmingly Catholic, usually from an M.R.P. background, and indeed from higher-than-average social positions.[13] By the late seventies the movement had come a long way from its progressive beginnings and had ended up as the reformist alibi for a government of the Right which, as Chirac harried Giscard's ministers in what has been described as a 'corrida portugaise', was less and less capable of reform.

Some symptoms of dissatisfaction within the ranks were becoming apparent. The fusion of the two groups of Centrists (the followers of Pompidou and Giscard respectively) had taken place in May 1976 when the C.D.S. was set up; Dreyfus regarded this as an attempt in some sense to return to roots.[14] The new party aimed to function as a specific Christian Democrat group within the new Giscardian majority. Certainly, as Dreyfus remarks, its electorate in the 1977 municipal and 1978 legislative elections bore a remarkable resemblance to that of the M.R.P. circa 1962, confirming the image of the party as a Catholic, rural and, to some extent, regional force. But activists were content to follow Lecanuet's line of alliance with Giscardism, even to the extent of accepting the party's joining the U.D.F., an electoral cartel pulled together by Giscard to fight the 1978 elections against the united Left and, less visibly, against Chirac's R.P.R. This helped keep the party's seats intact at least and the tactic was pursued until the 1981 presidential defeat of Giscard.

Whatever hopes of realignment or autonomy may have existed at this juncture were soon dissipated as the Left government got down to its attempt at Keynesianism in one country. The consequences of the failed dash for economic growth were increased social polarization and, politically, a recementing of the old majority which had so acrimoniously lost the presidency. The Socialists did their best to help this process with the catastrophic attempt to take the private schools into public ownership in 1983–84; despite Savary's pragmatism at Education, Prime Minister Mauroy wrecked hopes of a realistic deal with the Catholic education lobby by agreeing to demands from deputies of the *Parti Socialiste* (P.S.) for the insertion into the bill of unacceptable clauses, by P.S. deputies of

[13] C. Ysmal, 'Adhérents et dirigeants du centre démocrate', *Revue française de science politique*, 32 (1972), pp. 77–88.

[14] Dreyfus, *Histoire*, p. 379 ff.

old fashioned secularist persuasion and usually from an F.E.N. background.[15] The million-strong demonstrations and the brusque withdrawal of the bill by Mitterrand are ancient history now, but for purposes of our enquiry we need to imagine the effect which such an episode must have had on the C.D.S. It can only have been confirmed in its conclusion that for the present at least there was no other option but alliance with the Right given the sectarianism of 'l'alliance socialo-communiste'. This was confirmed not just on a tactical level but doctrinally; it was now that the C.D.S. began to discover the virtues of market liberalism and sing its praises in a manner unthinkabl in the days of the M.R.P.[16] Hence the party's enthusiastic participation in the Right's 1986 election win and its occupation of some strategic portfolios in the Chirac government of 1986–88. Some C.D.S. leaders were indeed among the more enthusiastic privatizers and deregulators, particularly Méhaignerie at Housing (where he reversed the Quilliot law to favour landlords at the expense of tenants) and Arthuis (keen to bring competitive tendering into the public sector).

The Chirac interlude did not however allow C.D.S. to become just another party of the Right. The government's promise of an economic revival was not fulfilled, and growing social tensions were evident, as seen in the rise of the *Front National* (F.N.) and the less than firm attitude taken to it by some of the C.D.S. coalition partners. Towards the end of the Chirac interlude, as it became clear that Mitterrand had a very good chance of being reelected, one senses a fundamental reappraisal of the whole C.D.S. strategy taking place, both on the level of activists and – in a somewhat different perspective, it will be argued – of leaders. All felt increasingly uncomfortable in the conservative coalition, which was probably going to lose anyway. None were happy about the rise of a new and brutal segment of the Right, and all suspected that the 'end of Gaullism' might finally be in the offing, once Chirac was beaten again and the now limited audience of this particular variety of populism was revealed. This latter factor should never be underestimated in analyzing the motives of Christian Democrats; they consider, rightly, that Gaullism is one of the major reasons for the failure of their tradition to take a bigger

[15] A. Prost, 'The Educational Maelstrom', in G. Ross, S. Hoffman and S. Malzacher (eds.), *The Mitterrand Experiment* (London, 1987), pp. 217–33; J. Ambler, 'Equality and the Politics of Education' in J. Ambler (ed.), *The French Socialist Experiment* (Philadelphia, 1985), pp. 116–44.

[16] F. Bayrou, 'Libéralisme et démocratie personnaliste: différences et convergences', *France-Forum*, 1982, pp. 13–18. See also the chapter 'Vouloir' of the C.D.S. 1986 election manifesto written by Bayrou and Barrot.

role in French politics and they know that Gaullists have seldom concealed the contempt in which they hold them. Thus breaking out of an alliance of necessity must have begun at last to look plausible. All the more so as noises began to emerge from the other side of politics (mainly the Elysée palace) about possible realignments. Between ballots the fatal and highly ambiguous word *ouverture* was duly pronounced.

The C.D.S. has prepared for some kind of new scenario by endorsing and indeed actively suscitating the presidential candidacy of Raymond Barre. Although considered as a man of either liberal or Gaullist tradition (depending on which parts of his career one took) Barre did his best to present an image that was more Christian Democrat than anything else. In particular his stressing of the need for social justice amid his market-orientated discourse and his references to personalism showed how far he was leaning towards this tradition. [17] But although Barre was to draw an electorate which was basically a Christian Democrat one, it was soon clear that he would lose on the first ballot and that therefore Mitterrand would remain President. Thus the whole business of reappraisal could no longer be put off; hence the gradual moves towards some kind of autonomy within the Right listed above. The crucial moment in this process was undoubtedly the constitution of the separate list for the Euroelections, as this marks the furthest limit to which C.D.S. was ready to go. We will examine it in some detail.

Although strong hints had been given after the round of elections in 1988 that the C.D.S. might run its own list for the European elections, this possibility was brought sharply to the fore by an event which happened outside that party. This was the emergence of the *rénovateurs*, who first came to notice in March 1989. This group of young deputies of the Right spanned all the parties of the coalition and included many of the rising stars of the opposition – Noir and Carignon from the R.P.R., Millon from the P.R. and individuals such as Baudis, Bayrou and Bosson from the C.D.S. What this apparently heterogenous group had in common was their desire to renew the Right (not that they would use this term) from within, if need be at the cost of disbanding the existing parties and moving towards some broad new single formation on the lines of the German Christlich-Demokratische Union (C.D.U.) or British Conservatives. [18] The platform of such a catch-all formation would be suitably vague but it

[17] R. Barre, 'Ce que je crois' *La Croix* 11 December 1987, pp. 13–15.

[18] For a blow by blow account of the abortive campaign of the renovators see G. Bresson and J.-M. Thénard, *Les 21 jours qui ébranlèrent la droite* (Paris, 1989).

would be anchored more towards the centre ground, a clear aim of the group being to demarcate its project unambiguously from Le Pen and his supporters. An image of modernity and efficiency would be presented. Such a united formation with a single agreed candidate would have a good chance of winning the presidency. The sub-text of this discourse was clearly that the existing generation of leaders, particularly presidential losers Giscard and Chirac (but also perhaps P.R. boss Léotard?) would have to go, as they were by now unelectable and a millstone around the Right's neck. It should be pointed out here that what really triggered the *rénovateur* offensive was the news that there would be a combined R.P.R./U.D.F. list for the Euroelection, led by none other than Giscard.

This modernizing offensive by a part of the Right, including some powerful figures from its own ranks, put the C.D.S. leaders in a quandary. There were now likely to be three lists on the Right and Centre, not two; the C.D.S., if it put up a list, would be accused of dividing the Right. Also if the *rénovateur* project was not unsuited to the thinking of some C.D.S. leaders, as we will argue, then its timing and the fact that it originated from outside the party made it hard to sell to the activists. In our view it is pressure from the latter that made Méhaignerie go ahead with the party congress at Lille to discuss the European election.[19] In the meantime his task was facilititated by the climb-down of the renovators, who were either bullied or cajoled by their party leaders into sticking with the official list. But Méhaignerie sensed that the C.D.S. as a party would not willingly support this list and hence reluctantly sanctioned an independent C.D.S. one.

The manner in which this list came about was highly informative as to the leadership's real thinking. Rather than ask the congress to approve outright a list of names in ranking order, the leadership simply sought approval for an autonomous list, but one which it would be free to compose after the congress. What they wanted, of course, was the freedom to put at the head of the list the name of Simone Weil, recently evicted from leadership of the R.P.R./U.D.F. list to the advantage of Giscard, and who in fact appeared at the congress to a less than rapturous reception. It was clear that none of the C.D.S. leaders wanted to lead a list which needed to score better than the polls foresaw if its credibility (and that of the party) was to be maintained. The ever shrewd Jean Lecanuet, having failed to get support for the official R.P.R./U.D.F. list, was ready to quantify exactly what the

---

[19] *Libération* 24 April 1988; *Le Monde* 23–24 April 1988.

stakes were.[20] But when confronted with the question of the *tête de liste*, Méhaignerie pleaded the weight of his other responsibilities, in the manner of an unfortunate activist cornered in a ward meeting and rapidly running out of excuses. Barrot did likewise. The trio of *rénovateurs*, all good media performers and thus credible as *tête de liste*, sat on their hands, happy to help scupper a project which could only stand in the way of their own, despite some very direct appeals from senior members like André Diligent. Even Bernard Stasi, the man believed to be keenest on an autonomous approach for the C.D.S., was not tempted. So in due course the list was announced, led by a woman who is most definitely not, either by religion or political tradition, from the Christian Democrat family, with in second place J.-L. Borloo, a non-member of the party. No stipulation was made that successful candidates join the P.P.E. (*Parti Populaire Européen*), the Christian Democrat grouping in the European Parliament, whose manifesto the C.D.S. had made its own. Nor did they, as Weil remained with the Liberal group and Borloo refused to join any. Given the furtive and reluctant way in which the whole operation was conducted, with highly contradictory signals being sent to the electorate, it is not surprising that Lecanuet's credibility threshold was nowhere near attained; in fact it could be considered surprising that as many as 8 per cent actually bothered to turn out. But Christian Democracy has always had that bedrock at least.

It is my belief that the C.D.S. leadership was not too worried by this outcome, in that it seemed to block the door once and for all for any chance of autonomy for the party. Henceforth it would be forced to seek a role within the Right and logically to play the same game as the *rénovateurs* (though just what the relationship between these and the C.D.S. might be was far from certain). At this point it is now possible for us to evaluate in more depth just what was involved in this failed attempt at autonomy.

In Seiler's view Christian Democrat parties may well have to take one of two routes, both distasteful in their way. On the one hand, they may seek to preserve their Christian identity; by doing this in a climate of progressive religious dealignment, they may be condemning themselves to electoral decline. On the other hand, they may abandon their Christian characteristics, seeking to become a loose catch-all party of the Centre-Right, mopping up Conservatives, Liberals and sundry Right-wingers. Such a tactic may

---

[20] For Lecanuet even 16 per cent would not be enough to become viable in a bipolarized system (see newspapers quoted in note 18).

well lead to electoral success but at the cost of losing the party's soul. Seiler sees the German *Christlich-Demokratische Union/Christlich-Soziale Union* (C.D.U./C.S.U.) or the Austrian *Österreichische Volkspartei* (Ö.V.P.) as typical of the second alternative; but he sees M.R.P. as typifying the first.

However, in our view the decline of M.R.P./C.D.S. is due in part to its progressive shredding of its Christian identity, especially under Lecanuet, without of course any compensatory electoral gain. Over the years the party has played down a number of its characteristic features, the first of which is the doctrine of Personalism. Originally elaborated by philosophers such as Mounier, it aimed specifically to be distinct from liberalism with its stress on the individual. This latter is seen as a rather arid and inhuman entity by Personalists, being driven by competitive urges; the dimension of solidarity or belonging to any sort of community seems to them to be absent from mainstream liberalism. But it is precisely through this notion of the person as someone needing to be fulfilled in different contexts and to a large extent via fruitful contact with his fellows that the sociable and indeed solidaristic aspects of Christian Democracy take root. Or, to put it less pompously, this is why this type of politics still has a bridge to the Left. Yet although internal C.D.S. texts may still recall the older doctrine,[21] the movement's public profile has become increasingly one of a moderate Centre-Right party in whose discourse market liberalism sounds ever more stridently.[22] It seems clear that the C.D.S. leadership has been pursuing, albeit fairly unsuccessfully, more of a C.D.U.-type strategy, hence its convergence with the *rénovateurs*. Or at least it seems to have accepted J.-L. Parodi's advice that in politics Centrist groups cannot have any real existence except as a dynamic ginger group within a coalition of either Right or Left.[23] Clearly Méhaignerie and his group believe that C.D.S. can only play such a role in a coalition of the Right. I believe that there are several reasons for this pessimistic acceptance of a downgraded role for the Christian Democrat current and that some of them are flawed.

The first of these is what can only be called institutional pessimism. The electoral system, with its two ballots for major contests, seems to

---

[21] The C.D.S. founding text, *L'autre solution* (Paris, 1977), for instance devotes its first forty pages to the philosophical positions and ancestry of the movement.

[22] P. Letamendia, 'La démocratie chrétienne en France', *Etudes*, 370 (June 1989), 745–53.

[23] J.-L. Parodi, 'Carrefour au centre du paysage politique', *La Croix* 2 June 1988. For a similar view see C. Ysmal, 'Destin des centrismes', *Projet*, 64 (September–October 1972).

generate bipolarized behaviour on an increasing scale; whatever the pre-election relationship between Socialists and Communists, voters of either camp feel drawn to vote for the other's candidate on the second ballot. The C.D.S. knows this and knows that it must accept the corrollary that its own candidates must have similar support from voters of the Right. Hence its chances of breaking free of the Right are minimal. This would be the end of the argument, were it not for one other possibility, that the system of alliances be changed and that in particular the P.S. ditch the P.C.F. and move positively towards Christian Democracy. At the time when *ouverture* was in the air, speculation was rife about such a move, with its attendant possibility of a hegemonic Socialist/Centre alliance which would have left the P.C.F. and the harder elements of the Right in the cold for a long time. Were such a deal to have materialized, it might also have involved changing the electoral system more in the direction of proportional representation, which would have loosed institutional constraint in no small way.

Unfortunately an acceptable offer never came, for a variety of cultural and instrumental factors. The keenest elements in the P.S. for a realignment were the Rocard group, unsurprisingly given that many originate from the leftish tendencies within the Catholic Action movement.[24] Clearly the majority of the party were less keen, given that their culture has been so strongly influenced by the knee-jerk anti-Catholicism of the traditional French Left and that they are in many cases still emotionally committed to Left unity.[25] But what matters here is probably less cultural gaps, though these should never be underestimated, than material considerations. The present alliance of convenience guarantees many deputies their seats and many mayors their town halls; if a new alliance were to come in, these politicians would need to be convinced that it could be at least as productive electorally. In the short time available between the 1988 elections and the 1989 campaigns it was never really possible to embark on this task. The most that could be done was what actually happened: a few powerful notables (not all Christian Democrats even) did their calculations and threw in their lot with Mitterrand. For any more serious realignment to have taken place on a party basis the attitudes of elites on both sides would have needed to be much bolder.

[24] L.A. Bell, 'The Modernist Left in France: A Political and Intellectual History', Unpublished Ph. D. thesis, University of Reading, 1988.
[25] For a good discussion of stereotypes see the debate in *La Croix* 24 July 1986: 'Barrot-Rocard: le dialogue est ouvert' (reprinted in the edition of 13 May 1988).

Clearly C.D.S. leaders were – and here is another factor – much more cautious than their activists. The grassroots/elite tension is a commonplace of all party life, but recently it seems to have been very strong here. The C.D.S. congress is probably a good guide to grassroots feeling.[26] Considering the erosion which the movement has suffered over the years in terms of activists (and voters) going, via the *deuxième gauche*, towards the Rocardian end of the P.S., we may be surprised that there was still such a demand for C.D.S. autonomy. The leadership had other visions. Central to its calculation was the increasing difficulty within the Right and the growing unpopularity of its traditional leaders, to which could be added from 1988 onwards the growing irrelevance of Barre. In this context the chances for youngish C.D.S. bosses within a hopefully revamped Right began to look more promising, especially when, as with Méhaignerie, their recent ministerial careers had given ample reassurance to right-wing voters. How else are we to understand Méhaignerie's bid for the premiership in the next Right government?[27] Behind Matignon stands the Elysée. In fact, long-term career perspectives as well as shorter-term electoral expediency helped turn leaders in a different direction from their followers.

A final consideration was doubtless the long-term anxiety about the future of the Christian Democrat vote. If religious identification is declining, then presumably there is less and less justification for trying to appeal to voters on the basis of a specifically Christian message. It is true that this view involves believing that voters need a high degree of identification with religion in order to be mobilized by an appeal on Christian Democrat lines; many would challenge such a view. If the C.D.S. leaders did see it thus, then it was one more reason for watering down their autonomy and seeking a place in a bigger, looser Right. Yet for all the apparent rationality of this choice, which indeed seems to some so overdetermined as to merit no argument, it may be asked whether from the point of view of the movement's future Méhaignerie's decision was the correct one.

It is true that bipolarization is powerfully entrenched in the French system. But this does not necessarily mean that the P.S. has to be wedded to Left unity forever. There is little to suggest that the P.C.F. can do anything more than hang on, and with increasing difficulty at that. It can also be

---

[26] For a typical grassroots view see R. Linaudière, 'La lente émergence du centre', *La Croix* 30 December 1988.

[27] *Le Monde* 3–4 September 1989.

asked if at the second ballot P.C.F. voters are really going to resist voting for a Socialist/Centrist candidate when the alternative might be to let in the Right. They have after all shown their readiness to *voter utile* for some years now, not least in the first round of presidential contests, as P.C.F. candidates know to their cost. In other words the P.C.F. bogey might not be so great as feared.

Nor should too much be made of the cultural differences which have stood in the way of a Socialist/C.D.S. rapprochement. To begin with, little was heard of these as late as the mid seventies when, it will be recalled, the new Socialist party, at the height of its radicalism, was still governing towns such as Nantes, Nancy and Marseille in partnership with ex-members of the M.R.P. Even in the more stressed climate of the Fourth Republic the two families had shared in several governments of course. Where there has been a will there has usually been a way. In any case the point is that cultural tensions within the French body politic are now measurably less than they were.[28] The episode of the failed schools nationalization showed that the old anticlerical appeal cannot mobilize large numbers of voters and indeed that it may have the opposite effect (though it is not intended to imply that all the anti-government protesters of 1984 were motivated by purely religious or ideological considerations). The P.S. cannot escape drawing this conclusion (which is not to say that the *laïc* tradition cannot serve purposes of internal party mobilization, but that is an entirely different issue). If secularism is indeed dead in electoral terms, then one of the major bones of ideological contention disappears.

This consensus on schools is symptomatic of a wider consensus within French society. More than ever before it now appears that French people want an efficient economy, where private enterprise has a major role but where the state plays the role of guarantor of social justice. They want a more European identity (while remaining French). They are less and less interested in ideology (witness their increasing refusal to categorize themselves in terms of Left or Right)[29] and are fairly tolerant of diversity in others' lifestyles. They are in general sceptical about how much governments can actually influence their life, particularly via the economy. In short there seems considerable mileage for parties who present themselves with a fairly

---

[28] F. Furet, J. Julliard and P. Rosanvallon, *La république du centre* (Paris, 1988); A. Duhamel, *Les habits neufs de la politique* (Paris, 1988).

[29] E. Schweisguth, *La dimension droite/gauche en France* (paper given to I.P.S.A. congress, Washington, 1988). I am grateful to the author for allowing me to see this paper.

low ideological profile as discreetly reformist or left of centre, committed to a dynamic economy but with guarantees for those who fall behind in the race; certainly the P.S. has moved sharply towards this stance in its recent declarations.[30]

Culturally then there would seem to be little in the way of a P.S./Centrist *rapprochement*. Certainly voters would not fear it, and indeed Cayrol is correct to say that in this respect they are ahead of the party leaders.[31] By studying the electorate of Barre in the presidential campaign and the U.D.F. in the legislatives he has built up a picture of the typical Centrist voter, a group which accounts in his view for some 15 per cent of the electorate, with a hard core of some 8 per cent. This latter seems very much to be made up of C.D.S. support. Although Centrist voters are sociologically closer to the Right and can be described as modernizers, for example in their Europeanism and attachment to economic dynamism, they are more sympathetic than R.P.R. voters to issues such as a wealth tax or increased educational expenditure. They are much less fearful on issues such as law and order or immigration. Politically, though a majority of them voted for the Right in the second ballot of both elections in 1988, few rule out the possibility of one day voting P.S. (only one eighth of C.D.S. voters). These voters support the entry of Centrists into the Rocard government, with 66 per cent of the CDS voters wanting this as of now. On the other side of the coin, Socialist voters have moved in a convergent direction; only 28 per cent are hostile to opening the government towards the Centre, while 50 per cent would even be prepared to give Raymond Barre a place in it. On this evidence it would seem difficult to hide behind the old excuse of previous Republics, that leaders would like to be bolder in their alliances but that voters would never allow them to do it. Voters are now more 'dealigned' than ever.[32]

The problem clearly lies with the leaders, especially within the Socialist party where much will depend on how the ideological and programmatic profile of the party develops. This will be inseparable from the leadership struggle, which is resolving itself into a contest between Rocard (the most favourable to the kind of evolution postulated here), Jospin (instinctively the most hostile and around whom the traditionalist forces will gather) and Fabius

---

[30] Parti Socialiste, *Propositions pour la France* (Paris, 1988); F. Mitterrand, *Lettre à tous les Français* (manifesto for presidential campaign, Paris, 1988).

[31] R. Cayrol, 'Les citoyens centrés', *Politique aujourd'hui*, 3 (June 1989), 72–83.

[32] P. Habert and A. Lancelot, 'L'émergence d'un nouvel électeur', *L'élection présidentielle de 1988* (Paris, 1988), pp. 16–23.

who, as ever, will wait as long as possible to see which way the cat jumps. If the C.D.S. is to enjoy some kind of autonomous role again then one of these men will have to come up with a proposition which aims at more than detaching one or two leaders to act as figleaves for P.S. rule.

The C.D.S. leadership too will have to think very carefully. In particular it may ask itself whether the career hopes invested in its 'C.D.U.' strategy are realistic. Arguably these leaders can obtain as much in partnership with the moderate Left as they can from the rising *rénovateurs* whose numbers and appetites are big enough to leave even privileged allies with *la portion congrue*. They should also ask themselves just how much of their traditional ethic can be saved in partnership with these young and hungry liberals, whose political options point fairly unerringly towards a dual society with a large underclass of losers. Whatever else it has stood for, Christian Democracy has always refused that.

It is probably correct to say that in the 1990s French Christian Democracy can never be the force it once was; certainly it can never hope to win France over to its whole political project. But it still has a structure and an electorate, an electorate which has evolved considerably. The best bet for its future might well be as the conscience of a broad Centre-Left grouping, an arrangement which would also leave some options open. Whether the leaders will dare to go down this road, and how far their potential partners will encourage them remains to be seen. Christian Democracy has neither died nor managed a successful resurrection; for the moment it is still on the life-support machine.

Index

Index

Index

Ultramontanism, x, 59, 62, 91, 97, 116, 120

Ultraroyalism, 76, 78, 90, 100–3, 105, 114–5

Union du Centre, 204

Union pour la Démocratie Française (U.D.F.), 203–4, 209, 212, 218

Union Sacrée, x, 150, 154, 159, 174

Verdier, Cardinal, 157–8

Verdun, battle of (1916), 168

Veuillot, Louis, 69

Vichy regime, x–xi, 150, 153, 158–62, 164, 167–86, 189, 193

Waldeck-Rousseau, René, 141–2, 150–2, 164–5

Weil, Simone, 204, 212–3

Weber, Max, 68–75

Zeldin, Theodore, 63, 85, 107–8, 117

Zola, Emile, 108, 114, 139, 141–2